The English Dramatists

THOMAS MIDDLETON

VOLUME THE FIRST

Vera Effigies
Tho Midletoni Gent.

THE WORKS

OF

THOMAS MIDDLETON

EDITED BY

A. H. BULLEN, B.A.

IN EIGHT VOLUMES

VOLUME THE FIRST

AMS PRESS INC.
New York
1964

Published by
AMS PRESS INC.
56 E. 13th Street, N.Y. 10003
Printed in United States of America

TO

ALGERNON CHARLES SWINBURNE,

GREAT AS SCHOLAR AND CRITIC,

GREATER AS POET,

THESE VOLUMES ARE INSCRIBED

BY THE EDITOR.

PREFACE.

THE works of Thomas Midddleton were collected in 1840 by Alexander Dyce. This edition has long been out of print, and the need of a new edition has been keenly felt. Of Dyce's editorial work it would be difficult to speak too highly; he was a man of wide and accurate reading, and his critical acumen was considerable. I have, of course, made a very free use of his notes.

In the present edition are included some pieces that were unknown to Dyce. These are: (1) a prose tract entitled *The Peace-Maker, or Great Britain's Blessing*, 1618, which has been erroneously ascribed to James I.; (2) *A Musical Allegory*, 1622 (printed for the first time), from a MS. preserved among the Conway Papers; (3) *The Triumphs of Honour and Virtue*, 1622, reprinted from the Shakespeare Society's Papers. I have also included a slight tract relating to Sir Robert Sherley, which Dyce rejected on insufficient information. The two parts of *The Honest Whore* will be printed hereafter among Dekker's works.

VOL. I.   *b*

The etched portrait of Middleton is from a rough woodcut prefixed to *Two New Plays*, 1657.

I have to return my warmest thanks to my friend Mr. C. H. Firth for his great kindness in reading the proof-sheets of the present volumes and aiding me with valuable suggestions throughout. My friends Mr. S. L. Lee and Mr. W. J. Craig have also given me occasional help.

13th May 1885.

CONTENTS OF VOL. I.

INTRODUCTION.

———◆———

IT should be an editor's aim to cultivate a nice sense of proportion and eschew exaggeration. Uncritical eulogy has the effect of irritating or repelling the reader; and when a poet has stood the test of time for nearly three centuries, his position needs no strengthening by violent displays of editorial zeal. Middleton's most recent critic[1] has not hesitated to affirm that "in daring and happy concentration of imagery, and a certain imperial confidence in the use of words, he of all the dramatists of that time is the disciple that comes nearest to the master." The reader who gives to these volumes the study they deserve will discover that this statement is not made at random, but is the mature judgment of a balanced mind. The comedies of intrigue show ready invention and craftsmanlike skill, though the plots are sometimes thin and the humour often gross; for dignity of moral senti-

---

[1] The writer of the anonymous article on Middleton in the ninth edition of the *Encyclopædia Britannica*.

ment the serious scenes of *A Fair Quarrel* have hardly been surpassed ; *The Changeling, Women beware Women,* and *The Spanish Gipsy* are among the highest achievements of the English drama.

Thomas Middleton was the only son[1] of William Middleton,[2] gentleman, who settled in London, and there married Anne, daughter of William Snow. The date of the dramatist's birth may be fixed *circ.* 1570; and it is probable that he was born in the metropolis. There is no' evidence to show whether he received an academical training. A Thomas Middleton was admitted member of Gray's Inn in 1593, and another in 1596; the earlier entry probably refers to the dramatist.

In 1597 Middleton began his literary career with *The*

---

[1] There was also a daughter, Avicia, who married (1) John Empson, (2) Alan Waterer. From C 2 *Vis. Surrey,* 1623, p. 328, Coll. Arms, Dyce gives the following pedigree, which is also found (translated) in Harl. MS. 1046, fol. 209 :—

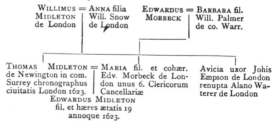

WILLIMUS = ANNA filia   EDWARDUS = BARBARA fil.
MIDLETON | Will. Snow   MORBECK | Will. Palmer
de London | de London | de co. Warr.

THOMAS MIDLETON = MARIA fil. et cohær.   Avicia uxor Johis
de Newington in com. | Edv. Morbeck de Lon-   Empson de London
Surrey chronographus | don unus 6. Clericorum   renupta Alano Wa-
ciuitatis London 1623. | Cancellariæ   terer de London
EDWARDUS MIDLETON
fil. et hæres ætatis 19
annoque 1623.

[2] His arms were : *Argent on a saltier, engrailed, sables, a castle of the first.* On 23d April 1568 Sir Gilbert Dethick, Garter king-at-arms, assigned him as his crest : *On his torce, argent and sables, an ape passant and chain, gold mantled, argent, double gules.—Dethick's Guifts, Vincent,* 162, fol. 215, Coll. Arms (quoted in full by Dyce).

Wisdom of Solomon Paraphrased. As we know of no other writer of the same name, I fear we must hold the dramatist responsible for this intolerable and interminable performance. The fluency of the versification is aggravating to the last degree. Through stanza after stanza and page after page we plod, vainly hoping to find something to reward us, some flash of inspiration; and when we reach the end, we are too dejected to congratulate ourselves on our release. It is extraordinary that a man of Middleton's brilliant ability should have perpetrated so insipid a piece of work. When the dramatists turned their hands to sacred subjects, the result was seldom satisfactory; but few have shown themselves so ill-fitted as Middleton for this class of composition.

Middleton was again before the public In 1599 with *Microcynicon, Six Snarling Satyres.* His name is not on the title-page, but some preliminary stanzas, headed *His Defiance to Envy*, are signed "T. M. Gent.;" and there is no reason to doubt that the initials belong to the dramatist. These satires call for little comment. "Brief, but tedious," will be the censure of most readers, and I dare not question the justice of the finding. Following in the steps of Marston and Hall, Middleton thought it necessary to adopt a rugged rhythm and barbarous phraseology. At the time of publication these "snarling satyres" may have interested a small esoteric circle of readers, who were able to read between the lines and applaud the hits; but the salt has long since lost its savour.

We cannot determine at what date Middleton began

to write for the stage. The earliest reference to him in Henslowe's Diary (ed. Collier, p. 221) is an entry dated 22nd May 1602, from which it appears that he was then engaged with Munday, Drayton, Webster, and some others not named, in writing a play called *Cæsar's Fall*, for which Henslowe advanced five pounds on account. Under date 29th May (ibid. p. 222) is an entry recording the payment of three pounds to Dekker, Drayton, Middleton, Webster, and Munday for a play called *too harpes, i.e. Two Harpies*. On 21st October (ibid. p. 227) Middleton received four pounds in part payment for *The Chester Tragedy*, and on 9th November two pounds " in fulle paymente of his playe called *Randowlle earlle of Chester*" (ibid. p. 228), which was doubtless the same piece as *The Chester Tragedy*. From an entry dated 14th December 1602 (ibid. p. 228) we learn that Middleton was paid five shillings for writing a prologue and epilogue to Greene's *Friar Bacon*, when that play was revived at court. There is another entry (ibid. p. 241), dated 2d October 1602, recording the payment of twenty shillings to Middleton on account of an unnamed play written for Lord Worcester's company. Time, which " hath an art to make dust of all things," has spared neither *Cæsar's Fall*, nor the *Two Harpies*, nor *The Chester Tragedy* (which Malone in a moment of forgetfulness identified with the *Mayor of Queenborough*), nor the prologue and epilogue to *Friar Bacon*.

In 1602, then, Middleton was closely employed in dramatic writing; but it is fairly certain that he had begun work a few years earlier. The date 1599 has

Introduction. XV

been assigned to the excellent comedy *The Old Law*, which was first published in 1656 as the work of Massinger, Middleton, and Rowley. If the play was written in 1599[1] (a point on which we cannot speak with certainty), Massinger could have had no hand in the original composition, for in 1599 he was a youth of fifteen. Probably Massinger did no more than revise the play on the occasion of its revival at the Salisbury Court Theatre; I doubt whether he added a single scene. Rowley's share was certainly considerable. When he is writing at his best, Rowley is one of the drollest of writers. He was a poor hand at constructing plots; he was often guilty of the most atrocious absurdities; his verse hobbled badly when it came from his pen, and in its passage through the press was reduced by the old printers to a *rudis indigestaque moles ;* he roared like a bull of Bashan when he ought to have been dignified. But he had a genuine gift of humour; and at times (as in *A Woman never Vext* and passages of *All's Lost by Lust*) he could wring our heart-strings with pity. I would unhesitatingly assign to him the scene (iii. 1) where Gnotho, anxious to put away his old wife Agatha and take a younger, bribes the parish-clerk to alter the date in the register. The conclusion of *The Old Law* is the drollest

---

[1] In iii. 1, the Clerk, after reading from the parish-register, "*Agatha, the daughter of Pollux*, born in an. 1540," observes, "and now 'tis 99." At first sight we should feel inclined to pronounce that 1599 *must* be the date of the production of the play. But it is well to tread cautiously, remembering that the play was not printed until 1656, that it has descended in a very corrupt state, and that both copyists and printers constantly blunder over dates.

of all drolleries. To the relief of the old courtiers and
the dismay of their gaping heirs, Evander, the Duke, has
just pronounced void the law which condemned to death
all men of fourscore years and all women of threescore.
At this moment Gnotho and his friends are seen approaching in riotous mirth, preceded by a band of fiddlers
and followed by the sorrowing wives, who are being conducted to execution. Gnotho, more forward than the
rest, has a double business in hand ; he is provided with
his new bride, and when he has seen Agatha despatched
by the hangman, he will proceed to church to solemnise
the second marriage. "Crowd on afore !" he shouts
impatiently to the fiddlers. The Duke calls a halt and
inquires the meaning of the procession. Gnotho,
anxious to make an end of the business, very briefly
explains, and then shouts again to the fiddlers "Crowd
on !" Evander demands more light on the matter, but
Gnotho is in no mood for parleying. "A lusty woman,
able-bodied, and well-blooded cheeks," says Evander,
eyeing Agatha ; "sure I cannot think that she be so
old,"—to which Gnotho replies that he will bet Evander
two to one she is of the full age. Evander commits the
case to the consideration of the old courtiers. Gnotho
listens with amused pity while they sternly denounce his
conduct, and when they have ended exclaims, "A
mess of wise old men ! ye are good old men, and talk
as age will give you leave." But at length, by slow
degrees, he is brought to realise the true state of affairs.
There is nothing in Massinger's or Middleton's plays to
match the drollery of this scene ; but whoever has read

Rowley knows what a rich vein of whimsical humour he could sometimes discover. Yet in this very scene Middleton's presence is plainly visible; the humour is Rowley's, but without Middleton's help the Duke and old courtiers would not have preserved so dignified a demeanour. To Middleton probably belong all the serious parts of the play. The scenes in which the wantonness of the young court-gallants and Eugenia is so spiritedly represented are unquestionably by Middleton, and the talk of the lawyers in the opening scene is quite in his manner. *The Old Law* was a favourite with Charles Lamb, who wrote of it—"There is an exquisiteness of moral sensibility, making one to gush out tears of delight, and a poetical strangeness in all the improbable circumstances of this wild play, which are unlike anything in the dramas which Massinger wrote alone. The pathos is of a subtler edge. Middleton and Rowley, who assisted in this play, had both of them finer geniuses than their associate." Whether the plot was original or borrowed I cannot say. A few years ago Anthony Trollope constructed a slight novel, *The Fixed Period*, with a plot of somewhat similar character. There is only one quarto of *The Old Law*, published in 1656, and the text is deplorably corrupt. Numerous emendations, sometimes excellent and sometimes needless, were made by Monk Mason and Gifford. Perhaps I ought to have allowed myself more freedom in the matter of emendation. Among my corrections there are two I regard as tolerably certain. Hippolita pleading before the

young courtiers for the life of her old father-in-law, says
(v. 1) :—

> " For yet, methinks, you bear the shapes of men,
> (Though nothing more than *merely beautifeaus*
> To make you appear angels)," &c.

Gifford converted the italicised words into "*merely
beauty serves,*" and this emendation was adopted by
Dyce ; but Gifford's reading is quite unintelligible. My
own correction, "*mercy beautifies,*" is, I venture to think,
unassailable. Again : Leonides, admiring his daughter-
in-law's devotion, exclaims—

> " That the *stronger* tie of wedlock should do more
> Than nature in her nearest ligaments
> Of blood and propagation ! I should ne'er
> Have begot such a daughter of my own."

Gifford and Dyce read "*strong*" for "*stronger.*" The
true reading is certainly "*stranger,*" which gives us the
desired antithesis.

Dyce considered the tragi-comedy of *The Mayor of
Queenborough* (first printed in 1661) to be one of Middleton's earliest plays. I do not follow him in laying
stress on dumb-shows as evidence towards fixing the
date. We have a dumb-show in *The Changeling,* which
is certainly one of Middleton's maturest works. Webster gives us dumb-shows in *The White Devil.* My own
view is that *The Mayor of Queenborough* was originally
an early play, but that it underwent considerable revi-
sion at a later date, and has descended in its revised
form. In iv. 3 (see vol. ii. p. 86) there are some lines

which contain a resemblance, too close to be accidental, to a passage in *The Tempest.* Middleton frequently imitates Shakespeare, but it is hardly likely that Shakespeare (as Reed supposed) was on this occasion returning the compliment. Many passages are so strikingly fine that I cannot but believe them to have been written when Middleton's genius was in its full maturity. What a grip there is in such lines as these !—

> "We are all, my lord,
> The sons of fortune ; she has sent us forth
> *To thrive by the red sweat of our own merits.*"

Or take these lines on woman's lust :—

> "'Tis her cunning,
> The love of her own lust, which makes a woman
> Gallop down hill as fearless as a drunkard."

Or these on Thong Castle :—

> "Why, here's a fabric that implies eternity ;
> The building plain but most substantial ;
> Methinks it looks as if it mock'd all ruin,
> Saving that master-piece of consummation,
> The end of time, which must consume even ruin,
> And eat that into cinders."

Again and again we are arrested by the bold utterance, the fine dramatic ring of the verse. Yet the play as a whole leaves little impression on the mind, and has the appearance of being an immature production. The odd confusion of chronology is a mark of youthful treatment. Only at an early stage of his career would Middleton have ventured to introduce a Puritan into a chronicle play which deals with Hengist and Horsus. Rowley, who wrote *The Birth of Merlin,* would have had

not the slightest hesitation in the matter, and Heywood
was equally indifferent; but Middleton in his mature
work shows due respect for chronology. The plot is
repulsive. Vortiger is a monster of iniquity, and his
brutality towards his gentle wife, Castiza, is peculiarly
disgusting. Roxana is a creature of lust, effrontery,
and guile. Middleton's later studies of depraved feminine character are among his highest achievements;
but Roxana cannot for a moment compare with Bianca
in *Women beware Women* or Beatrice in *The Changeling.*
The comic scenes were doubtless effective on the stage;
they are somewhat tiresome by the fireside. In Rowley's hands the Mayor would have been a more amusing
figure. It is for the detached passages of noble poetry
that students will value this tragi-comedy, which is
admirably adapted for purposes of quotation. Lamb
has introduced one short extract from it into his essay
The Superannuated Man:—" I no longer hunt after
pleasure; I let it come to me. I am like the man

> 'that's born and has his years come to him
> In some *green* desert.'" [1]

The extract is from i. 1, where Constantius seeks to be
relieved from assuming the cares of royalty :—

> " I know no more the way to temporal rule
> Than he that's born and has his years come to him
> In a *rough* desert."

---

[1] It is also given in the *Fragments* appended to *Extracts from the
Garrick Plays* in Hone's *Table Book.* These *Fragments* are unpardon-
ably omitted from collected editions of the *Specimens* and *Extracts.*

It will be perceived that by the change of *rough* into *green*, Lamb has given a novel significance to the passage.

First on the list of Middleton's printed plays is *Blurt, Master Constable*, 1602, a sprightly, well-written play, containing some charming poetry. The scene is laid in Venice. Hippolito and Camillo, returning from the wars, are received by Hippolito's sister, Violetta. Camillo, a suitor to Violetta, has brought with him as prisoner a French gentleman, Fontinelle, whom he delivers into his mistress's hands as a trophy of war. Charmed with his grace of manner, Violetta falls in love with her prisoner at first sight; and her passion is reciprocated. The lovers contrive to baffle the machinations of Hippolito and Camillo, and at length are secretly married. Severe censure has been passed, quite undeservedly, on the conclusion of the play. Professor A. W. Ward, who usually takes pains to be scrupulously accurate, observes in his account of Middleton (*Engl. Dram. Lit.*, ii. 74) :—" The lightness and gaiety of writing in *Blurt, Master Constable* (printed 1602), cannot render tolerable a play with so vile a plot. Beginning pleasantly, and indeed prettily enough, with the sudden passion of a lady for the prisoner brought home from the wars by her lover, *it ends offensively with the unfaithfulness of the prisoner*, who has escaped and married the lady, and is finally brought back to her by a device which resembles a parody on the plot of *All's Well that Ends Well*." But, if I have read the play rightly, Mr. Ward has misstated the matter. Hippolito and Camillo, in their anxiety to effectually sunder the

young lovers, endeavour to clap up a match between
Fontinelle and the courtesan Imperia. Hippolito
broaches the matter to Imperia, and—that she may not
buy a pig in a poke—sends her Fontinelle's portrait;
she is delighted with the portrait and welcomes the
proposal. In iii. 1, Hippolito and Camillo offer Fontinelle his liberty if he will marry Imperia, but he indig-
nantly rejects the proposal and is sent back to prison.
Frisco, the courtesan's page, is then employed to visit
the prisoner and use his powers of persuasion. At this
point the plot is not so plain as we could have wished,
and it is probable that a scene between Frisco and
Fontinelle has been lost. A plan of escape is devised
during the prison conference: Fontinelle is to change
clothes with Frisco and repair to the courtesan's house.
Meanwhile Fontinelle sends by Frisco a letter to
Violetta, bidding her come at midnight to Saint
Lorenzo's monastery, and bring a friar to conduct the
marriage. The poet leaves us to fill in details. When
the marriage had been solemnised, it remained for the
bride and bridegroom to seek a place of shelter. What
was to be done, for the hour was late? The course they
took is as plain as day. It was agreed that Fontinelle
should go to the courtesan's house, pretending that he
had come to carry out his engagement, and that Violetta
should presently follow to claim her husband. It is a
violent absurdity to suppose that Fontinelle's speech to
Imperia in v. 2 is the language of genuine passion:—

> " Now, by the heart of love, my Violet
> Is a foul weed (*O pure Italian flower !*)

She a black negro, to the white compare
Of this unequalled beauty. O most accurst,
That I have given her leave to challenge me !
But, lady, poison speaks Italian well,
And in her loath'd kiss I'll include her hell."

The parenthesised words ought to be enough for any
reader; but we have, besides, the explicit statement of
Violetta at the close of the play :—

" My Fontinelle ne'er dallied in her arms ;
She never bound his heart with amorous charms :
My Fontinelle ne'er loathed my sweet embrace :
She never drew love's picture by his face :

.   .   .   .

*With prayers and bribes we hired her both to lie
Under that roof."*

Of course I do not deny that it would have been more
decorous for the marriage-night to have been spent
under some other roof than the courtesan's ; but it must
be remembered that the young lovers were not in a
position to pick and choose their lodging.   Helena's
device in *All's Well* seems to me far less defensible than
Violetta's.   Fontinelle's conduct throughout is the conduct of an honourable gentleman.   I am sorry that Mr.
Ward should have misrepresented the plot ; but I allow
that Middleton ought to have rendered such misrepre-
sentation impossible by supplying more details and
leaving less to the reader's imagination.   It is not easy
to carry in one's head the plots of several hundreds of
plays ; and so careful a stage-historian as Mr. Ward may
well claim indulgence for occasional lapses.

We may assume that Middleton's marriage with Mary,

daughter of Edward Morbeck,[1] one of the six clerks in Chancery, took place in 1602 or 1603 ; for his son Edward was born in 1604. There were no other children of the marriage.

In 1604 were published two interesting tracts, *Father Hubbard's Tale, or the Ant and the Nightingale,* and *The Black Book ;* the former was entered in the Stationers' Books on 3rd January 1603–4, and the latter on 22nd of the following March. The address *To the Reader* prefixed to *Father Hubbard's Tale* is signed T. M., and the *Epistle to the Reader* prefixed to *The Black Book* bears the same initials. There cannot be the slightest doubt [2] that these initials belong to the dramatist. With a light hand the writer exposes the foibles and vices of the time. He was evidently a great admirer of Nashe—to whom he makes many allusions—and reflects in his own

---

[1] See pedigree on p. xii. In Harl. MS. 1046, fol. 209, the name is written *Marbecke.*

[2] Mr. Carew Hazlitt has the hardihood to assert "there is no pretence whatever for assigning this volume [*Father Hubbard's Tale*] to Middleton," whose claim to *The Black Book* he denies with equal emphasis. Middleton, according to Mr. Hazlitt, "usually put his name to anything that came from his pen ; " but *A Mad World, my Masters* and *A Trick to Catch the Old One* bear merely the initials " T. M." Mr. Hazlitt assigns these tracts to Thomas Moffat (or Moufet or Muffet), a medical writer and author of a curious poem on the management of silkworms. There is a good life of Muffet in Cooper's *Athen. Cantab.*, ii. 400–402. He spent his closing days in retirement at Bulbridge, near Wilton, in the capacity of retainer to the Earl of Pembroke. That this man at the end of his career (he died in 1605) should have abandoned scientific studies to attack the vices of the town is *prima facie* unlikely ; and Mr. Hazlitt adduces not a grain of evidence in support of his extraordinary theory.

pages something of Nashe's marvellous brilliancy. To
students of the social life of the early seventeenth century these tracts—and similar writings of Dekker and
Rowlands—are invaluable. In *Father Hubbard's Tale*
we are shown how a rich young spendthrift squanders
in dicing and debauchery the hard-earned fruits of his
father's parsimony, until at length he is driven to join
the ranks of the sharpers who have fleeced him, and
assists in ruining other young heirs. The elaborate
description of the young prodigal's apparel is quite in
Nashe's vein of whimsical extravagance. We are conducted in *The Black Book* through the rowdiest parts of
the metropolis, Turnbull Street and Birchin Lane, the
haunts of drabs and thieves. Middleton's knowledge of
London, like Sam Weller's, was extensive and peculiar.

In the same year (1604) Middleton assisted Dekker
in the composition of *The Honest Whore.* We find
in Henslow's Diary (ed. Collier, p. 232) the following
entry :—

"Lent unto the company, to geve unto Thomas Deckers and
Middelton, in earnest of ther Playe called the pasyent man and the
onest hore, the some of v^li 1604."

The First Part of *The Honest Whore* was issued in
1604, and the Second Part in 1630 : on the title-pages
of both parts only Dekker's name is found. I agree
with Dyce that Middleton's share in this play was
inconsiderable. Dekker had, as Lamb says, "poetry
enough for anything." His sympathy with sinful and
sorrowing humanity was genuine and deep; but his

poignant feelings sometimes found expression in language which seems to have the air of insincerity. In
the fine scenes where Hippolito implores Bellafront to
abandon her vicious course of life, and again where he
strives to undo the effect of his former teaching, one
feels that the arguments and illustrations are enforced
with over-heated vehemence. This note of exaggeration
is never absent from Dekker's work; he let his fancy
have full swing and did not write "with slower pen."
But he was the most natural of writers, lovable at all
points, full of simplicity and tenderness. The character
of Orlando Friscobaldo is drawn in Dekker's cheeriest,
sunniest manner. I would ascribe to Middleton the
scenes (i. 5 and iii. 1) where the gallants endeavour to
irritate the patient Candido. Bellafront's preparations
for receiving visitors, and the conduct of the gallants on
their arrival (ii. 1), closely recall a scene in *Michaelmas
Term* (iii. 1). In these scenes, and in a few comic
scenes of the Second Part, we recognise Middleton's
hand, but hardly elsewhere.

About the time when the First Part of *The Honest
Whore* was composed, Dekker went out of his way to
acknowledge a slight obligation under which he lay
towards Middleton. On the 15th March 1603–4, King
James, with the Queen and Prince Henry, paid a state
visit to the City, and Dekker was employed to write
a pageant for the occasion. When the pageant was
printed (1604), he appended to the speech of Zeal the
following note:—"If there be any glory to be won by
writing these lines, I do freely bestow it, as his due, on

Tho. Middleton, in whose brain they were begotten, though they were delivered here: *quæ nos non fecimus ipsi, vix ea nostra voco."* As the speech is only sixty lines long, it is curious—considering how indifferent the dramatists were to literary etiquette—that he should have made this acknowledgment. Had Middleton's share in *The Honest Whore* been at all considerable, we may be tolerably sure that his name would not have been omitted from the title-page.

After 1604 Middleton published nothing until 1607, in which year appeared *The Phœnix*[1] and *Michaelmas Term.* Both these comedies are full of life and movement. Phœnix, son of the Duke of Ferrara, is solicited by his father, at the instance of some disaffected courtiers, to travel in foreign parts that he may gain observation and experience. He agrees to the proposal, but requests that he may be accompanied only by a single attendant, Fidelio ; for he suspects treachery, and is determined to outwit the courtiers. Instead of travelling abroad, he disguises himself and travels in his own kingdom, with the intent not only to keep a sharp eye on the courtiers, but to detect what abuses are rife throughout the land. In the course of his perambulations he discovers notable roguery. There is Tangle, an "old busy turbulent fellow, a villainous maltworm, that eats holes into poor men's causes,"

---

[1] In vol. i. p. 101, I say that *The Phœnix* "was licensed by Sir George Buc, 9th May 1607." I ought to have said "licensed *for printing.*" So on p. 213 in regard to *Michaelmas Term.*

who talks in a legal jargon that becomes somewhat
tedious. Then there is Falso, a justice of the peace,
who takes bribes on all sides, and keeps a set of rascally
serving-men, who employ their leisure in committing
highway robberies. We are also introduced to a worth-
less sea-captain, who has grown tired of his wife, and
signs a bond for the sale of her ; and to a wanton city
madam, who by robbing her husband supports a needy
knight for her pleasure. In this nest of villainy there
is found one honest man, Quieto, who (like Candido
in *The Honest Whore*) is at peace with everybody and
allows nothing to ruffle his equanimity. There is an
abundance of amusing intrigue and lively situations.
The poetry put into the mouth of Phœnix is of a
high order. Genuine eloquence is shown in the apos-
trophes to " sober Law, made with meek eyes, persuading action " (i. 4), and to "reverend and honourable
Matrimony" (ii. 2). The latter passage, as Dyce re-
marked, bears some resemblance to the lines beginning
" Hail, wedded Love !" in the fourth book of *Paradise
Lost.*

In *Michaelmas Term* we see a young gentleman,
Master Easy, caught in the snares of a griping usurer,
Quomodo. Tighter and tighter in each successive
scene the meshes close round the victim. In the end
all comes right ; villainy overreaches itself, and Master
Easy not only gets back his lands, but is left in lawful
possession of the bloodsucker's wife, a spirited woman.
Michaelmas Term is full of excellent fun, and the reader
has only himself to blame if he fails to find amusement.

Quomodo's one ambition was to be a landed proprietor·
When he sees that his dream is about to be realised,
his exultation is delightfully comic. He dwells with
gusto on the prospect of the Whitsun holidays, when
he will ride down to his estate in Essex " with a number
of citizens and their wives, some upon pillions, some
upon side-saddles," his son, Sim, riding ahead in a
peach-coloured taffeta jacket. There will be good store
of logs for Christmas ; and he intends to astonish the
citizens' wives by the quality of the fruit from his
orchard. His parting words to the victim whom he
has fleeced of everything are drolly cordial :—" If it
please you, sir, you know the house ; you may visit us
often, and dine with us once a quarter."

A Trick to Catch the Old One[1] and *The Family of
Love* were published in 1608 : the former had been
entered in the Stationers' Registers on 7th October 1607,
and the latter on the 12th of the same month. I do
not hesitate to endorse Langbaine's brief but emphatic
judgment on *A Trick to Catch the Old One :*—" This
is an excellent old play." The plot is as follows. An
improvident young gallant, Witgood, who has mortgaged
all his property to his usurious uncle, Lucre, repents of
his evil courses and is anxious to make a new start. He
pretends that he is the accepted suitor to a rich widow
from the country. The so-called widow is a courtesan,

---

[1] A kind of proverbial saying. Cf. Day's *Isle of Gulls*, ii. 5 :—
" We are in the way to *catch the old one.*"

who throws herself into the scheme with uncommon
zest. A shrewd innkeeper is engaged as her serving-
man and despatched to Lucre's house to make inquiries
on his mistress's behalf about Witgood's fortunes. He
feigns to be unaware that he is addressing Witgood's
uncle ; he wants to hear from some sober citizen whether
the match contemplated by his mistress is desirable, and
whether Witgood is a man of substance. Lucre pricks
up his ears at once. Poor relatives are a nuisance, but
when a timely stroke of luck promotes them to afflu-
ence, then the case is altered, and those who formerly
neglected them are ready with suit and service, even
where little or no personal advantage is to be derived.
Lucre is the more pleased to hear of his nephew's good
fortune because he anticipates that the widow's lands
may eventually pass from Witgood's possession to his
own. For some months he had refused to see Witgood,
but he now sends a messenger to say that his nephew
would be a welcome visitor. Witgood replies that he
is very much occupied, and he begs to be excused.
Lucre's eagerness is doubled ; he renews the invitation
in a more cordial manner. Presently Witgood arrives
and is congratulated by his uncle, who cheerfully under-
takes to supply his present necessities and stop the
mouths of importunate creditors. Then Witgood in-
troduces the widow, with whose appearance Lucre is
charmed. Meanwhile the news of the engagement has
been noised abroad, and the prodigal's creditors assemble
to congratulate him, vying with each other in pressing
their services upon him. The rumour reaches the ears

of Onesiphorous Hoard, Lucre's mortal enemy; and Hoard determines to endeavour to supplant Witgood in the widow's affections. Taking with him some trusty companions to substantiate his statements, he goes to the widow, exposes Witgood's former extravagances and present poverty, and proposes himself as a more eligible suitor. The widow professes herself vastly indignant against Witgood and accepts Hoard in his stead. On that very day she was to meet Lucre and Witgood in order to make final arrangements for the marriage. There is no time to be lost; so it is agreed that under some pretext she shall slip from Witgood's company, whereupon Hoard and his friends will surprise her and carry her by boat to the sanctuary of Cole Harbour, where a parson shall be in attendance. Lucre is furious when he discovers that the prize has been carried off by his hated antagonist. Away he hies with his nephew and friends to Cole Harbour. Hoard has no objection to discuss the situation, for the marriage has just been secretly performed. The courtesan and Lucre converse apart; she pays him home soundly: did he expect that she would marry a beggar? let him restore the lands and then she will marry his nephew. To thwart his adversary he gladly catches at the proposal, and volunteers besides to make his nephew his heir. When the mortgage has been given up, Lucre learns that he has made the sacrifice too late. Meanwhile Witgood is still exercising his brain, anxious to reap the full benefit of the situation. He asserts that there was a pre-contract between himself and the widow, and threatens to bring the matter into a court of law. Hoard is violently alarmed, and eagerly adopts his wife's proposal that Witgood should be bought off. At first Witgood is inexorable—he will have law; but finally he consents to abandon his claim on condition that his creditors' demands are satisfied. When this difficulty is settled, Hoard prepares a marriage feast and invites his friends, including Lucre and Witgood (who has meanwhile secretly married Hoard's niece) among the guests. The *dénouement* is exceedingly amusing. Hoard's brother, on being introduced to the bride, recognises Witgood's mistress, and a scene of some confusion follows; but finally Hoard puts a good face on the matter and reminds the guests that "the wedding dinner cools." It will be seen that in writing this comedy Middleton was more anxious to amuse than to teach a moral lesson. Grave moralists may argue that it is reprehensible for a man to fasten his cast-off mistress on his bride's uncle; nor am I inclined to dispute the reasonableness of the contention. But we must not bring the squint looks of "budge doctors of the stoic fur" to bear on these airy comedies of intrigue. Middleton could moralise severely enough when the occasion required; but in the present instance his aim was to provide entertainment, and he succeeds admirably. It is impossible not to admire the happy dexterity with which the mirthful situations are multiplied. The interest never flags for a moment, but is heightened at every turn.

The Family of Love is written with Middleton's usual freedom and facility. As he had been before the public

for some years, it is curious to note the modesty with
which he refers to himself in the prologue :—

> "If, for opinion hath not blaz'd his fame,
> Nor expectation filled the general round,
> You deem his labours slight," &c.

In the Address to the Reader he mentions that the play
was in the press before he had notice of it, "by which
means some faults may escape in the printing;" and
he adds that "it passed the censure of the stage with
a general applause."

Your Five Gallants was entered in the Stationers'
Registers on 22d March 1607–8, under the title of
Fyve Wittie Gallants. The quarto, which is very care-
lessly printed, bears no date, but was probably published
in 1608. The five gallants are "the broker gallant,"
"the bawd gallant," "the cheating gallant," "the pocket
gallant," "the whore gallant,"—a choice fraternity of
vagabonds, whose manner of life is described with much
gusto. There is an allusion in iv. 2 to the closing of
playhouses in time of plague. The year 1607 was a
plague-year. On 12th April the Lord Mayor in a letter
to the Lord Chamberlain announced that the plague was
increasing in the skirts and confines of the city; and
suggested that orders should be given to the justices of
Middlesex to interdict the performance of stage-plays
at Whitechapel, Shoreditch, Clerkenwell, and other out-
lying districts.[1]

---

[1] See *Analytical Index of the Series of Records known as the
Remembrancia*, p. 337.

A Mad World, my Masters,[1] licensed on 12th October 1608 and printed in the same year, is a pleasanter play than the preceding. The characters of Sir Bounteous Progress, the liberal knight who keeps open house for all comers, and Harebrain, the jealous husband, yoked to a demure light-o'-love, are very ably drawn; and the situations are worked out with the adroit briskness that we admired in *A Trick to Catch the Old One*. The deception practised by the counterfeit players recalls the similar incident in the *Mayor of Queenborough*. Middleton seems to have been tickled with the notion of converting wanton wagtails into wives. In *A Trick to Catch the Old One*, Witgood succeeded in marrying his mistress to his wife's uncle; in *A Mad World* the tables are turned, and Follywit finds himself united to his uncle's mistress. The victims in both cases submit with a good grace. A large part of Mrs. Behn's *City Heiress*, 1681, was conveyed from *A Mad World*.

In 1609 Middleton published a slight tract commemorating the exploits of the adventurous Sir Robert Sherley, the youngest and most remarkable of the Three English Brothers.[2] As the dedication to Sir Thomas

---

[1] A pamphlet by Nicholas Breton, printed in 1603, bears the same title. I suppose that "A mad world, my masters," was a sort of proverbial expression.

[2] An excellent account of these remarkable men is given in *The Sherley Brothers, an historical memoir of the lives of Sir Thomas Sherley, Sir Anthony Sherley, and Sir Robert Sherley, Knights. By one of the same house* [the late Evelyn Philip Shirley, Esq.] Roxburghe Club, 1848. The play of *The Three English Brothers* by Day, Wilkins, and William Rowley, is reprinted in my edition of Day's Works, 1881.

Sherley is subscribed "Thomas Middleton," I have felt
bound, against my inclination, to include this uninterest-
ing tract among our author's works.

The Roaring Girl, written in conjunction with Dekker,
was published in 1611.[1] Of Mary Frith, the Roaring
Girl, whose adventures are so graphically described by
the dramatists, I have given some account in a pre-
fatory note to the play (iv. 3–6). In the Address to the
Reader Middleton says:—"Worse things, I must needs
confess, the world has taxed her for than has been
written of her;" and he concludes with the very proper
observation—"We rather wish in such discoveries,
where reputation lies bleeding, a slackness of truth than
fulness of slander." Under this judicious treatment the
Amazon of the Bankside becomes an attractive figure.
She moves among rowdies and profligates without suffering any contamination; she has the thews of a giant
and the gentleness of a child. Secure in her "armed
and iron maidenhood," and defying the breath of
scandal, she daffs the world aside and chooses a life
of frolic freedom. She can converse with rogues and

---

[1] Mr. Fleay confidently fixes the date of composition before November 1604. "The date is proved by the allusion in it to *Westward
Ho*. This play was revised by Dekker about 1610–11." I need hardly
say that the allusion to *Westward Ho* proves nothing, for it would
have been quite as intelligible to the audience in 1611 as in 1604.
Besides, I strongly doubt whether Mary Frith had come into notoriety
so early as 1604. At the earliest computation she was not born before
1584–85. When Mr. Fleay says "this play was revised by Dekker,"
he is of course merely expressing his own belief,—not an ascertained
fact. My view is that the two authors worked on the play together,
and this view is clearly supported by internal evidence.

cheats in their cant language, and knows all their tricks
and subterfuges.   Her hand is heavy on swaggerers, but
she has a woman's ear for a tale of lovers' distress, and
is quick to render efficient aid.   The conception is
strikingly fresh and original.   We can distinguish, I
think, with some approach to exactness, Middleton's
share from Dekker's.   Throughout the first act Dekker's
hand is clearly traceable.   The description of the fur-
niture in Sir Alexander Wengrave's house is quite in
Dekker's vein of fantastic extravagance, and is closely
paralleled by similar descriptions in the *Wonder of a
Kingdom.*   When Sir Alexander says—

> " Then, sir, below
> The very floor, as 'twere, waves to and fro,
> And like a floating island seems to move
> Upon a sea bound in with shores above,"

we are at once reminded of Torrenti's boast in a *Wonder
of a Kingdom*—

> " I'll pave my great hall with a floor of clouds,
> Wherein shall move an artificial sun,
> Reflecting round about me golden beams,
> Whose flames shall make the room seem all on fire."

The dullest reader must perceive that the same fancy
was at work in both instances.   Middleton never in-
dulged in these airy extravagances.   Sir Bounteous in
A Mad World has far homelier notions of magnificence.
The second act opens precisely in Middleton's manner.
The very names of the characters—Laxton, Goshawk,
Greenwit, Gallipot, &c.—are evidence in his favour.

This style of nomenclature, which Middleton commonly adopted in his comedies, was not affected by Dekker. Then the characters are just such as we find in other plays of Middleton.   Mistress Gallipot may be compared with Mistress Purge in *The Family of Love* or with Falso's Daughter in *The Phœnix ;* and Mistress Openwork, the jealous scold, is a repetition of Mistress Glister in *The Family of Love.*   The dialogue is conducted with Middleton's usual smartness and rapidity.   The second scene of act ii., where Sir Alexander, having overheard his son courting Moll, implores him to abandon the suit, has Dekker's naturalness of sentiment and fluency of metre, a not unpleasing mixture of blank verse and rhyme.   Act iii. is mainly by Middleton : the feigning of the precontract in the second scene is a repetition of the device in *A Trick to Catch the Old One ;* the conduct of Laxton and Gallipot is precisely the same as that of Witgood and Hoard.   As to iv. 1, where young Wengrave brings the *Roaring Girl* to his father's house, I am not at all sure about the authorship, but I incline to Middleton ; the next scene, before Gallipot's house, is evidently Middleton's for the most part, but the rhymed speeches at the end seem to belong to Dekker.   The whole of the fifth act I would ascribe to Dekker.   Those who have read Dekker's *Bellman of London* and *Lanthorn and Candlelight* are aware that he made a special study of the cant language of thieves.   He has turned this knowledge to account very largely in the last act of the present play.

We next hear of Middleton in 1613, when he was

employed to write a pageant, *The Triumphs of Truth*, to celebrate the Mayoralty of Sir Thomas Middleton.[1] There are two editions of the pageant, and to the second is appended the " manner of his lordship's entertainment " at the opening of the New River Head.   Pageants are usually tedious, and *The Triumphs of Truth* is no exception to the rule.   The speeches are smoothly written, but the songs are poor.   The pageant seems to have been mounted on a costly scale, and some of the emblematic inventions are curious.   Envy was represented " eating of a human heart, mounted on a rhinoceros, attired in red silk, suitable to the bloodiness of her manners."   One of the chief features of the pageant was an emblematic representation of the Grocers' Company (to which Sir Thomas Middleton belonged) in a water-spectacle :—" Then . . . his Lordship and the worthy company are led forward toward the water-side, where you shall find the river decked in the richest glory to receive him ; upon whose crystal bosom stands five islands, artfully garnished with all manner of Indian fruit-trees, drugs, spiceries and the like ; the middle island with a fair castle especially beautified ; " the castle representing the newly-established forts of the East-India Company. It must have been peculiarly gratifying to the Lord Mayor to read the following exordium, in which modern readers will find a spice of satirical humour :—" Search all chronicles, histories, records, in what language or

---

[1] Judging from the dedication, there appears to have been no relationship between the dramatist and Sir Thomas Middleton.

letter soever; let the inquisitive man waste the dear
treasures of his time and eyesight, he shall conclude his
life only in this certainty, that there is no subject upon
earth received into the place of his government with the
like state and magnificence as is the Lord Mayor of the
city of London." What eloquence! what a climax! That
sentence ought to be written in letters of gold and set
up in the Mansion House as a monument *in perpetuum.*
Middleton then proceeds to impress on the civic authorities the necessity of employing a competent pageant-
writer, one whose invention can match the brilliancy of
the scenic shows. I am sorry to add that he takes the
opportunity to deal a blow at Anthony Munday :—" It
would heartily grieve any understanding spirit to behold,
many times, so glorious a fire in bounty and goodness
offering to match itself with freezing art, sitting in darkness with the candle out, looking like the picture of
Black Monday." Munday came in for plenty of knocks,
but his poetical credit stood high in the city; and, in
spite of Middleton's sneer, he was employed as pageant-
maker during the next three years.

On 4th January 1613-14, a masque by Middleton,
The Mask of Cupid, which was never printed, and of
which no MS. is known to exist, was performed at the
Merchant Tailors' Hall, as we learn from the following
entry in the City Records (under date 18th January
1613-14) :—" Item: it is ordered by the Court that
Thomas Middleton Gent. shall be forthwith allowed
upon his bill of particulars such recompense and charges,
as the committees lately appointed for the ordering of

the late solemnities at Merchant Tailors' Hall shall think meet, for all his disbursements and pains taken by him and others in the last *Mask of Cupid*, and other shows lately made at the aforesaid Hall by the said Mr. Middleton."[1] The solemnities were in honour of the recent marriage of Robert Kerr, Earl of Somerset, to Lady Frances Howard. In Howes' continuation of Stowe's *Annales* (ed. 1615, p. 928) there is an account of the magnificent reception of the infamous pair at Merchant Tailors' Hall.

The comedy *No Wit, No Help like a Woman's*, published in 1657, bears some indications of having been written *circ.* 1613. Weatherwise, in iii. 1, says:—"If I, that have proceeded in five and twenty such books of astronomy [*i.e.* almanacs], should not be able to put down a scholar now in one thousand six hundred and thirty-eight, the dominical letter being G, I stood for a goose." Among Shirley's *Poems*, 1646, is a prologue to a play (acted in Dublin) called *No Wit to a Woman's.* This play was without doubt Middleton's, and the passage quoted above—which suggests the date 1613–14 —was introduced by Shirley on the occasion of the revival of the play at Dublin. Of course Shirley may have been reckoning in round numbers; and perhaps we ought not to put too literal a construction upon the words. From Weatherwise's references to his almanac, we gather that the play was produced in June. It is one of Middleton's ablest comedies, but it leaves a

---

[1] Quoted by Dyce from Rep. No. 31 (Part II.) fol. 239 *b*.

somewhat unpleasant taste in the mouth. The characters have more variety than in the earlier comedies. Sir Oliver Twilight is a very humorous and original creation. He will not part with a penny-piece to his son and daughter at their marriage; but they are welcome to live with their partners under his roof and have all their wants supplied :—

> " 'Tis his pride
> To have his children's children got successively
> On his forefathers' feather-beds."

Equally original is Weatherwise, who regulates all his actions by the signs of the zodiac. Savourwit, Sir Oliver's servant, is a fellow of infinite resources and matchless impudence. The deception practised by Mrs. Low-water, in assuming man's apparel and going through a mock marriage with the wealthy Lady Goldenfleece, would be a hazardous experiment on the modern stage ; but Elizabethan audiences were accustomed to such exhibitions. Philip Twilight is an unsatisfactory character. His mother and sister on their passage to Guernsey had fallen into the hands of privateers, had been separated and sold. After nine years comes a letter from the mother—

> " Which related all
> Their taking, selling, separation,
> And never meeting ; and withal requir'd
> Six hundred crowns for ransom."

Philip Twilight is sent by his father with the ransom ; but instead of applying the money to its proper uses he spends it on his own pleasure. While thus employed he meets with "a sweet young gentlewoman, but one that would not sell her honour for the Indies." He secretly marries her, and brings her home to his father's house as his long-lost sister, pretending that he has received sure intelligence abroad of his mother's death. With the fortunes of a damnable young scoundrel who shows such heartless disregard for his mother's suffering it is difficulty to have any sympathy. Probably Middleton was following some Italian novel, but it is a pity that he did not represent young Twilight under a pleasanter aspect.

A Chaste Maid in Cheapside, printed in 1630, is stated on the title-page to have been performed by the Lady Elizabeth's servants at the Swan on the Bankside. I take it on the authority of Mr. Fleay [1] (who has made a special study of the perplexing history of the theatrical companies between 1576 and 1642), that there was no Princess Elizabeth's company before 1611, and that before 1617 the company had removed to the Cockpit in Drury Lane. Mr. Fleay reminds me (in a private communication) of the statement made by John Taylor, that early in 1613 "all the players except the King's men had left their usual residency in the Bankside and played in Middlesex, far remote from the Thames." But as the Princess Elizabeth's company may have acted occasionally at the Swan after this date, I am not inclined to think that we are justified in saying that the *Chaste Maid* must have been produced in or before 1613.

---

[1] See his privately printed tract *On the History of the Theatres in London*, 1882.

The company appears to have left the Bankside because it was unable to compete with the King's men. After the destruction of the Globe (June 1613), when their too powerful rivals repaired to Blackfriars, the Princess Elizabeth's company may have returned to their old quarters. The *Chaste Maid* is the only extant play that we know to have been acted at the Swan. The play is exceedingly diverting, but I cannot conscientiously commend it *virginibus puerisque*, for the language and situations occasionally show an audacious disregard for propriety. Lamb quoted the exquisitely droll soliloquy in which Master Allwitt, the contented cuckold, describes the blessedness of his lot. If the reader, disregarding the anathemas of virtuous critics, gives the *Chaste Maid* a hearing, I can promise him plenty of entertainment.

Civitatis Amor was written to celebrate Charles's assumption of the title of Prince of Wales (4th November 1616). As the signature "Thomas Middleton" is found in the middle of the pageant, after the song of Peace, it is not improbable that another hand wrote the later part. We may dismiss without comment *The Triumphs of Honour and Industry*, 1617; *The Inner Temple Masque*, 1619; and *The Triumphs of Love and Antiquity*, 1619.

In 1617 appeared the admirable play *A Fair Quarrel*, in which Middleton was assisted by Rowley; a second edition with additional comic matter followed in the same year. Lamb quoted in his *Specimens* the duel scene and the scene where Captain Ager before the duel seeks to be resolved of his mother's honour from her own lips. The exquisite criticism which Lamb passed upon those scenes will be familiar to every reader. It may be said without hesitation that, outside Shakespeare's highest works, there is nothing in the English drama more affecting, nothing nobler, than the colloquy between Captain Ager and his mother. That scene and the duel scene I believe to belong to Middleton. To such a height of moral dignity and artistic excellence Rowley never attained. We may safely assign to Rowley the boisterous comic scenes. Middleton's humour is of a quieter character ; he had little liking for noisy horse-play. Apart from the scenes where Captain Ager and the Colonel are concerned, I cannot trace Middleton's hand with any clearness. At the end of the first act Rowley's metrical harshness strikes upon the ear, and throughout the scenes relating to Fitzallen and Jane we seldom escape from it. The incident of the Physician tempting Jane is very unpleasant, but powerfully treated. Rowley was a writer of high ability, but he was sadly wanting in artistic form and refinement.[1] He is too blunt and emphatic,—there is too much of the *fortiter in modo.*

In *Calendar of Domestic State Papers*, under date 19th July 1618, I find—" Licence to Wm. Alley, at nomina-

---

[1] "The plot of Fitzallen, Russell, and Jane," says Langbaine, " is founded, as I believe, on some Italian novel, and may be read in English in the *Complaisant Companion*, octavo, p. 280. That part of the Physician tempting Jane and then accusing her, is founded on a novel of Cynthio Giraldi. See Dec. 4, Nov. 5."

tion of Thomas Middleton, of the sole printing and publishing of a book by Middleton called *The Peacemaker, or Great Britain's Blessing.*" The pamphlet here mentioned was printed anonymously in the same year by Thomas Purfoot, and a second edition appeared in 1619. In the British Museum Catalogue it is ascribed to King James; and the mistake is not surprising, for Middleton was hoaxing his readers—posing before the public as his royal master. The preliminary address "to all our true-loving and peace-embracing subjects" reads like James's *ipsissima verba.* There is an attempt throughout to keep up the deception; but occasional hints show clearly enough that James was not the writer. In sig. B. 1 we have "Let England then (the seat of our Salomon) rejoice in her happy government." It is too absurd to suppose that James would refer to himself as "our Salomon." A great part of the pamphlet is taken up with a tirade against the practice of duelling, which had been denounced five years earlier in "A Publication of His Majesty's Edict and severe Censure against private Combats and Combatants." The circumstances connected with the publication of *The Peacemaker* are most mysterious. Perhaps Middleton applied to James to allow the pamphlet to be issued with the royal imprimatur, and it is possible that James complied by writing the preliminary address; but more probably the whole business was an elaborate joke on Middleton's part. The virtuous indignation expressed against tobacco must have pleased James:—"That witch Tobacco, which hath quite blown away the smoke of Hospitality and turned the chimneys of their forefathers into the noses of their children." The vein of pedantry (assumed for the nonce) must have been equally gratifying to the wise fool. I am puzzled by the pamphlet.

Much more trouble than usually went to the writing of masques appears to have been spent on *The World Tost at Tennis*, 1620.[1] Ben Jonson said that "next himself only Fletcher and Chapman could make a masque ;" but Middleton and Rowley have amply proved their ability on the present occasion. The invention is ingenious, the speeches are finely written, and the songs are smooth. First comes an Induction, consisting of a lively colloquy between the "the three ancient and principal receptacles," Richmond, St. James's, and Denmark House. Richmond is jealous of the prestige acquired by Denmark House, who in very graceful language quiets her fears by the assurance that all three sisters shall be held in equal honour :—

> " The round year
> In her circumferent arms will fold us all,

---

[1] " In all the copies, says Dyce, "of this masque that I have seen, a portion of the letterpress has been cut off from the bottom of the title-page by the binder." The copy before me has the letterpress cut away at the top, but preserves the date 1620 at the bottom : on the title-page is an emblematic engraving. This copy, which is bound up with some quartos of Rowley's plays, belongs to the library of Worcester College, Oxford. I take this opportunity of thanking the Provost and Fellows of that society for their generosity in lending me at various times rare quartos from the fine dramatic collection in the College Library. There are three copies of *The World Tost at Tennis* in the British Museum. In one the title-page is plain and bears the date 1620 ; in the other two—which have the emblematic engraving—the date has been cut away.

And give us all employment seasonable.
I am for colder hours, when the bleak air
Bites with an icy tooth : when summer has sear'd,
And autumn all discolour'd, laid all fallow,
Pleasure taken house and dwells within doors,
Then shall my towers smoke and comely show :
But when again the fresher morn appears,
And the soft spring renews her velvet head,
St. James's take my blest inhabitants,
For she can better entertain them then,
In larger grounds, in park, sports and delights :
Yet a third season, with the western oars,
Calls up to Richmond, when the high-heated year
Is in her solstice ; then she affords
More sweeter-breathing air, more bounds, more pleasures ;
The hounds' loud music to the flying stag,
The feathered talenter to the falling bird,
The bowman's twelve-score prick even at the door,
And to these I could add a hundred more."

The masque opens with a dialogue, marked in the early
parts by Rowley's metrical irregularity, between a soldier
and a scholar. While they are deploring the neglect
shown to men of their profession, Pallas descends and
chides them for their discontent. She begins by affirm-
ing that there should be no divorce between arts and
arms,—

"For he's the complete man partakes of both,
The soul of arts join'd with the flesh of valour,
And he alone participates with me."

She then proceeds to preach a homily in praise of
poverty. The soldier ventures to respectfully reply,
"there's yet a competence which we come short of."
To this Pallas rejoins that the cause may be as much

"in your own negligence as our slow blessings;" but they shall prefer their complaints to Jupiter, who presently descends to the sound of music. Jupiter delivers his views after a very trenchant fashion :—

> "'Tis more than Jupiter
> Can do to please 'em : unsatisfied man
> Has in his ends no end ; not hell's abyss
> Is deeper gulf'd than greedy avarice ;
> Ambition finds no mountain high enough
> For his aspiring foot to stand upon :
> One drinks out all his blessings into surfeits,
> Another throws 'em out as all were his,
> And the gods bound for prodigal supply :
> What is he lives content in any kind ?
> That long-incensèd Nature is now ready
> To turn all back into the fruitless chaos."

Then to show the malcontents what in old time "arts and arms commixt . . . did in the world's broad face," Pallas calls on the Muses to lead in the Nine Worthies. When this show is ended and Jupiter is again beginning to chide his petitioners, Time enters weeping and explains the causes of his sorrow,—how landlords and usurers greedily long for his coming, but when he arrives they bend their plodding heads over their money-bags, let him pass unnoticed and then instantly sigh for his return ; the lawyer drives him off from term to term ; the prodigal sickens him with surfeits; the drunkard sets him on his head topsy-turvy; all the women hate him, and with "gloss and pencilry" wipe off the impression that he sets upon their cheeks. Time having retired, Jupiter denounces vain-glorious pride, and to rebuke

modern extravagance in the matter of apparel, summons
the Five Starches (daughters of Deceit), who perform a
grotesque dance, and after a short dispute for precedency
retire. Jupiter now descends from his aerial machine,
and "to show the strange removes of the world, places
the orb, whose figure it bears, in the midst of the stage;"
whereupon Simplicity enters, takes up the orb and
moralises on the changes that have been effected in the
world. While he is thus engaged Deceit enters; a
dialogue follows, in which Deceit strives to gain the
good graces of Simplicity, but is obliged to retire dis-
comfited. Then is heard within a reaper's song in
praise of Simplicity. Presently Deceit re-enters in company with a King. Simplicity resigns the orb to the
king; Deceit offers to relieve the king of the burthen,
but his offer is rejected with scorn and he slinks away,
returning successively with a Land-captain, a Sea-captain,
a Flamen, and a Lawyer, who each in turn receive the
orb, and who are all equally resolute in refusing to
resign it to Deceit. Finally the orb is given back to the
king; Deceit, in company with the Devil (who arrived at
a late stage of the proceedings), finding himself baffled at
all points, withdraws not to return; and the others, after
an exhortation from the king, presently follow, leaving the original characters in possession of the stage.
Jupiter then delivers a valedictory address to the soldier
and scholar, impressing upon them that it will be their
own fault if they fail to prosper, for never was a brighter
career open for soldiers and scholars. He alludes
specially to James' patronage of learning, and to the

opportunities offered by the war in the Palatinate. The malcontents recant and the masque closes. There is one great merit in *The World Tost at Tennis ;* it is not tedious, as masques so frequently are. The verse was something more than a peg on which to hang the costumes. By the fireside it can be read with pleasure, and, handsomely mounted, it must have been received on the stage with applause.

On 6th September 1620 Middleton was appointed to the office of City Chronologer. His appointment is thus recorded [1] in the City Records :—

" 1620, 6th September, 18th James I.—Thomas Middleton, admitted City Chronologer. Item, this day was read in Court (of Aldermen) a petition of Thomas Middleton, Gent., and upon consideration thereof taken, and upon the sufficient testimony this Court hath received of his services performed to this City, this Court is well pleased to entertain and admit the said Thomas Middleton to collect and set down all memorable acts of this City and occurrences thereof, and for such other employments as this Court shall have occasion to use him in ; but the said Thomas Middleton is not to put any of the same acts so by him to be collected into print without the allowance and approbation of this Court; and for the readiness of his service to the City in the same employments this Court does order that he shall receive from henceforth, out of the Chamber of London, a yearly fee

---

[1] *Analytical Index to the Series of Records known as the Remembrancia* (printed for the Corporation in 1878), p. 305, n. The exact date of Middleton's appointment was unknown to Dyce.

of 6*l.* 13*s.* 4*d.*" On 20th November [1] of the same year
his salary was raised to ten pounds. On 17th April
1621 a Freedom was granted to him towards his expenses,
and on 7th May 1622 another Freedom was granted
for his better encouragement in his labours. On 17th
September 1622, for his further encouragement, he
received a gift of fifteen pounds, and on 6th February
1622–23 another gift of twenty pounds. On 24th April
1623 another Freedom was granted to him, and on
2d September 1623, for his services at the shooting
on Bunhill and at the Conduit Head before the Lord
Mayor and Aldermen, he was rewarded with twenty
marks. We learn from Oldys' annotated copy of Langbaine (preserved in the British Museum) that Middleton's
MS. City Chronicle was extant in the last century.
"There are two MSS. of this Author's [Middleton's] in
being which have never been taken notice of in any
Acco[t] of him. They were sold in an Auction of Books
at the Apollo Coffee House in Fleet Street ab[t] the year
1735 by Edw Lewis, but puff'd up to a great price, bought
back, & coud not afterw[ds] be recovered. They are
entitled I. *Annales :* or a Continuation of Chronologie ;
conteyninge Passages and Occurrences proper to the
Honno[ble] City of London : Beginninge in the Yeare of
our Lorde 1620. By Thomas Midleton then received
by their Honno[ble] Senate as Chronologer for the Cittye.

---

[1] This is the date given in *Remembrancia*, p. 305, n. According to
the extract which had been furnished to Dyce, the increase of salary
was granted on 23d January 1620–21.

There are in it these Articles under the year 1621.—On Good Fryday in the Morn died John (King) Lord Bp. of London.—28 May Fra. Ld Verulam committed to the Tower. (Seal taken from him the last day of April).—27 Decr. Sr Edwd Coke Committed to the Tower.—Decr. The Fortune Play House, situate between White Cross Street and Golding Lane, burnt, &c. II. *Middleton's Farrago:* In which there is—The Earl of Essex his Charge agt^t Visc^t Wimbleton, & the Visc^ts Answ^r.—The Treaty and Articles of Marriage between Pr. Cha : & Hen : Maria. — Parliamentary Matters, 1625–26.— Habeas Corpus 1627, &c."

Before we come to the consideration of the final group of tragedies and romantic comedies in which Middleton's genius was shown at its highest, it will be convenient to discuss *The Witch.* This tragi-comedy (first printed by Isaac Reed in 1770, from a MS. then in the possession of Major Pearson, and now preserved in the Malone Collection at Oxford) has received, owing to its Shakespearean interest, more attention than it deserves on its own merits. It is strangely ill-constructed and is not by any means one of Middleton's finest works, though uncritical writers have absurdly advanced it to the first place. In the MS. the play is stated to have been "long since acted by his Majesty's servants at the Blackfriars." We must not lay too much stress on the words "long since," as though they carried us back for many years. The King's men were not acting regularly at the Blackfriars before June 1613, when, at the destruction of the Globe, they had to seek fresh quarters. After the rebuilding of the Globe, they kept both houses for their own use.[1] This external evidence does not amount to much; for the King's men, though not regularly employed at the Blackfriars before 1613, may have acted there occasionally in earlier years. But looking at *The Witch* in connection with Middleton's other plays (and this is what previous critics have neglected to do), I should certainly refer it to the later part of his career,—to the period when he was no longer content with composing lively comedies of intrigue, but was turning his attention towards subjects of deeper moment. We have seen that (with the doubtful exception of *The Mayor of Queenborough,* which I consider to be a revised version of an early play) *A Fair Quarrel,* 1616–17, is the first of Middleton's plays in which the serious interest predominates. Without attempting to fix the exact date of *Macbeth,* we can with confidence refer it to 1606–10. In April 1610 Dr. Simon Forman witnessed a performance of *Macbeth* at the Globe. Now between the years 1606 and 1610 Middleton wrote *The Phœnix, Michaelmas Term, A Trick to Catch the Old One, The Family of Love, Your Five Gallants, A Mad World my Masters,* and a portion of *The Roaring Girl* (published in 1611). He had established his position as a writer of comedies of intrigue, and there is not a shred of evidence to show that he made during those years any essay in the direction of tragedy or tragi-comedy. Let us next consider the relation between *Macbeth* and *The Witch.* It is only in

---

[1] I am again relying on Mr. Fleay's *History of Theatres,* p. 4.

the incantation scenes that the resemblance [1] appears.
As to the essential difference between the witches of
Shakespeare and Middleton, it would be presumption in
an editor to attempt to add anything to Lamb's ex-
quisite criticism.   The hags in Ben Jonson's *Masque of
Queens* (1609) conduct their rites after much the same
fashion as Shakespeare's weird sisters.   But to guide
him in selecting the ingredients for Hecate's hell-broth,
Shakespeare needed not the wealth of learning which
Ben Jonson displayed in the footnotes of his masque.
The reports of the trials of the Scotch witches and
Scot's *Discovery of Witchcraft* would have furnished him
with all the details that he required.   It is not at all
surprising that the incantation scenes in *Macbeth* should
bear a general resemblance to the similar scenes in *The
Witch ;* indeed, it would be more extraordinary *not* to
find such resemblance.   But the difficulty lies in this fact,
that the stage-directions in *Macbeth* contain allusions to
two songs which are found in Middleton's *Witch.*   At
the close of Hecate's speech in iii. 5, after the words

> " And you all know Security
> Is mortals' chiefest enemy,"

the folio gives the stage-direction "*Music and a Song.*"
Hecate them exclaims—

> " Hark, I am called, my little spirit, see
> Sits in a foggy cloud and stays for me ; "

---

[1] Middleton frequently imitates in other plays Shakespearean expres-
sions ; so we need not be surprised to find echoes from *Macbeth*
in occasional passages of *The Witch.*   These petty larcenies prove
nothing.

and another stage-direction follows, " *Sing within.* ' Come away, come away,' &c." I quote in full the passage of *The Witch* (iii. 3.) where this song occurs :—

" *Song above.*

        Come away, come away,
        Hecate, Hecate, come away !
Hec. I come, I come, I come, I come,
        With all the speed I may,
        With all the speed I may.
        Where's Stadlin ?
        [*Voice above.*] Here.
Hec. Where's Puckle?
        [*Voice above.*] Here ;
        And Hoppo too, and Hellwain too ;
        We lack but you, we lack but you ;
        Come away, make up the count.
Hec. I will but 'noint, and then I mount.
               [*A Spirit like a cat descends.*
        [*Voice above.*] There's one comes down to fetch his dues,
        A kiss, a coll, a sip of blood ;
        And why thou stay'st so long
            I muse, I muse,
        Since the air's so sweet and good.
Hec. O, art thou come ?
            What news, what news ?
Spirit. All goes still to our delight :
        Either come, or else
            Refuse, refuse.
Hec. Now I'm furnish'd for the flight.
Fire. Hark, hark, the cat sings a brave treble in her own
language.
Hec. [*Going up.*] Now I go, now I fly,
        Malkin my sweet spirit and I.
        O what a dainty pleasure 'tis
        To ride in the air
        When the moon shines fair,

> And sing and dance and toy and kiss !
> Over woods, high rocks, and mountains,
> Over seas, our mistress' fountains,
> Over steep[y] towers and turrets,
> We fly by night, 'mongst troops of spirits :
> No ring of bells to our ears sounds,
> No howls of wolves, no yelps of hounds ;
> No, not the noise of cannons' breach,
> Or cannons' throat our height can reach.
> [*Voices above.*] No ring of bells," &c.

Again, in *Macbeth,* iv. 1, after Hecate's words—

> " And now about the cauldron sing,
>   Like elves and fairies in a ring,
>   Enchanting all that you put in,"

occurs the stage-direction " *Music and a Song.* ' Black Spirits,' " &c.   In *The Witch,* v. 2, we find—

" *Hec.* Stir, stir about, whilst I begin the charm.

A charm-song about a vessel.

> Black spirits and white, red spirits and gray,
> Mingle, mingle, mingle, you that mingle may !
>   Titty, Tiffin,
>   Keep it stiff in ;
>   Fire-drake, Puckey,
>   Make it lucky ;
>   Liard Robin,
>   You must bob in.
> Round, around, around, about, about !
> All ill come running in, all good keep out."

It is to be noticed that the songs found in the MS. of *The Witch* occur (with slight variations) in Davenant's alteration of *Macbeth,* 1674.   Now, looking at the first passage (" Come away, come away," &c.), it is plain to

the dullest reader that, though the first five lines are in
every way appropriate, what follows before we reach
Hecate's airy song is grotesquely out of keeping with the
solemnity of Shakespeare's Hecate. The fantastic lines
" Now I go, now I fly," &c., are undoubtedly fine as we
read them in *The Witch*, but, transferred to *Macbeth*, they
wantonly disturb our conception of the awful personage
who has just announced—

> " This night I'll spend
> Unto a dismal and a fatal end."

In regard to the second passage, it is equally clear that
only the two first lines and the two last could be attri-
buted to Shakespeare,—and the two last lines may be
dismissed without difficulty. It would be reasonable to
assume that five lines of the first passage and two (or
four) of the second belong to *Macbeth*, and were omitted
from the copy used by the editors of the First Folio.
It was not unusual to omit songs from the printed copies
of plays : none of Lyly's charming songs, for example,
are included in the first editions of his plays. But the
editors of the First Folio were more careful in this respect, and I can only suppose that the copy from which
they printed was slightly imperfect. *Macbeth* bears other
traces of having been printed from a faulty transcript.
Certainly no competent critic would deny that the
second scene of the first act has descended in an imperfect state. If my view is correct that *The Witch*
was written after *Macbeth*, Middleton would of course
have studied Shakespeare's play; and it is not at all

surprising that he should have taken these songs and expanded them. Nor, again, need we be amazed at the fact that Davenant was in possession of a playhouse copy of *Macbeth* containing additions from Middleton's play. The players dealt with Shakespeare's text as with any ordinary playwright's; they saw an opportunity of giving more " business " to Hecate and the witches by conveying passages from Middleton, and they were indifferent to the fact that they were degrading Shakespeare's creations. It is only, I repeat, in the incantation scenes that there is any resemblance between Middleton's poor play and Shakespeare's masterpiece. Yet, strange to relate, there have been found in our own day scholars [1] who have proposed to hand over to Middleton some of the finest passages in *Macbeth*. It will be enough for me to say that there is not a shadow or tittle of evidence, whether internal or external, to support these assertions.

Among the Conway papers in the Record Office is a MS. " Invention by Thomas Middleton, being a musical allegory performed for the service of Edward Barkham, Lord Mayor of London, when he entertained his brother aldermen at a feast in the Easter holidays, Ap. 22, 1622." I have printed it for the first time; it has little merit. In the same year Middleton produced the " Triumphs of Honour and Virtue " for the mayoralty of Peter Probyn. It was reprinted in 1845 among the

---

[1] Mr. Fleay in a private communication tells me that he has largely modified the views put forward in his *Shakespeare Manual.* I trust that Mr. Aldis Wright has also repented of his temerity.

Shakespeare Society's Papers from an unique exemplar. This and the preceding piece were unknown to Dyce.

Middleton, like many of his contemporaries, appears to have had no desire for posthumous fame. His finest works—*The Changeling, Women beware Women,* and *The Spanish Gipsy*—were not published in his lifetime. *The Changeling* was issued by Humphrey Mosely in 1653; and to the same publisher, whom all students of the English drama should respect, we owe *Women beware Women,* published (with *No Wit, no Help like a Woman's*) in 1657. *The Spanish Gipsy* was printed for Richard Marriot in 1653. Had these plays been destroyed, the loss to our dramatic literature would have been serious, for only here is Middleton's genius seen in its full maturity. Rowley assisted in the composition of *The Changeling* and *The Spanish Gipsy; Women beware Women* was written wholly by Middleton.

The Changeling is partly founded on Book I. Hist. 4 of Reynolds' *God's Revenge against Murder,* of which the earliest edition is dated 1621. A "Note of such plays as were acted at court in 1623 and 1624," in Sir Henry Herbert's office-book (Malone's *Shakespeare,* 1821, iii. 227) contains the entry—"Upon the Sunday after, being the 4 of January 1623, by the Queene of Bohemia's Company, *The Changeling,* the Prince only being there. At Whitehall." The play must have been written circ. 1621–23. I agree with Dyce in thinking that Middleton had the chief share in *The Changeling.* Rowley was probably responsible for the conduct of the

underplot. The wild extravagance of the madhouse
scenes is quite in his manner. I have little doubt that
the last scene of the play is by Rowley. The violence
of the language and the introduction of ill-timed comic
touches remind us of *All's Lost by Lust;* and the
metrical roughness is painfully prominent. There are
also occasional traces of Rowley in the opening scenes.

Regarded as an artistic whole, *The Changeling* cannot
challenge comparison with *The Maid's Tragedy, The
Broken Heart,* or *The Duchess of Malfi.* It has not the
sustained tragic interest of these masterpieces ; but there
is one scene in *The Changeling* which, for appalling
depth of passion, is not merely unsurpassed, but, I
believe, unequalled outside Shakespeare's greatest tragedies. Dismissing the underplot, let us follow the *summa
fastigia rerum.* Alsemero, seeking employment in the
wars, has arrived at Alicant on his way to Malta. In a
church at Alicant he sees Beatrice-Joanna, daughter to
Vermandero, governor of the castle, and is so smitten
with her beauty that he forgets the wars and thinks only
of making her his bride. A few days before Alsemero's
arrival Beatrice had been contracted to Alonzo de
Pivacquo, and the marriage was to be solemnised without delay ; but at first sight of Alsemero she falls pas-
sionately in love with him and loathes her contracted
husband. Alonzo's brother, Tomaso, notices the strangeness of her demeanour and endeavours to dissuade
Alonzo from the marriage ; but his counsel is ill-received.
In the service of Vermandero is a hard-favoured attendant, De Flores, a man of gentle birth but broken for-

tunes. He is possessed by an over-mastering passion
for Beatrice, who is disgusted with his attentions and
shrinks from him as from a poisonous creature, openly
scoffing at him, but in her inmost heart stirred with a
vague dread of him. As the marriage-day draws near
and she ponders over the situation, she can see help
only from one quarter—from the man whom she detests,
De Flores. She knows his devotion, and she knows also
his poverty. She changes her treatment towards him,
and greets him with smiles instead of frowns. De Flores
is ravished with delight :—

> " Her fingers touch'd me !
> She smells all amber."

Gradually she proceeds to discover to him her hatred
of Alonzo. He kneels to her and implores to be employed in her service. She imagines that his eagerness is
prompted by greed, and to spur his resolution gives him
gold, promising more when Alonzo is despatched :—

> "When the deed's done
> I'll furnish thee with all things for thy flight ;
> Thou may'st live bravely in another country."

When she retires he exclaims—

> "O my blood !
> Methinks I feel her in mine arms already ;
> Her wanton fingers combing out this beard,
> And, being pleased, praising this bad face.
> Hunger and pleasure, they'll commend sometimes
> Slovenly dishes, and feed heartily on 'em.
> Nay, which is stranger, refuse daintier for 'em.
> Some women are odd feeders."

At this moment he sees Alonzo approaching :—

> " Here comes the man goes supperless to bed,
>   Yet shall not rise to-morrow to his dinner."

Alonzo, who is the guest of Vermandero, has come to ask De Flores to conduct him over the castle and show him the strength of the fortifications. It is agreed that they shall make their tour of inspection immediately after dinner. To secure himself from interruption, Alonzo, before joining his guide, announces that he is going to take a gondola. The doomed man and De Flores, after passing through labyrinthine passages, reach a vault, the entrance to which is so narrow that they disencumber themselves of their rapiers in order to make freer progress. De Flores hangs up the weapons on hooks fitted in the wall for that purpose ; but he has previously concealed a naked rapier behind the door. While Alonzo is looking through a casement which affords a full view of the castle's strength, De Flores snatches the hidden weapon and stabs him several times in the back. On Alonzo's finger is a diamond ring which sparkles in the dimness of the vault. De Flores tries to draw the ring from the finger, that he may show it to Beatrice as evidence that the deed has been accomplished : but it clings obstinately, and to obtain it he has to cut off the finger. The meeting that presently follows between De Flores and Beatrice is the most powerful scene in the play. Hearing that Alonzo is despatched, she exclaims—

> "My joys start at mine eyes ; our sweet'st delights
> Are evermore born weeping."[1]

But at the sight of the dead man's ringed finger she retreats with a cry of horror, " Bless me, what hast thou done ? " De Flores observes grimly—

> "Why, is that more
> Than killing the whole man ? I cut his heart-strings.
> A greedy hand thrust in a dish at court
> Hath had as much as this."

Looking at the ring, she muses, " 'Tis the first token my father made me send him ; " but there is no touch of pity in her heart for the dead man. She bids De Flores bury the finger and keep the ring for himself; "at the stag's fall the keeper has his fees," and that ring is worth three hundred ducats. De Flores remarks—

> " Twill hardly buy a capcase for one's conscience though,
> To keep it from the worm, as fine as 'tis."

Beatrice hastens to add that she did not intend the ring to be his sole recompense ; then noticing his clouded countenance, she protests that it would be misery in

---

[1] Cf. *The Phœnix*, vol. i. p. 198 :—

> " Our joy breaks at our eyes ; the prince is come."

Again, in *The Old Law*, vol. ii. p. 204 :—

> " I've a joy weeps to see you, 'tis so full,
> So fairly fruitful."

In *The Changeling* we have the image presented in its final and faultless form.

her to give him cause for offence.   Sharp and significant
is the reply—

> " I know so much, it were so ; misery
> In her most sharp condition."

But Beatrice has not the least suspicion of the meaning
conveyed by the words.   She sees before her only a
man of broken fortunes, who for gold has stained his
hand with blood.   She offers him three thousand golden
florins.   He puts them by scornfully, with the remark
that he could have hired a journeyman in murder at
that rate.   Thinking that he is dissatisfied with the
amount, she offers to double it, but is met by the retort
that she is taking a course to double his vexation.   Still
not a hint of De Flores' purpose crosses her mind.   She
is anxious to bring the interview to an end ; the man's
obstinacy—his inordinate greed—is embarrassing ; she
must act with decision.   Alarmed but resolute, she
fronts him :—

> " For my fear's sake,
> I prithee, make away with all speed possible ;
> And if thou be'st so modest not to name
> The sum that will content thee, paper blushes not :
> Send thy demand in writing, it shall follow thee ;
> But, prithee, take thy flight."

He answers quietly, "You must fly too then."   With
astonishment she inquires his meaning.   He coolly reminds her that she is his partner in guilt, and points out
that his flight would at once draw suspicion on her.
Watching the effect of his words, he proceeds—

> " Nor is it fit we two, engag'd so jointly,
>   Should part and live asunder ; "

Then with a gesture of impatience as she shrinks from him—

> " What makes your lip so strange ? [1]
>   This must not be betwixt us."

At length she grasps the reality of the situation. But the man is her father's servant ; her dignity shall awe him into shame. As he presses forward for her embrace, she draws herself to her full height—

> " Speak it yet farther off, that I may lose
>   What has been spoken, and no sound remain on't ;
>   I would not hear so much offence again
>   For such another deed."

But she utterly miscalculates her power. Calm, through very intensity of passion, and keen as a knife's edge, is De Flores' answer—

> " Soft, lady, soft !
>   The last is not yet paid for : O, this act
>   Has put me into spirit ; I was as greedy on't
>   As the parch'd earth of moisture when the clouds weep :
>   Did you not mark, I wrought myself into't,
>   Nay, sued and kneeled for't ? Why was all that pains took ?
>   You see I've thrown contempt upon your gold ;
>   Not that I want it [not], for I do piteously ;
>   In order I'll come to't, and make use on't,
>   But 'twas not held so precious to begin with,
>   For I place wealth after the heels of pleasure ;

---

[1] So in Middleton's *Women beware Women*, iii. 1 :—

> " Speak, what's the humour sweet,
>   *You make your lip so strange !* "

> And were I not resolv'd in my belief
> That thy virginity were perfect in thee,
> I should but take my recompense with grudging,
> As if I had but half my hopes I agreed for."

Still she will not abandon all hope, but tries desperately to retain her self-possession :—

> "Thy language is so bold and vicious,
> I cannot see which way I can forgive it
> With any modesty."

Here De Flores loses patience :—

> "Push! you forget yourself;
> A woman dipp'd in blood and talk of modesty!"

She bids him remember the barrier that her birth had set between them. "Push! fly not to your birth!" he retorts :—

> "You must forget your parentage to me;
> You are the deed's creature; by that name
> You lost your first condition, and I challenge you,
> As peace and innocency has turn'd you out
> And made you one with me."

She prostituted her affections when she abandoned her affianced husband for Alsemero, and she shall never enjoy Alsemero unless she first yields her body to the murderer's embraces. De Flores has no care for his own life; he will confess all if she refuses. Her pride is crushed, and she kneels at the feet of the man whom she was wont to spurn :—

> "Stay, hear me once for all; I make thee master
> Of all the wealth I have in gold and jewels;
> Let me go poor unto my bed with honour
> And I am rich in all things."

The last spark of hope is quenched by the relentless answer :—

> "Let this silence thee ;
> The wealth of all Valencia shall not buy
> My pleasure from me ;
> Can you weep Fate from its determin'd purpose?
> So soon may [you] weep me."

Neither Webster nor Cyril Tourneur nor Ford has given us any single scene so profoundly impressive, so absolutely ineffaceable, so Shakespearean as this colloquy between Beatrice and De Flores. In *A Fair Quarrel* Middleton showed how nobly he could depict moral dignity ; but this scene of *The Changeling* testifies beyond dispute that, in dealing with a situation of sheer passion, none of Shakespeare's followers trod so closely in the master's steps.

The latter part of the play contains some powerful writing, but there is no scene that can be compared for a moment with the terrible colloquy. Vermandero construes Alonzo's disappearance as a dishonourable flight. Resenting the supposed insult, he lends a willing ear to Alsemero's suit, and is anxious to have the match concluded without delay. Beatrice is in perplexity as the marriage day draws near ; but I must be excused for passing over the device by which she conceals the loss of her virginity from Alsemero. Meanwhile Tomaso has a shrewd suspicion of foul play, but knows not on whom to fasten the guilt. By a sort of instinct he suspects De Flores—"honest

De Flores," as men call him. Honest De Flores! a
queen would as soon fix her palace in a pest-house as
Honesty would seek a lodging in this ill-favoured fellow.
De Flores is uncomfortable in Tomaso's presence, and
seeks to avoid him. On one occasion Tomaso strikes
him, but he has no power to draw :—

> "I cannot strike ; I see his brother's wounds
> Fresh bleeding in his eye as in a chrystal."

But the catastrophe is at hand. Alsemero's friend,
Jasperino, has observed passages of familiarity between
De Flores and Beatrice. He reports what he has seen
to Alsemero. A powerful scene follows, in which Beatrice confesses to Alsemero that she procured the murder of Alonzo, but denies the charge of unchastity.
Alsemero will not act rashly ; he locks her in a closet
while he ponders his plan of conduct. At this moment
De Flores enters. Confronted with Beatrice's confession,
he proceeds to disclose what she had suppressed. " He
lies ! the villain does belie me !" cries Beatrice from
within. Alsemero unlocks the closet and sends in De
Flores. At this point Vermandero and Tomaso enter
with two prisoners who have been seized on suspicion
of having murdered Alonzo. As Vermandero is pro-
ceeding to explain the circumstances of their arrest, cries
are heard issuing from the closet, and presently De
Flores re-enters dragging in Beatrice. Wounded to the
death, she has just strength enough to confess her guilt
and declare her penitence. But there is no touch of

shame in De Flores. He has had his enjoyment of Beatrice and is content to die :—

> "I thank life for nothing
> But that pleasure : it was so sweet to me
> That I have drunk up all, left none behind."

An attempt is made to lay hands on him that he may be reserved for torture, but he frustrates the intention by dealing himself a mortal stab—"it is but one thread more, and now 'tis cut."

The Changeling was revived at the Restoration. Under date 23d February 1660–61, Pepys entered in his Diary —"To the Playhouse and there saw *The Changeling*, the first time it hath been acted these twenty years, and it takes exceedingly." From Downes' *Roscius Anglicanus* we learn that Betterton, about the age of twenty-two, sustained the character of De Flores.[1]

A "Note of such playes as were acted at court in 1623 and 1624," in Sir Henry Herbert's office-book, contains the entry : "Upon the fifth of November at Whitehall, the Prince being there only, *The Gipsye*, bye the Cockpitt company" (Malone's *Shakespeare*, 1821, iii. 227). From a passage in ii. 1 we may conjecture that *The Spanish Gipsy* was a later play than *The Changeling*, and that the part of Constanza was taken by an actor who had given satisfaction as Antonio.

---

[1] The part of the pretended madman, Antonio (in the underplot), from which the play takes its name (*Changeling* = idiot), was sustained with success before the Revolution by Robbins, and at the Restoration by Sheppy (see Collier's *Hist. of Engl. Dram. Lit.*, ii. 107, ed. 1).

The Spanish Gipsy is an admirable example of a well-contrived and well-written romantic comedy. It is at once fantastic and pathetic, rippling with laughter and dashed with tears ; a generous, full-blooded play. The introductory scenes are peculiarly impressive, filling the reader with wonder as to how a tragic issue is to be averted. Roderigo, son of the corregidor of Madrid, has fallen in love with a girl whom he has casually seen, and with whose name he is unacquainted. He has noticed her walking a few paces behind an old gentleman and his wife, but he knows not whether she is their daughter or servant. Whoever she may be, he has determined to possess her. He communicates to his friends Louis and Diego his intention of forcibly carrying her off, and requests their assistance, which (with some reluctance on Louis' part) they agree to render. An opportunity is presently offered : the old couple is seen approaching in the dusk of evening, followed by the maiden. Roderigo secures his prize and hurries away, while the elders are firmly held by Louis and Diego. But when the old man exclaims, " Do you not know me ? I am De Cortes, Pedro de Cortes," Louis quickly looses his hold, and bidding Diego follow, takes to flight. Louis is the accepted of De Cortes's daughter, whom he has unwittingly betrayed to dishonour. Meanwhile Roderigo by a private garden-way has conveyed his victim to his father's house. A noble scene ensues, in which the dishonoured lady confronts her unknown ravisher :—

> " Though the black veil of night hath overclouded
> The world in darkness, yet ere many hours

The sun will rise again, and then this act
Of my dishonour will appear before you
More black than is the canopy that shrouds it :
What are you, pray ? what are you ? "

The ravisher's spirit is quelled; he can but answer in
monosyllables. " Not speak to me ? are wanton devils
dumb ? " she cries; women's honour would be safe if
men could plead no better than " this untongued piece of
violence." Then she flings herself upon him and clutches
him fast : " You shall not from me." He offers her gold,
but she replies—

> " I need no wages for a ruin'd name
> More than a broken heart."

Impatiently shaking her off, he retires and locks the
door. Left alone in the darkness, she gropes her way
towards the window, invoking the " lady-regent of the
air, the moon," to light her to some brave vengeance.
As she draws aside the window-curtains, she sees by the
starlight a fair garden, in the centre of which is an
alabaster fountain. Then her glance wanders round the
richly furnished chamber and lights upon a crucifix,
which she conceals in her bosom. Just when she has
concluded these rapid observations, by which she will
be able to identify that room hereafter, Roderigo returns.
He professes penitence for his sin and offers all repara-
tion in his power. She will not disclose her name ; she
will take her shame with her to the grave ; but she has
two requests to make of him : first, that neither in riot
of mirth nor in privacy of friendship nor in idle talk he

shall mention the wrong that he has done; and, secondly, that he shall lead her back, before the morning rise, to the place where he met her. He solemnly promises to fulfil the conditions, and she passes veiled from the house.

It is indeed a sombre introduction, preparing us to expect some tale of blood and vengeance. I leave the reader to discover by what smooth channels the argument is conducted to a peaceful issue. *The Spanish Gipsy* [1] has all the interest of a novel; stripped of its poetry and reduced to a mere prose narrative, it would hold the reader's attention. In the gipsy scenes (which were, doubtless, largely the work of Rowley) we breathe the fresh air of the woodlands, and the songs have the genuine ring of rollicking freedom. There are few more charming figures than that of the young maiden, Constanza, who in gipsy guise follows her exiled father in his wanderings, singing and dancing in the booths of fairs, sportive as a squirrel and maidenly as Rosalind.

The Spanish Gipsy opened gloomily and ended cheerfully, but in *Women, beware Women*, the reverse process is adopted. The introduction to this powerful tragedy is singularly sweet. Leantio, a young factor, has married without her parents' consent a Venetian beauty, Bianca, and brings her to his mother's house at Florence. Bianca

---

[1] "Two stories," says Professor Ward, "taken from Cervantes are here—not very closely—interwoven, that of Roderigo and Clara being drawn from *La Fuerze de la Sangre* (The Force of Blood), that of the Gipsies from *La Gitanilla*."

has cheerfully abandoned her rich home to share her lover's slender fortunes. She is devoted to him, and he to her. The widowed mother is fearful that the house will afford poor entertainment for so high-born a lady, but Bianca with winning grace professes herself perfectly happy. In a few days Leantio's affairs oblige him to leave his wife. He gives his mother directions that Bianca should not be seen abroad, for he is jealous of her beauty, and dreads lest his treasure should be snatched from him. The leave-taking is most charmingly described. "But this one night, I prithee," whispers Bianca imploringly, and it must have been difficult indeed to resist such an appeal; but his affairs will brook no delay, and he knows that one night will mean twenty, and then forty more, if he stays; besides, he is to return in five days. Bianca acquiesces, but cannot control her tears when she perceives that he is really gone. While the widow is cheering and consoling her as they sit by the window, a crowd of sightseers gathers in the streets. The widow remembers that it is the day on which the Duke and nobles hold their solemn annual procession. Presently the procession draws near with music and song: in front are six knights bare-headed, then two cardinals, followed by the Lord Cardinal and his brother the Duke, in whose train come the nobles two by two. Bianca is enchanted with the magnificence of the spectacle; her vanity also is flattered, for she assures the widow that the Duke cast a glance at the window as he passed; whereupon the old lady sensibly remarks—

> " That's every one's conceit that sees a duke;
>   If he look steadfastly, he looks straight at them,
>   When he, perhaps, good, careful gentleman,
>   Never minds any, but the look he casts
>   Is at his own intentions, and his object
>   Only the public good."

But Bianca is right; the Duke did notice her, and he determines to make prize of her beauty. To effect his purpose he employs the services of a clever and abandoned court lady, Livia, who sets to work with devilish cunning. She invites the widow to her house, pleasantly chides her for living so much in seclusion, and hopes she will be a frequent guest. The poor widow, anxious about her daughter-in-law, who is sitting lonely at home, endeavours to bring the visit quickly to a close; but Livia insists that she shall stay, and they sit down to play chess. Attracted by Livia's sympathetic manner, the widow discloses the secret of her son's marriage, and without much persuasion is induced to send for Bianca, who presently arrives and is cordially welcomed. While Livia and the widow continue their game, Guardiano (a creature of the Duke's) shows Bianca round the picture-gallery. As she is expressing her delight at the wonders of the gallery, Guardiano tells her that the fairest piece yet remains; he draws aside a curtain and the Duke steps from his concealment. At first she makes a bold stand against the Duke's solicitations; but when to adroit flattery he adds dazzling promises of the greatness that he will confer upon her (not without hints of violence in case of her refusal), soon her resistance is weakened, and after no severe struggle she capitulates. As she returns, outwardly calm, from the Duke's embraces to her protectress's side, she is filled with loathing for the infamous creatures who have betrayed her. But she is not of the stuff of which heroines are made, and when the first feeling of shame is past, she treads the path of sin unblushingly. Her change of manner perplexes and distresses the unsuspecting widow :—

> " She was but one day abroad, but ever since
> She's grown so cutted there's no speaking to her:
> Whether the sight of great cheer at my lady's,
> And such mean fare at home, work discontent in her,
> I know not; but I'm sure she's strangely alter'd.
> I'll ne'er keep daughter-in-law i' th' house with me
> Again, if I had an hundred."

On the fifth day Leantio returns. His heart is brimming with love for his young bride ; as he draws near his home and deliciously muses on the contentment that his marriage has brought him, the very air around the house seems laden with blessings. But at the first sight of Bianca his joy is dashed to the ground. No loving arms are stretched out to welcome him ; a few cold words of greeting, and then Bianca proceeds to complain of the meanness of her lodging and protest that she will not be mewed up from society. While Leantio is endeavouring to pacify his wife, a knocking is heard at the door. Bianca is hurried into another room and a messenger enters; he has come from the Duke with a message to Bianca. Leantio protests that there is no such person in the house, that he has never heard the name before ; and with this answer the messenger retires.

When Bianca hears from her distracted husband that
she has been summoned to the palace, she hastens, to
his amazement, to obey the summons.   Left alone, he
muses bitterly, converting into curses the blessings that
he had lately pronounced on marriage.   Presently the
messenger returns, summoning him to the Duke's presence.   Arrived at the palace, he sees the Duke whispering in Bianca's ear, and knows that his last hope
is gone.   To be rid of Leantio's presence, the Duke
appoints him to the captaincy of some distant castle.
Leantio retains his composure and expresses his grati-
tude, but his heart is being riven in twain.   He is
no tame cuckold ; he has loved deeply and he can hate
deeply :—

> " She's gone for ever, utterly ; there is
> As much redemption of a soul from hell
> As a fair woman's body from his palace.
> Why should my love last longer than her truth ?
> What is there good in woman to be lov'd,
> When only that which makes her so has left her ?
> I cannot love her now, but I must like
> Her sin and my own shame too, and be guilty
> Of law's breach with her, and mine own abusing ;
> All which were monstrous : then my safest course,
> For health of mind and body, is to turn
> My heart and hate her, most extremely hate her."

It is a pitiful, thrice-pitiful story, worked out with relentless skill to a ghastly catastrophe.   The passionate
energy and concentrated bitterness of the language is as
remarkable as in *The Changeling.*

The comedy *More Dissemblers besides Women* was

licensed by Sir Henry Herbert to the King's Company on 17th October 1623, without fee, as being an "old play," which had been previously licensed by Sir George Buc (Chalmers' *Supplem. Apol.*, p. 215). Dyce thought that the word "old" proves the play to have been "produced a considerable time previous to the year 1623;" but it is, I think, merely a term applied to such plays as had been previously licensed. Sir George Buc ("by reason of sickness and indisposition of body wherewith it had pleased God to visit him") resigned the post of Master of the Revels in May 1622. Before that date the comedy must have been written; but it is evidently a late work, more elaborate and substantial than the early comedies. The guileless Cardinal, with an inexhaustible stock of moral reflections and an implicit belief in the purity of his scapegrace nephew, Lactantio, is drawn with tenderness and care. Equally successful is the character of the Duchess, who, having vowed "ne'er to know love's heat in a second husband," after seven years of widowhood suddenly has her resolution shaken, but quickly checks the course of her affections when she finds that the man whom she admires is devoted to another mistress, and, after composing differences all round, returns to the strictness of her former life. A witty serving-man, Dondolo, contributes not a little to the entertainment. The girl-page who accompanies the profligate Lactantio is a pathetic little figure; but it is a pity that Middleton adopted so intolerably gross a device for discovering her condition to the Duchess.

In 1623 Middleton composed the pageant *The Tri-*

umphs of Integrity for Sir Martin Lumley's mayoralty.
It was mounted on an elaborate scale, the chief feature
in the spectacle being the Chrystal Sanctuary, styled the
Temple of Integrity, "where her immaculate self, with
all her glorious and sanctimonious concomitants, sit,
transparently seen through the chrystal." The columns
were of gold and the battlements of silver, and "the
whole fabric for the night-triumph [was] adorned and
beautified with many lights, dispersing their glorious
radiance on all sides through the chrystal."

We have now to consider the most curious incident
in Middleton's career—the circumstances attending the
production of *A Game at Chess.* When the proposed
Spanish marriage, which had been very unpopular with
the English people, was broken off in the autumn of
1623, Middleton in *A Game of Chess* gave voice to the
satisfaction of his countrymen at the failure of negotia-
tions and their detestation of Spanish intrigues. The
play was acted with great applause in August 1624
for nine days continuously; then a strong protest from
Gondomar, the Spanish Ambassador, caused 'its with-
drawal, and both author and actors were summoned to
appear before the Privy Council. The official correspondence in regard to the matter has been preserved.
On 12th August 1624 Mr. Secretary Conway addressed
the following letter to the Privy Council :—

"May it please your Lordships,—His Majesty hath received
information from the Spanish Ambassador of a very scandalous
comedy acted publickly by the King's players, wherein they take
the boldness and presumption, in a rude and dishonourable fashion,

to represent on the stage the persons of his Majesty, the King of Spain, the Conde de Gondomar, the Bishop of Spalato, &c. His Majesty remembers well there was a commandment and restraint given against the representing of any modern Christian kings in those stage-plays; and wonders much both at the boldness now taken by that company, and also that it hath been permitted to be so acted, and that the first notice thereof should be brought to him by a foreign ambassador, while so many ministers of his own are thereabouts, and cannot but have heard of it. His Majesty's pleasure is, that your Lordships presently call before you as well the poet that made the comedy as the comedians that acted it : And upon examination of them to commit them, or such of them as you shall find most faulty, unto prison, if you find cause, or otherwise take security for their forthcoming; and then certify his Majesty what you find that comedy to be, in what points it is most offensive, by whom it was made, by whom licensed, and what course you think fittest to be held for the exemplary and severe punishment of the present offenders, and to restrain such insolent and licentious presumption for the future. This is the charge I have received from his Majesty, and with it I make bold to offer to your Lordships the humble service of, &c. From Rufford, August 12th, 1624."

Their Lordships on 21st August sent the following answer :—

"After our hearty commendations, &c.—According to his Majesty's pleasure signified to this Board by your letter of the 12th of Aug., touching the suppressing of a scandalous comedy acted by the King's players, we have called before us some of the principal actors, and demanded of them by what license and authority they have presumed to act the same ; in answer whereto they produced a book being an original and perfect copy thereof (as they affirmed) seen and allowed by Sir Henry Herbert, Knt., Master of the Revels, under his own hand, and subscribed in the last page of the said book : We demanding further, whether there were not other parts or passages represented on the stage than those expressly contained in the book, they confidently protested they added or varied from the same nothing at all. The poet, they tell us, is one Middleton, who shifting out of the way, and not attending the Board with the rest, as was expected, we have given warrant to a messenger for the apprehending of him. To those that were before us we gave a round[1] and sharp reproof, making them sensible of his Majesty's high displeasure herein, giving them strait charge and commands that they presumed not to act the said comedy any more, nor that they suffered any play or interlude whatsoever to be acted by them or any of their company until his Majesty's pleasure be further known. We have caused them likewise to enter into bond for their attendance upon the Board whensoever they shall be called. As for our certifying to his Majesty (as was intimated by your letter) what passages in the said comedy we should find to be offensive and scandalous ; we have thought it our duties for his Majesty's clearer information to send herewithal the book itself subscribed as aforesaid by the Master of the Revels, that so either yourself or some other whom his Majesty shall appoint to peruse the same, may see the passages themselves out of the original, and call Sir Henry Herbert before you to know a reason of his licensing thereof, who (as we are given to understand) is now attending at court. So having done as much as we conceived agreeable with our duties in conformity to his Majesty's royal commandments, and that which we hope shall give him full satisfaction, we shall continue our humble prayers to Almighty God for his health and safety ; and bid you very heartily farewell."

On the 27th Conway wrote again :—

"Right Honourable,—His Majesty having received satisfaction in your Lordships' endeavours, and in the signification thereof to him by yours of the 21st of this present, hath commanded me to signify the same to you. And to add further, that his pleasure is, that your Lordships examine by whose direction and application the personating of Gondomar and others was done ; and that being found out, the party or parties to be severely punished, his Majesty

---

[1] Dyce (following Chalmers) printed "sound," but "round" is the reading in the register.

being unwilling for one's sake and only fault to punish the innocent or utterly to ruin the company. The discovery on what party his Majesty's justice is properly and duly to fall, and your execution of it and the account to be returned thereof, his Majesty leaves to your Lordships' wisdoms and care. And this being that I have in charge, continuing the humble offer of my service and duty to the attendance of your commandments, &c. From Woodstock, the 27th August 1624."[1]

On the same day the following letter[2] was addressed by the Lord Chamberlain to the Lord President of the Council :—

"To the right hon^ble my very good Lord, the Lord Viscount Maundeville, Lord President of his Majesty's most hon^ble Privy Counsell, theis.

My very good Lord

Complaynt being made unto his Majesty against the Company of his Comedians, for acting publiquely a Play knowne by the name of a Game at Chesse, contayning some passages in it reflecting in matter of scorne and ignominy upon the King of Spaine, some of his Ministers and others of good note and quality, his Majesty out of the tender regard hee had of that King's honor and those of his Ministers who were conceived to bee wounded thereby, caused his letters to bee addressed to my Lords and the rest of his most hon^ble Privy Council, thereby requiring them to convent those his Comedians before them, and to take such course with them for this offence as might give best satisfaction to the Spanish Ambassador and to their owne Honnors. After examination that hon^ble Board thought fitt not onely to interdict them playing of that play, but of any other

---

[1] This correspondence was first printed in Chalmers' *Apology for the Believers in the Shakespeare Papers*, p. 497, sqq.

[2] "The original is in the State Paper Office : for the transcript I am indebted to Mr. J. P. Collier."—*Dyce.* But in the second edition of his *Hist. of Eng. Dram. Lit.* Collier says that the original was in possession of the late Mr. F. Ouvry.

also, untill his Majesty should give way unto them.   And for their
obedience hereunto they weare bound in 300^li bondes.   Which
punishment when they had suffered (as his Majesty conceives) a
competent tyme, upon their petition delivered heere unto him, it
pleased his Majesty to comaund mee to lett your Lordship understand (which I pray your Lordship to impart to the rest of that
hon^ble Board) that his Majesty now conceives the punishment, if
not satisfactory for that their insolency, yet such as since it stopps
the current of their poore livelyhood and mainteanance, without
much prejudice they cannot longer undergoe.   In consideration
therefore of those his poore servants, his Majesty would have their
Lordships connive at any common play lycensed by authority, that
they shall act as before.   As for this of the Game at Chesse, that
it bee not onely antiquated and sylenced, but the Players bound as
formerly they weare, and in that point onely never to act it agayne.
Yet notwithstanding that my Lords proceed in their disquisition to
fynd out the originall roote of this offence, whether it sprang from
the Poet, Players, or both, and to certefy his Majesty accordingly.
And so desireing your Lordship to take this into consideration, and
them into your care, I rest

Yo^r Lo^ds most affectionate

Cousin to serve you,

PEMBROKE."

Under date 30th August 1624 the Council register
contains the entry :—

"This day Edward Middleton of London, gent. being formerly
sent for by warrant from this Board, tendred his appearance,
wherefor his indemnitie is here entered into the register of counceil
causes ; nevertheless he is enjoyned to attend the Board till he be
discharged by order from their Lordships."

Dyce inserts "Thomas" in brackets after "Edward,"
supposing that the clerk of the Privy Council made an
error in the name.   But Dyce had not personally in-

spected the register; he relied entirely on Chalmers. It was pointed out by a writer in the Shakespeare Society's Papers that the person who tendered his appearance was the poet's son. Under date 27th August 1624 is the following entry in the register : [1]— "A warrant directed to Robert Goffe, one of the Messengers of His Ma^ts Chamber to bring one Middleton *sonne to Midleton the Poet* before their Llo^ps to answer," &c.

A copy of *A Game at Chess*, formerly in the possession of Major Pearson, and now preserved in the Dyce Library at South Kensington, has the following MS. note in an old hand :—

"After nyne dayse wherein I have heard some of the acters say they tooke fiveteene hundred Pounde the spanish faction being prevalent gott it supprest the chiefe actors and the Poett Mr. Thomas Middleton that writt it committed to prisson where hee lay some Tyme and at last gott oute upon this petition presented to King James.

> 'A harmles game : coynd only for delight
> was playd betwixt the black house and the white
> the white house wan : yet still the black doth bragg
> they had the power to put mee in the bagge
> use but your royall hand. Twill set mee free
> Tis but removing of a man thats mee.'"

Dyce, following Malone, gave his opinion that the statement in regard to the receipts was a gross exaggeration; but he did not sufficiently realise the intense

---

[1] My thanks are due to the Clerk of the Council, C. Lennox Peel, Esq., C.B., for his courtesy in allowing me to consult the register.

excitement caused by the performances. If Dyce had
seen the following letter of Chamberlain to Carleton,
dated 21st August 1624, he would probably have modified his opinion :—" I doubt not but you have heard
of our famous play of Gondomar, which hath been
followed with extraordinary curiosity, and frequented
by all sorts of people, old and young, rich and poor,
masters and servants, papists, wise men, &c., church-
men and Scotsmen, as Sir Henry Wotton, Sir Albert
Morton, Sir Benjamin Rudyard, Sir Thomas Lake, and
a world besides. The Lady Smith would have gone
if she could have persuaded me to go thither. I am
not so sour nor so severe but that I would willingly
have attended her, but I could not sit so long, for we
must have been there before one o'clock at farthest to
find any room. They counterfeited his person to the
life, with all his graces and faces, and had gotten, they
say, a cast suit of his apparel for the purpose, and his
letter, wherein the world says there lacked nothing but
a couple of asses to carry it, and Sir George Petre or
Sir Tobie Matthew to bear him company. But the
worst is, playing him, they played somebody else, for
which they are forbidden to play that or any other play
till the King's further pleasure be known ; and they may
be glad if they can so escape Scot-free. The wonder
lasted but nine days, for so long they played it " (*Court
and Times of James I.*, ii. 472–473).

A Game at Chess contains some very caustic satire
against Gondomar (the Black Knight), whose fair-seem-
ing hypocrisy is exposed with masterly power, while his

bodily infirmities are ridiculed with provoking persistence.
The satirist's lash falls heavily on the apostate Bishop of
Spalato[1] (the Fat Bishop), who is represented as a swag-
bellied monster of gluttony — and lecherous withal.
There is abundant evidence to show that the satire was
keenly appreciated. Three editions—without date, but
probably printed in 1624—have come down, and Collier
possessed a title-page of an edition dated 1625. A
MS. copy is preserved in the British Museum, another
at Trinity College, Cambridge, and a third (imperfect)
at Bridgewater House. It is curious to note that Sir
Thomas Browne possessed a MS. of the play (Browne's
Works, ed. Wilkin, 1835, iv. 470). Howel, in a letter [2]
to Sir John North from Madrid, writes :—"I am sorry
to hear how other nations so much tax the English
of their incivility to public Ministers of State ; and
what ballads and pasquils and fopperies and plays
were made against Gondomar for doing his master's
business" (*Letters*, ed. 1678, p. 123). Ben Jonson in
iii. 1 of *The Staple of News* (acted in 1625) has a
passage—too indelicate to quote—about Gondomar and
"the poor English play was writ of him." Fletcher in
the prologue to *Rule a Wife and Have a Wife* makes
an allusion to *A Game at Chess* :—

---

[1] In a note prefixed to the play I shall endeavour to identify some of
the other characters.

[2] The letter is dated "August 15, 1623 ; " but Oldys in his annotated
copy of Langbaine remarks :—"The first edition [of Howel's *Letters*]
in 4to, 1645, is in six parts or sections ; but no dates to any of the
letters ; hence so many errors when he did date them."

"Do not your looks let fall,
Nor to remembrance our late errors call,
Because this day we're Spaniards all again,
The story of our play and our scene Spain :
The errors, too, do not for this cause hate ;
Now we present their wit, and not their state."

The extraordinary applause that the play won was remembered as a stage-tradition for many years. In Davenant's *Playhouse to be Let* (first acted in 1663) an actor brings word to his fellows—"There's such a crowd at doors as if we had *a new play of Gondomar*."

Two comedies, *The Widow* and *Anything for a Quiet Life*, remain for consideration. *The Widow* was published in 1652 by Humphrey Moseley as the work of Jonson, Fletcher, and Middleton. I must confess, with Gifford, that I cannot discover any traces of Jonson's hand. Collier was surprised that Gifford "did not trace his pen through the whole of the fourth act;" but to me the scene where Latrocinio disguises himself as an empiric and dispenses his nostrums in a hired room of an inn, seems rather to be imitated from Ben Jonson than written by him. Nor can I discover Fletcher's hand, unless the songs be his. Dyce pointed out that a conceit in iv. 2 is found in *The Honest Lawyer*, a play by "S. S.," printed in 1616. "S. S." is a very poor writer, and it is hardly probable that Middleton would have taken the trouble to borrow from such a source.[1]

---

[1] I follow Dyce in spite of Mr. Fleay's assertion that "the argument from the 'imitation' in *The Honest Lawyer* is imbecile. It is not possible to say which author was the imitator." Mr. Fleay's own views about *The Widow* may be seen in his article on Middleton in *Shakespeariana*, No. xii.

In v. 1 we have a mention of "yellow bands" as "hateful,"—an evident allusion to the execution (Nov. 1615) of the infamous Mrs. Turner, the poisoner, who invented yellow bands and wore a yellow ruff at the gallows. In i. 2 ("You play a scornful woman") there appears to be an allusion to Beaumont and Fletcher's *Scornful Lady*, which was written some time between 1609 and 1615. From internal evidence I should be inclined to group *The Widow* with a *Mad World, my Masters*, and *A Trick to Catch the Old One*, assigning 1608–9 as the date of original production. It was revised at a later date—not improbably by Fletcher.

Anything for a Quiet Life was printed in 1662. According to Malone, "it appears from internal evidence to have been written about the year 1619" (*Shakespeare*, ed. 1821, xv. 425). Mr. Fleay, without giving any reason for his judgment, assigns *circ.* 1623 as the date of production. In i. 1 we have mention of "the late ill-starred voyage to Guiana." Dyce supposed that a reference was intended to the first voyage under Raleigh in 1595, but Middleton must certainly have been alluding to something more recent—probably to the voyage of 1617. In ii. 1 there may perhaps be a reference to *The Changeling* ("You shall see me play the Changeling"). The project, ridiculed in i. 1, of "devising new water mill[s]for the recovery of drowned lands" is mentioned in Ben Jonson's *The Devil is an Ass*, ii. 1, acted in 1616. I suspect that the play in its present shape has been revised by another hand. The character of Lady Cressingham is drawn very much in the manner of

Shirley, who delighted to ridicule the whims and extravagances of high-bred ladies. Perhaps Middleton left the play unfinished and Shirley completed it.

In 1626 Middleton composed the pageant *The Triumphes of Health and Prosperity* for the mayoralty of Sir Cuthbert Hacket. The first speech makes allusion to the devastations (so graphically described in Thomas Brewer's *Weeping Lady*) caused by the plague in the previous year.

We have seen that in 1623 (*vide* note 1, p. xii.) Middleton was living in Newington Butts. He was buried there on 4th July 1627, as Dyce discovered from an entry in the register of the parish church.[1] On 7th February 1627–28 his widow, Magdalen Middleton, applied to the civic authorities for pecuniary assistance, and received twenty nobles. The entry (Rep. No. 42, f. 89) runs :—

---

[1] Chetwood in his account of Middleton, prefixed to a reprint of *Blurt, Master Constable*, in a *Select Collection of Old Plays*, Dublin, 1750, tells us that Middleton "lived to a very great age. . . . We may judge of his longævity by his works ; since his first play was acted in 1601 and his last in 1665. . . . That he was much esteem'd by his brother poets we may judge by four lines of Sir William Lower upon his comedy call'd *A Michaelmas Term*, 1663." The four lines given by Chetwood are :—

> "Tom Middleton his numerous issue brings,
> And his last Muse delights us when she sings ;
> His halting age a pleasure doth impart,
> And his white locks show Master of his Art."

Chetwood took a pride and pleasure in gulling his readers : *Michaelmas Term* was printed in 1607, and there is no edition of 1663. The ingenious lines ascribed to Sir William Lower (who died in 1662) are of course a forgery.

"Item : this day, upon the humble petition of Magdalen Middleton, late wife of Thomas Middleton, deceased, late Chronologer of this City, it is ordered by this Court that Mr. Chamberlain shall pay unto her as the gift of this Court the sum of twenty nobles." A " Mrs. Midelton " was buried at Newington Butts on 18th July 1628 (as appears from an entry in the parish register) : she was doubtless the dramatist's widow. Ben Jonson succeeded Middleton in the post of City Chronologer.

There can be little doubt that Middleton was concerned in the authorship of more than one of the plays included among the works of Beaumont and Fletcher. I reserve that point for consideration hereafter in my Introduction to Beaumont and Fletcher. Mr. Fleay attributes to Middleton *A Match at Midnight* and *The Puritan.* The first of these comedies was printed in 1633, and is ascribed on the title-page to " W. R." *i.e.* William Rowley. I strongly favour Mr. Fleay's view that Rowley merely altered it (*circ.* 1622) for a revival, and that the real author was Middleton. It is written very much in the style of Middleton's early comedies of intrigue. *The Puritan* was published in 1607, and the title-page states that it was "written by W. S.,"—a fraudulent attempt to induce the public to believe that Shakespeare was the author, though Dyce and others suppose the initials to belong to Wentworth Smith. Middleton wrote a play called *The Puritan Maid, Modest Wife and Wanton Widow* (entered in the Stationers' Registry, 9th September 1653) ; but this title will hardly suit *The Puritan,* which, nevertheless, I believe to be by Middleton. One curious expression in *The Puritan* (C 3), "by yon Bear at Bridge-foot in heaven," re-occurs in Middleton's *No Wit, No Help like a Woman's* (vol. iv. p. 415). Steevens, not understanding the joke, altered the word "heaven" to "even" in *The Puritan.* Throughout the play we are reminded of Middleton. The satire on the Puritans is what we find in *The Family of Love;* and the picture of town-life that the play gives is quite in the manner of Middleton's early comedies. George Pyeboard is an inferior Witgood. It is the poorest of Middleton's plays, unless we except *Your Five Gallants,* but it is not unamusing. George Pyeboard is evidently George Peele, the hero of the *Merry Conceited Jests,* which were published in the same year (1607) as the play, and furnished the playwright with hints.[1] Pyeboard's references to his almanac (sig. F 4) recall several passages in other plays of Middleton.

There are not many allusions to Middleton in the writings of his contemporaries.[2] Jonson told Drummond of Hawthornden in 1619 "that Markham (who added his English Arcadia) was not of the number of the Faithful, *i.e., Poets,* and but a base fellow. That such were Day and Middleton." I should like to think that this was but

---

[1] Mr. Fleay discovers in *The Puritan* some satirical references to Shakespeare, but my eyes cannot see through a millstone. It is a pity that Mr. Fleay injures his own credit by his habit of jumbling fact and fiction together.

[2] A poet of our own time has paid to Middleton's genius the highest tribute that it has yet received. See Mr. Swinburne's Sonnets on the English Dramatists, No. IX.

the expression of a passing gust of discontent ; but we have seen that six years afterwards Jonson went out of his way to sneer at *A Game at Chess.* To the *Duchess of Malfi* Middleton contributed commendatory verses (in 1623), but Webster in the Address to the Reader prefixed to *The White Devil* (1612), while complimenting Chapman, Dekker, Heywood, &c., made no mention of Middleton. In Taylor's *Praise of Hempseed,* 1620, are the lines :—

> " And many there are living at this day
> Which do in paper their true worth display,
> As Davis, Drayton, and the learned Dun,[1]
> Johnson, and Chapman, Marston, Middleton,
> With Rowley, Fletcher, Withers, Massinger,
> Heywood, and all the rest where'er they are,
> Must say their lines but for the paper sheet
> Had scarcely ground whereon to set their feet."

In a well-known passage of Heywood's *Hierarchy of Blessed Angels,* 1635, Middleton is mentioned :—

> " Fletcher and Webster, of that learned pack
> None of the mean'st, yet neither was but Jack.
> Decker's but Tom ; nor May nor Middleton,
> And he's now but Jack Ford that once were John."

His name is also found on the list of poets in Howes' continuation of Stow, 1615, p. 811. In *Wit's Recreations* is the following epigram :—

> "To Mr. Thomas Middleton.
>
> Facetious Middleton, thy witty Muse
> Hath pleased all that books or men peruse.

---

[1] So Donne's name is frequently spelled.

> If any thee despise, he doth but show
> Antipathy to wit in daring so:
> Thy fame's above his malice, and 'twill be
> Dispraise enough for him to censure thee."

The anonymous author of *On the Time-Poets* in the *Choice Drollery*, 1656, is not complimentary:—

> " The *squibbling* Middleton[1] and Haywood sage,
> Th' apologetick Atlas of the stage."

There are critics who station poets in order of merit as a schoolmaster ranges his pupils in the classroom. This process I do not intend to adopt with Middleton. The test of a poet's real power ultimately resolves itself into the question whether he leaves a permanent impression on the mind of a capable reader. A poet may carve cherry-stones with exquisite skill; but mere artistry, though a man might have the very touch of Meleager, soon palls. It becomes more and more a relief to turn from the χελιδόνων μουσεῖα of this refined age to the Elizabethans. Middleton may be charged with extravagance and coarseness. True: but he could make the blood tingle; he

---

[1] In the ballad on the pulling down of the Cockpit by the prentices (Shrove Tuesday 1616–17) we find:—

> " Books old and young on heap they flung
> And burnt them in the blazes,
> Tom Dekker, Haywood, Middleton,
> And other wandering crazes."

But I am not at all sure that the ballad is genuine. It is given in Collier's *Hist. of Eng. Dram. Lit.*, ed. 2, pp. 386–388, "from a contemporary print."

could barb his words so that they pierce the heart through and through. If *The Changeling, Women beware Women, The Spanish Gipsy,* and *A Fair Quarrel* do not justify Middleton's claims to be considered a great dramatist, I know not which of Shakespeare's followers is worthy of the title.

ADDENDA.

VOL. I. *p.* 129, *note* 1.—"*Steaks* of velvet" are probably panels or squares of velvet inserted in the cloth. In *Your Five Gallants* (iv. 5) we have "white blankets cut out in *steaks*," *i.e.* in square pieces.

VOL. I. *p.* 217, *note* 1.—Besides the allusion to the tipple of "lambswool," there is certainly a reference to lamb-skin (*i.e.* parchment) bonds. See vol. iv. p. 391, ll. 9–12.

VOL. II. *p.* 273, *note* 2.—Mr. H. C. Hart, of Dublin, supplies me with an apposite quotation from Sharpham's *Fleire*, 1607, in regard to the (temporary?) disuse of blue coats by serving-men :—

"*Flo.* By this light I'll never suffer serving-men come near me again . . . unless the rogue kiss his hand first.

"*Fleire.* O madam! why? since *blue coats were left off*, the kissing of the hand is the serving-man's badge : you shall know him by't."

VOL. II. *p.* 320, *note* 2.—I withdraw my suggestion that *froating* = *fretting*, *embroidering*. Mr. Hart has convinced me that the meaning is "rubbing in a perfumed oil to sweeten the garment." He refers me to Ben Jonson's *Cynthia's Revels*, v. 2 :—"Taste, smell : I assure you, sir, pure benjamin, the only spirited scent that ever awaked a Neapolitan nostril. You would wish yourself all nose for the love on't. I *frotted a jerkin* for a new-revenued gentleman yielded me three-score crowns but this morning, and the same titillation."

In *England's Parnassus*, 1600, are two quotations (pp. 281, 321) subscribed "Tho. Middleton" and "Th. Middl." They belong (as Dyce observed) to Christopher Middleton's *Legend of Humphrey Duke of Glocester*.

BLURT, MASTER-CONSTABLE.

Blvrt, Master-Constable.   Or   The Spaniards Night-walke.   As it hath bin sundry times priuately acted by the Children of Paules.

————————*Patresq ; severi*
Fronde comas vincti coenant, et carmina dictant.

London, Printed for Henry Rockytt, and are to be solde at the long shop vnder S. Mildreds Church in the Poultry.   1602. 4to.

"Blurt" was a contemptuous interjection ; and " Blurt ! Master Constable !" appears to have been a proverbial expression.   Dyce refers to *English Proverbs*, p. 14 (1st series), appended to Howell's *Lexicon Tetraglotton*, 1660.   In Ben Jonson's *Tale of a Tub* (ii. 1), Hilts calls the High Constable of Kentish Town " old Blurt."

DRAMATIS PERSONÆ.

DUKE OF VENICE.
HIPPOLITO, *brother to* VIOLETTA.
CAMILLO, *in love with* VIOLETTA.
BAPTISTA,
BENTIVOGLIO, } *Venetian gentlemen.*
VIRGILIO,
ASORINO,
CURVETTO, *an old courtier.*
FONTINELLE, *a French gentleman, taken prisoner by* CAMILLO.
LAZARILLO DE TORMES, *a Spaniard.*
DOYT, *page to* HIPPOLITO.
DANDYPRAT, *page to* CAMILLO.
TRUEPENNY, *page to* VIOLETTA.
PILCHER, *page to* LAZARILLO.
FRISCO, *servant to* IMPERIA.
BLURT, *master-constable.*
SLUBBER, *a beadle, his clerk.*
WOODCOCK, *a watchman.*
FRIAR.
Gentlemen, Servingmen, Watchmen, &c.

VIOLETTA, *sister to* HIPPOLITO.
IMPERIA, *a courtesan.*
TRIVIA, } *her attendants.*
SIMPERINA,
Ladies.

SCENE, VENICE.

BLURT, MASTER-CONSTABLE.

—o—

ACT I.

SCENE I.

A Room in CAMILLO'S *House ; a Banquet set out.*

Enter CAMILLO, HIPPOLITO, BAPTISTA, BENTIVOGLIO, *and* VIRGILIO (*with gloves*[1] *in their hats, as returning from war*), *leading in* VIOLETTA *and other Ladies :* DOYT *and* DANDYPRAT[2] *attending.*

Hip. Ay, marry, sir, the only rising up in arms is in the arms of a woman : peace, I say still, is your only paradise, when every Adam may have his Christmas

---

[1] It was the custom for gallants to wear their mistresses' gloves (or even garters) in their hats. Michael Drayton in the *Battaile of Agincourt*, describing the departure of the English troops for France, tells how
> " The nobler youth, the common rank above,
> On their curvetting coursers mounted fair,
> One ware his mistress' garters, one her glove,
> And he a lock of his dear lady's hair."

[2] "Dandyprat " is a term often applied to a dwarf or page. Cf. Middleton's *More Dissemblers besides Women*, iii. 1 :—
> " There's no good fellowship in this *dandyprat*."
There was a small coin of that name.

Eve. And [1] you take me lying any more by the cold sides of a brazen-face field-piece, unless I have such a down pillow under me, I'll give you leave to knock up both my golls [2] in my father's hall, and hang hats upon these tenpenny nails.

Viol. And yet, brother, when, with the sharpest hooks of my wit, I laboured to pull you from the wars, you broke loose, like a horse that knew his own strength, and vowed nothing but a man of war should back you— 12

Hip. I have been backed since, and almost unbacked too.

Viol. And swore that honour was never dyed in grain [3] till it was dipt in the colours of the field.

Hip. I am a new man, sister, and now cry a pox a' that honour that must have none but barber-surgeons to wait upon't, and a band of poor straggling rascals, that, every twinkling of an eye, forfeit their legs and arms into the Lord's hands! Wenches, by Mars his sweaty buff-jerkin (for now all my oaths must smell a' the soldado [4]), I have seen more men's heads spurned up and down like foot-balls at a breakfast, after the hungry cannons had picked them, than are maidenheads in Venice, and more legs of men served in at a dinner than ever I shall see legs of capons in one platter whilst I live.   28

---

[1] If.

[2] A cant term for hands.

[3] In Marsh's *Lectures on the English Language* (ed. 1862, pp. 55–62), the etymology and meanings of the word "grain" are elaborately discussed.

[4] Soldier.—The Spanish form.

First Lady. Perhaps all those were capons' legs you did see.

Virg. Nay, mistress, I'll witness against you for some of them.

Viol. I do not think, for all this, that my brother stood to it so lustily as he makes his brags for.

Third Lady. No, no, these great talkers are never great doers.

Viol. Faith, brother, how many did you kill for your share ?

Hip. Not so many as thou has done with that villanous eye by a thousand.   40

Viol. I thought so much ; that's just none.

Cam. 'Tis not a soldier's glory to tell how many lives he has ended, but how many he has saved : in both which honours the noble Hippolito had most excellent possession. Believe it, my fair mistress, though many men in a battle have done more, your brother in this equalled him who did most.   He went from you a worthy gentleman ; he brings with him that title that makes a gentleman most worthy, the name of a soldier ; which how well and how soon he hath earned, would in me seem glorious to rehearse, in you to hear ; but, because his own ear dwells so near my voice, I will play the ill neighbour and cease to speak well of him.   53

Viol. An argument that either you dare not or love not to flatter.

Cam. No more than I dare or love to do wrong ; yet to make a chronicle of my friend's nobly-acted deeds, would stand as far from flattery in me, as cowardice did from him.

Hip. 'S foot, if all the wit in this company have nothing to set itself about but to run division upon me, why then e'en burn off mine ears indeed. But, my little mermaids, Signior Camillo does this that I now might describe the Ninevitical motion[1] of the whole battle, and so tell what he has done;—and come, shall I begin ?   66

First Lady. O, for beauty's love, a good motion !

Hip. But I can tell you one thing, I shall make your hair stand up an end at some things.

Viol. Prithee, good brother soldier, keep the peace : our hair stand an end ! pity a' my heart, the next end would be of our wits. We hang out a white flag,[2] most terrible Tamburlaine, and beg mercy. Come, come, let us neither have your Ninevitical motions, nor your swaggering battles. Why, my lord Camillo, you invited me hither to a banquet, not to the ballad of a pitched field.   77

Cam. And here it stands, bright mistress, sweetly attending what doom your lips will lay upon it.

Viol. Ay, marry, sir, let our teeth describe this motion.

Second Lady. We shall never describe it well for fumbling i' th' mouth.

---

[1] Motion = puppet-show. The "motion of Niniveh" is frequently mentioned by old writers. Another popular "motion" was the "city of Norwich."

[2] Cf. Marlowe's *Tamburlaine*, pt. 1, iv. 2. l. 110, &c.

Hip. Yes, yes, I have a trick to make us understand one another, and [1] we fumble never so.

Viol. Meddle not with his tricks, sweetheart. Under pardon, my lord, though I am your guest, I'll bestow myself. Sit, dear beauties : for the men, let them take up places themselves. I prithee, brother fighter, sit, and talk of any subject but this jangling law at arms.　　90

[They seat themselves.

Hip. The law at legs then.

Viol. Will you be so lusty? no, nor legs neither; we'll have them tied up too. Since you are among ladies, gallants, handle those things only that are fit for ladies.

Hip. Agreed, so that we go not out of the compass of those things that are fit for lords.

Viol. Be't so : what's the theme then?

First Lady. Beauty; that fits us best.　　99

Cam. And of beauty what tongue would not speak the best, since it is the jewel that hangs upon the brow of heaven, the best colour that can be laid upon the cheek of earth? Beauty makes men gods immortal, by making mortal men to live ever in love.

Second Lady. Ever? not so : I have heard that some men have died for love.

Viol. So have I, but I could never see't. I'd ride forty miles to follow such a fellow to church; and would make more of a sprig of rosemary at his burial than of a gilded bride-branch at mine own wedding.[2]　　110

---

1 If.

2 "Rosemary, as being an emblem of remembrance, was used both

Cam. Take you such delight in men that die for love?

Viol. Not in the men, nor in the death, but in the deed. Troth, I think he is not a sound man that will die for a woman; and yet I would never love a man soundly, that would not knock at death's door for my love.

Hip. I'd knock as long as I thought good, but have my brains knocked out when I entered, if I were he. 117

Cam. What Venetian gentleman was there, that having this[1] in his burgonet did not (to prove his head worthy of the honour) do more than defy death to the very face? Trust us, ladies, our signiory stands bound in greater sums of thanks to your beauties for victory, than to our valour. My dear Violetta, one kiss to this picture of your whitest hand, when I was even faint with giving and receiving the dole of war, set a new edge on my sword, insomuch that

I singl'd out a gallant spirit of France,

---

at funerals and weddings. Compare *The Pleasant History of John Winchcomb, in his younger yeares called Jacke of Newberie:* "Then was there a faire bride cup of silver and gilt carried before her [the bride], wherein was a goodly *braunch of rosemarie gilded very faire,* hung about with silken ribonds of all colours: next was there a noyse of musitians that played all the way before her: after her came all the chiefest maydens of the countrie, some bearing great bride cakes, and some *garlands of wheate finely gilded,* and so she past unto the church." Sig. D 3, ed. 1633.—*Dyce.* Cf. Herrick's poem *To the Maids to walk abroad:*—

"This done, we'll draw lots who shall buy
And *gild* the bays and rosemary."

So in Morley's *Canzonets,* 1593:—

"Then run apace
And get a bride-lace
And *gilt* rosemary-branch the while there yet is catching."

[1] *i.e.* his mistress' glove in his helmet.

And charged him with my lance in full career;
And after rich exchange of noble courage,
(The space of a good hour on either side),   130
At last crying, Now for Violetta's honour!
I vanquished him and him dismounted took,
Not to myself, but prisoner to my love.

Viol. I have heard much praise of that French gallant: good my lord, bring him acquainted with our eyes.

Cam. I will.—Go, boy, fetch noble Fontinelle.
                                    [*Exit* DANDYPRAT.

Hip. Will your French prisoner drink well, or else cut his throat?

Cam. O, no! he cannot brook it.   140

Hip. The pox he can! 'S light, methinks a Frenchman should have a good courage to wine, for many of them be exceeding hot fiery whoresons, and resolute as Hector, and as valiant as Troilus; then come off and on bravely, and lie by it, and sweat for't too, upon a good and a military advantage.

Cam. Prithee, have done; here comes the prisoner.

Enter FONTINELLE *and* DANDYPRAT.

Viol. My Lord Camillo, is this the gentleman
Whose valour by your valour is subdued?

Cam. It is, fair lady; and I yield him up   150
To be your beauty's worthy prisoner.
Lord Fontinelle, think your captivity
Happy in this; she that hath conquered me
Receives my conquest as my love's fair fee.

Viol. Fair stranger, droop not, since the chance of
    wars
Brings to the soldier death, restraint, or scars.
    Font. Lady, I know the fortune of the field
Is death with honour, or with shame to yield,
As I have done.
    Viol. In that no scandal lies :
Who dies when he may live, he doubly dies.   160
    Font. My reputation's lost.
    Viol. Nay, that's not so ;
You fled[1] not, but were vanquish'd by your foe :
The eye of war respects not you nor him ;
It is our fate will have us lose or win ;
You will disdain if I you prisoner call?
    Font. No, but rejoice since I am beauty's thrall.
    Hip. Enough of this ; come, wenches, shake your
    heels.
    Cam. Music, advance thee on thy golden wing,
And dance division from sweet string to string.
    Font. Camillo, I shall curb[2] thy tyranny,   170
In making me that lady's prisoner :
She has an angel's body, but within't
Her coy heart says there lies a heart of flint.
              [*Music for a measure :*[3] *whilst* FONTINELLE
                  speaks, they dance a strain.
Such beauty be my jailor ! a heavenly hell !
The darkest dungeon which spite can devise

---

[1] Old ed. "flee."
[2] A friend of Dyce's proposed "curse."
[3] A stately dance, with measured steps.

To throw this carcass in, her glorious eyes
Can make as lightsome as the fairest chamber
In Paris Louvre.   Come, captivity,
And chain me to her looks !   How am I tost,
Being twice in mind, as twice in body lost !   180

         [VIOLETTA *on a sudden breaks off ; the rest stand*
            talking.

  Cam. Not the measure out, fair mistress ?

  Viol. No, fair servant, not the measure out : I have,
on the sudden, a foolish desire to be out of the
measure.

  Cam. What breeds that desire ?

  Viol. Nay, I hope it is no breeding matter.   Tush,
tush, by my maidenhead, I will not : the music likes me
not, and I have a shoe wrings me to th' heart ; besides,
I have a woman's reason, I will not dance, because I will
not dance.   Prithee, dear hero, take my prisoner there
into the measure : fie, I cannot abide to see a man sad
nor idle.   I'll be out once, as the music is in mine
ear.   193

  Font. Lady, bid him whose heart no sorrow feels
Tickle the rushes with his wanton heels : [1]
I've too much lead at mine.

  First Lady. I'll make it light.

  Font. How ?

  First Lady. By a nimble dance.

---

  1 Imitated from *Romeo and Juliet*, i. 4 :—
              " Let wantons, light of heart,
       Tickle the senseless rushes with their heels."
(Before the introduction of carpets, floors were strewed with rushes.)

Font. You hit it right.

First Lady. Your keeper bids you dance.

Font. Then I obey :

My heart I feel grows light, it melts away.·

> [*They dance ;* VIOLETTA *stands by marking*
> FONTINELLE.

Viol. In troth, a very pretty Frenchman : the carriage
of his body likes me well ; so does his footing ; so does
his face ; so does his eye above his face ; so does himself, above all that can be above himself.   203
Camillo, thou hast play'd a foolish part :
Thy prisoner makes a slave of thy love's heart.
Shall Camillo then sing Willow, willow, willow ?[1] not
for the world.   No, no, my French prisoner ; I will use
thee Cupid knows how, and teach thee to fall into the
hands of a woman.   If I do not feed thee with fair
looks, ne'er let me live ; if thou get'st out of my fingers
till I have thy very heart, ne'er let me love ; nothing but
thy life shall serve my turn ; and how otherwise I'll
plague thee, monsieur, you and I'll deal : only this because I'll be sure he shall not start, I'll lock him in a
little low room besides[2] himself, where his wanton eye
shall see neither sun nor moon.   So, the dance is done,
and my heart has done her worst,—made me in love.
Farewell, my lord ; I have much haste, you have many
thanks ; I am angered a little, but am greatly pleased.

---

[1] The burden of the ballad reprinted by Percy from a black-letter
copy in the Pepys' collection at Cambridge.   Everybody knows how
pathetically the old song is introduced in *Othello.*

[2] *i.e.* by himself.

If you wonder that I take this strange leave, excuse it
thus, that women are strange fools, and will take any
thing.   [*Exit.* 222

Hip. Tricks, tricks ; kerry merry buff![1] How now,
lad, in a trance ?

Cam. Strange farewell ! After, dear Hippolito.
O, what a maze is love of joy and woe !

       [*Exeunt* CAMILLO *and* HIPPOLITO.

Font. Strange frenzy ! After wretched Fontinelle.
O, what a heaven is love ! O, what a hell !   230

    [*Exit ; and then exeunt* LADIES, BAPTISTA, *&c.*

SCENE II.

A Street before BLURT'S *house.*

Enter LAZARILLO *melancholy, and* PILCHER.

Laz. Boy, I am melancholy, because I burn.

Pilch. And I am melancholy, because I am a-cold.

Laz. I pine away with the desire of flesh.

Pilch. It's neither flesh nor fish that I pine for, but for
both.

Laz. Pilcher, Cupid hath got me a stomach, and I
long for laced mutton.[2]

Pilch. Plain mutton, without a lace, would serve me.

Laz. For as your tame monkey is your only best, and

---

[1] " So Nash, 'Yea, without *kerry merry buffe* be it spoken,' &c.
Haue with you to Saffron-Walden, 1596, sig. F. 4 ; and Kempe, 'One
hath written Kemps farewell to the tune of *kery mery, Buffe.*' Dedication of the *Nine daies Wonder*, 1600."—*Dyce.*

[2] "Laced mutton " was a cant term for a whore.

most only beast to your Spanish lady; or, as your tobacco
is your only smoker away of rheum, and all other rheu-
matic diseases; or, as your Irish louse does bite most
naturally fourteen weeks after the change of your saffron-
seamed shirt; or, as the commodities which are sent out
of the Low Countries, and put in vessels called mother
Cornelius' dry-fats,[1] are most common in France; so it
pleaseth the Destinies that I should thirst to drink out
of a most sweet Italian vessel, being a Spaniard.   18

Pilch. What vessel is that, signior?

Laz. A woman, Pilcher, the moist-handed[2] Madonna
Imperia, a most rare and divine creature.

Pilch. A most rascally damned courtesan.

Laz. Boy, hast thou foraged the country for a new
lodging? for I have sworn to lay my bones in this chitty[3]
of Venice.

Pilch. Any man that sees us will swear that we shall
both lay our bones, and nothing but bones, and we stalk
here longer.   They tell me, signior, I must go to the
constable, and he is to see you lodged.

Laz. Inquire for that busy member of the chitty.   30

Enter DOYT *and* DANDYPRAT, *passing over the stage.*

Pilch. I will; and here come a leash of informers.
Save you, plump youths.

---

[1] An allusion to the sweating-tubs of Cornelius, used in the cure of
the *lues venerea.*

[2] A moist hand was supposed to indicate a wanton disposition.

[3] " *Chitty, i.e.,* perhaps, the Italian *città:* but Lazarillo afterwards
affectedly uses '*chick*' and '*chickness*' for *sick* and *sickness.*"—*Dyce.*

Dandy. And thee, my lean stripling.

Pilch. Which is the constable's house?

Doyt. That at the sign of the Brown-bill.[1]

Pilch. Farewell.

Dandy. Why, and farewell? The rogue's made of pie-crust, he's so short.

Pilch. The officious gentleman inherits here.

Laz. Knock, or enter, and let thy voice pull him out by the ears.

41

[PILCHER knocks at the constable's door.

Doyt. 'Slid, Dandyprat, this is the Spanish curtal [2] that in the last battle fled twenty miles ere he looked behind him.

Dandy. Doyt, he did the wiser; but, sirrah, this block shall be a rare threshold for us to whet our wits upon. Come, let's about our business; and if here we find him at our return, he shall find [3] us this month in knavery.

[Exit with DOYT.

Pilch. What, ho! Nobody speaks? Where dwells the constable?

50

Enter from the house BLURT *and* SLUBBER.

Blurt. Here dwells the constable.—Call assistance, give them my full charge,[4] raise, if you see cause.—Now, sir, what are you, sir?

---

[1] "A sort of pike with a hooked point, anciently carried by the English foot-soldiers, and afterwards by watchmen."—*Dyce.*

[2] "Curtal" was the name for a docked horse.

[3] Keep us supplied.

[4] Verges says to Dogberry, "Well, *give them* [*i.e.* the watch] *their*

VOL. I.

B

Pilch. Follower to that Spanish-leather gentleman.

Blurt. And what are you, sir, that cry out upon me? —Look to his tools.—What are you, sir? speak, what are you? I charge you, what are you?

Laz. Most clear Mirror of Magistrates,[1] I am a servitor to god Mars.

Blurt. For your serving of God I am not to meddle: why do you raise me?   61

Laz. I desire to have a wide room in your favour: sweet blood, cast away your name upon me; for I neither know you by your face nor by your voice.

Blurt. It may be so, sir: I have two voices in any company; one as I am master-constable, another as I am Blurt, and the third as I am Blurt master-constable.

Laz. I understand you are a mighty pillar or post in the chitty.

Blurt. I am a poor post, but not to stand at every man's door, without my bench of bill-men. I am (for a better) the duke's own image, and charge you, in his name, to obey me.   73

Laz. I do so.

Blurt. I am to stand, sir, in any bawdy-house, or sink of wickedness. I am the duke's own grace, and in any fray or resurrection am to bestir my stumps as well as he. I charge you, know this staff.

---

charge, neighbour Dogberry." In Glapthorne's *Wit in a Constable* there is a charge to the watch (evidently suggested by *Much Ado,* iii. 3).

[1] An allusion to the poem (or rather collection of poems) of that name.

Slub. Turn the arms to him.

Blurt. Upon this may I lean, and no man say black's
mine eye.   81

Laz. Whosoever says you have a black eye, is a camooch.[1] Most great Blurt, I do unpent-house the roof
of my carcass, and touch the knee of thy office, in
Spanish compliment. I desire to sojourn in your chitty.

Blurt. Sir, sir, for fault of a better, I am to charge
you not to keep a soldiering in our city without a pre-
cept:[2] besides, by my office, I am to search and examine you. Have you the duke's hand to pass?

Laz. Signior, no; I have the general's hand at large,
and all his fingers.   91

Blurt. Except it be for the general good of the
commonwealth, the general cannot lead you up and
down our city.

Laz. I have the general's hand to pass through the
world at my pleasure.

Blurt. At your pleasure! that's rare. Then, rowly,
powly, our wives shall lie at your command. Your
general has no such authority in my precinct; and there-
fore I charge you pass no further.   100

Laz. I tell thee I will pass through the world, thou
little morsel of justice, and eat twenty such as thou art.

---

[1] The term *camouccio* occurs in *Every Man out of his Humour.*
Gifford thought it might be a corruption of "camoscio, a goat or goat's
skin," and mean "clown or flatnose, or any other apposite term
which pleases the reader." *Camooch* must be connected with Fr. *camus.*

[2] A justice's warrant.

Blurt. Sir, sir, you shall find Venice out of the world :
I'll tickle you for that.

Laz. I will pass through the world as Alexander
Magnus did, to conquer.

Blurt. As Alexander of Saint Magnus did ! that's
another matter : you might have informed this at the
first, and you never needed to have come to your
answer.   Let me see your pass : if it be not the duke's
hand, I'll tickle you for all this : quickly, I pray ; this
staff is to walk in other places.   112

Laz. There it is.

Blurt. Slubber, read it over.

Laz. Read it yourself.   What besonian [1] is that ?

Blurt. This is my clerk, sir ; he has been clerk to a
good many bonds and bills [2] of mine.   I keep him only
to read, for I cannot ; my office will not let me.

Pilch. Why do you put on your spectacles then ?

Blurt. To see that he read right.   How now, Slubber?
is't the duke's hand ?   I'll tickle him else.   121

Slub. Mass, 'tis not like his hand.

Blurt. Look well ; the duke has a wart on the back
of his hand.

Slub. Here's none, on my word, master-constable, but
a little blot.

Blurt. Blot ! let's see, let's see.   Ho, that stands for
the wart ; do you see the trick of that ?   Stay, stay ; is
there not a little prick in the hand ? for the duke's hand

---

1 From Italian *besogno*—a beggar, rogue.

2 Of course a play on the words (" bonds and bills ") is intended.
See note 1, p. 17.

had a prick in't, when I was with him, with opening
oysters.   131

Slub. Yes, mass, here's one; besides, 'tis a goodly
great long hand.

Blurt. So has the duke a goodly huge hand; I have
shook him by it (God forgive me!) ten thousand times.
He must pass, like Alexander of Saint Magnus.—Well,
sir,—'tis your duty to stand bare,—the duke has sent his
fist to me, and I were a Jew if I should shrink for it.   I
obey; you must pass: but, pray, take heed with what
dice you pass; I mean, what company; for Satan is
most busy where he finds one like himself.   Your name,
sir?   142

Laz. Lazarillo de Tormes in Castile, cousin-german to
the adelantado [1] of Spain.

Blurt. Are you so, sir? God's blessing on your heart!
Your name again, sir, if it be not too tedious for you?

Laz. Lazarillo de Tormes in Castile, cousin-german
to the Spanish adelantado.

Slub. I warrant, he's a great man in his own country.

Blurt. Has a good name: Slubber, set it down:
write, Lazarus in torment at the Castle, and a cozening
German at the sign of the Falantido-diddle in Spain.
No, sir, you are ingrost: you must give my officer a
groat; it's nothing to me, signior.   154

Laz. I will cancel when it comes to a sum.

---

[1] The King's lieutenant of a country.   Cf. Fletcher's (?) *Love's Cure*,
ii. 1 :—" Nay, we are all signiors here in Spain, from the jakes-farmer to
the grandee or *adelantado*."

Blurt. Well, sir, well, he shall give you an item for't.
—Make a bill, and he'll tear it, he says.

Laz. Most admirable Blurt, I am a man of war, and
profess fighting.

Blurt. I charge you, in the duke's name, keep the
peace.   161

Laz. By your sweet favour, most dear Blurt, you
charge too fast : I am a hanger-on upon Mars, and have
a few crowns.

Pilch. Two ; his own and mine.   [*Aside.*

Laz. And desire you to point out a fair lodging for
me and my train.

Blurt. 'Tis my office, signior, to take men up a' nights ;
but, if you will, my maids shall take you up a' mornings.
Since you profess fighting, I will commit you, signior, to
mine own house.   But will you pitch and pay,[1] or will your
worship run—   172

Laz. I scorn to run from the face of Thamer Cham.[2]

Blurt. Then, sir, you mean not to run?

Laz. Signior, no.

Blurt. Bear witness, Slubber, that his answer is,
Signior No :[3] so now, if he runs upon the score, I have

---

[1] "Pitch and pay" = pay down immediately.   It has been suggested
that the expression originated from "pitching goods in a market and
paying immediately for their standing."

[2] Timur Khaun.

[3] "Signior No" = Nicholas Nemo, Mr. Nobody.   In Samuel Row-
ley's *Noble Soldier* one of the characters is named "Signior No."   Cf.
Day's *Isle of Gulls* (p. 59 of my reprint) :—
         "*Duke.* And you'll maintain that fashion ?
          Viol. Signior, No."
Day dedicates his *Humour out of Breath* to "Signior Nobody."

him straight upon Signior No.   This is my house, signior; enter.

Laz. March, excellent Blurt.   Attend, Pilcher.   180
            [*Exeunt* LAZARILLO, BLURT, *and* SLUBBER.

Re-enter DOYT *and* DANDYPRAT.

Pilch. Upon your trencher, signior, most hungerly.

Doyt. Now, sirrah, where's thy master?

Pilch. The constable has prest him.

Doyt. What, for a soldier?

Pilch. Ay, for a soldier; but ere he'll go, I think, indeed, he and I together shall press the constable.

Dandy. No matter; squeeze him, and leave no more
liquor in him than in a dried neat's tongue.   Sirrah
thin-gut, what's thy name?

Pilch. My name, you chops! why, I am of the blood
of the Pilchers.   191

Dandy. Nay, 's foot, if one should kill thee, he could
not be hanged for't, for he would shed no blood; there's
none in thee.   Pilcher! thou'rt a most pitiful dried one.[1]

Doyt. I wonder thy master does not slice thee, and
swallow thee for an anchovies.

Pilch. He wants wine, boy, to swallow me down, for
he wants money to swallow down wine.   But farewell;
I must dog my master.   199

Dandy. As long as thou dogst a Spaniard, thou'lt ne'er
be fatter: but stay; our haste is as great as thine; yet,

---

[1] *i.e.* dried pilchard.   "Dried pilcher," like "poor-john," was commonly used as a term of abuse.

to endear ourselves into thy lean acquaintance, cry, rivo[1] hoh! laugh and be fat; and for joy that we are met, we'll meet and be merry.   Sing.

Pilch. I'll make a shift to squeak.

Doyt. And I.

Dandy. And I, for my profession is to shift[2] as well as you: hem!   [*Music.*

SONG.

Doyt.   *What meat eats the Spaniard?*
Pilch.   *Dried pilchers[3] and poor-john.[4]*   210
Dandy. *Alas, thou art almost marr'd!*
Pilch.   *My cheeks are fall'n and gone.*
Doyt.   *Wouldst thou not leap at a piece of meat?*
Pilch.   *O, how my teeth do water! I could eat:*
              'Fore the heavens, my flesh is almost gone
              With eating of pilcher and poor-john.
                                                 [*Exeunt.*

---

[1] A bacchanalian exclamation, of doubtful origin.

[2] "Viz. trenchers, platters."—*Dyce.*

[3] Cf. Nashe's *Lenten Stuff:*—"If Cornish pilchards, otherwise called *Fumadoes*, taken on the shore of Cornwall from July to November, be so saleable as they are in France, *Spain* and Italy (which are but counterfeits to the red herring as copper to gold or ockamy to silver), much more their elbows itch for joy when they meet with the true gold, the true red herring itself."

[4] "Poor-john" was an inferior sort of dried hake.

ACT II.

SCENE I.

A Street.

Enter FONTINELLE *from tennis, and* TRUEPENNY.

Font. Am I so happy then ?

True. Nay, sweet monsieur—

Font. O, boy, thou hast new-wing'd my captiv'd soul !
Now to my fortune all the Fates may yield,
For I have won where first I lost the field.

True. Why, sir, did my mistress prick you with the Spanish needle[1] of her love, before I summoned you from her to this parley ?

Font. Doubts thou that, boy ?

True. Of mine honesty, I doubt extremely, for I cannot see the little god's tokens upon you : there is as much difference between you and a lover, as between a cuckold and a unicorn.   13

Font. Why, boy ?

True. For you do not wear a pair of ruffled, frowning,

---

[1] Cf. Nashe's *Anatomie of Absurditie* (Works, ed. Grosart, i. 25) :—
" She is more sparing of her *Spanish needle* than her Spanish gloves ;
occupies oftener her setting-stick than shears, and joys more in her
jewels than in her Jesus." The best needles were made in Spain.

ungartered [1] stockings, like a gallant that hides his small-
timbered legs with a quail-pipe boot: [2] your hose stands
upon too many points, [3] and are not troubled with that
falling sickness which follows pale, meagre, miserable,
melancholy lovers : your hands are not groping continually—   21

Font. Where, my little observer ?

True. In your greasy pocket, sir, like one that wants a
cloak for the rain, and yet is still weather-beaten : your
hat nor head are not of the true heigh-ho block, for it
should be broad-brimmed, limber like the skin of a white
pudding when the meat is out, the facing fatty, the felt
dusty, and not entered into any band : [4] but your hat is
of the nature of a loose, light, heavy-swelling wench, too
strait-laced. I tell you, monsieur, a lover should be all
loose from the sole of the foot rising upward, and from
the bases or confines of the slop [5] falling downward. If
you were in my mistress's chamber, you should find
othergates [6] privy signs of love hanging out there.   34

Font. Have your little eyes watched so narrowly ?

---

1 Truepenny is mentioning the ordinary symptoms of love-melancholy.
Cf. Overbury's character of *An Amorist :*—" He is untrust, unbutton'd,
and *ungarter'd,* not out of carelessness, but care."

2 So called from the plaits or wrinkles. Dyce quotes appositely from
the *Romaunt of the Rose* (v. 7212) :—

> " And high shewis knoppid with dagges,
>   That *frouncin* [*i.e.* wrinkle] *like a quale-pipe,*
>   Or botis riveling as a gipe."

3 The tagged laces by which the hose was fastened to the doublet.

4 " Band " was another form of " bond."

5 Loose breeches.

6 Otherways.

True. O, sir, a page must have a cat's eye, a spaniel's leg, a whore's tongue (a little tasting of the cog [1]), a catchpoll's hand,—what he gripes is his own ; and a little, little bawdy.

Font. Fair Violetta, I will wear thy love,   40
Like this French order, near unto my heart.
Via [2] for fate ! fortune, lo, this is all,
At grief's rebound I'll mount, although I fall !

Enter CAMILLO *and* HIPPOLITO *from tennis ;* DOYT *and* DANDYPRAT *with their cloaks and rapiers.*

Cam. Now, by Saint Mark, he's a most treacherous villain.
Dare the base Frenchman's eye gaze on my love ?

Hip. Nay, sweet rogue, why wouldst thou make his face a vizard, to have two loopholes only ? When he comes to a good face, may he not do with his eyes what he will ? 'S foot, if I were as he, I'd pull them out, and if I wist [3] they would anger thee.   50

Cam. Thou add'st heat to my rage. Away, stand back,
Dishonour'd slave, more treacherous than base !
This is the instance of my scorn'd disgrace.

Font. Thou ill-advis'd Italian, whence proceeds
This sudden fury ?

---

[1] Here, and in l. 39, a pun is intended :—*cog* and *keg*, *bawdy* and *body*.

[2] An expression of impatience or defiance.

[3] " And if I wist " = If I thought.

Cam. Villain, from thee.

Hip. Hercules, stand between them !

Font. Villain ? by my blood,
I am as free-born as your Venice duke !
Villain ? Saint Denis and my life to boot.
Thy lips shall kiss this pavement or my foot.   59

Hip. Your foot, with a pox ! I hope you're no pope,
sir : his lips shall kiss my sister's soft lip, and thine the
tough lips of this. Nay, sir, I do but shew you that I
have a tool. Do you hear, Saint Denis? but that we
both stand upon the narrow bridge of honour, I should
cut your throat now, for pure love you bear to my sister,
but that I know you would set out a throat.

Cam. Wilt thou not stab the peasant
That thus dishonours both thyself and me ?

Hip. Saint Mark set his marks upon me then ! Stab ?
I'll have my shins broken, ere I'll scratch so much as the
skins off a' the law of arms. Shall I make a Frenchman
cry O ! before the fall of the leaf ? not I, by the cross of
this Dandyprat.[1]   73

Dandy. If you will, sir, you shall coin me into a
shilling.

Hip. I shall lay too heavy a cross upon thee then.

Cam. Is this a time to jest ? Boy, call my servants.

Doyt. Gentlemen, to the dresser ![2]

Cam. You rogue, what dresser ?

---

[1] " Dandyprat " was a small coin. Many coins were marked with
crosses. The dramatists were constantly playing on the word *cross*.

[2] "When dinner was ready, the cook used to knock on the dresser
with his knife, as a signal for the servants to carry it into the hall. But

Enter Servingmen.

                                        Seize on Fontinelle,
And lodge him in a dungeon presently.   80

Font. He steps upon his death that stirs a foot.

Cam. That shall I try: as in the field before
I made thee stoop, so here I'll make thee bow.

Font. Thou playdst the soldier then, the villain now.

[CAMILLO *and his men set upon him, get him down,
        disweapon him, and hold him fast.*

Font. Treacherous Italians!

Cam. Hale him to a dungeon—
There, if your thoughts can apprehend the form
Of Violetta, doat on her rare feature;
Or if your proud flesh, with a sparing diet,
Can still retain her swelling sprightfulness,
Then court, instead of her, the croaking vermin   90
That people that most solitary vault.

Hip. But, sirrah Camillo, wilt thou play the wise and
venerable bearded master-constable, and commit him
indeed, because he would be meddling in thy precinct,

---

the words put into the mouth of the facetious Doyt appear to have been
those usually employed by the usher to the attendants on such occasions.
In the notes to the *Northumberland Household Book*, p. 423, are extracts from "Lord Fairfax's Orders for the servants of his household
[after the civil wars]," where, among "The Usher's Words of Direction," we find,—"Then he must warn to the Dresser, '*Gentlemen* and
Yeomen, *to the Dresser*.'" Gifford (Massinger's *Works*, vol. i. p. 166)
has cited from a note of Reed on Dodsley's *Old Plays* this passage of
Lord Fairfax's "Orders," &c., as if it contained the *warning* of the
cook; and Nares, in his *Glossary* (voc. *Dresser*), has made the same mistake."—*Dyce.*

and will not put off the cap of his love to the brown-bill [1]
of thy desires?   Well, thou hast given the law of arms a
broken pate already; therefore, if thou wilt needs turn
broker [2] and be a cut-throat too, do.   For my part, I'll
go get a sweet ball, and wash my hands of it.

Cam. Away with him! my life shall answer it.   100

Font. To prison must I then?   Well, I will go,
And with a light-wing'd spirit insult o'er woe;
For in the darkest hell on earth I'll find
Her fair idea to content my mind.
Yet France and Italy with blister'd tongue
Shall publish thy dishonour in my wrong.
O, now how happy wert thou, could'st thou lodge me
Where I could leave to love her!

Cam. By heaven, I can.

Font. Thou canst?   O, happy man!
This [is] a kind of new-invented law,   110
First feed the axe, after produce the saw.
Her heart no doubt will thy affections feel,
For thou'lt plead sighs in blood and tears in steel.
Boy, tell my love her love thus sighing spake,
I'll vail [3] my crest to death for her dear sake.

> [*Exit, guarded by the Servingmen.*

Cam. Boy? what boy is that?

Hip. Is't you, Sir Pandarus, the broking [4] knight of
Troy?   Are your two legs the pair of tressels for the
Frenchman to get up upon my sister?   119

---

[1] See note 1, p. 17.

[2] "A play on the word *broker*, which meant pander."—*Dyce.*

[3] *i.e.* lower.   [4] *i.e.* pandering.

True. By the Nine Worthies, worthy gallants, not I :
I a gentleman for conveyance ? I Sir Pandarus ? Would
Troy, then, were in my breeches, and I burnt [1] worse than
poor Troy ! Sweet signior, you know, I know, and all
Venice knows, that my mistress scorns double-dealing
with her heels.

Hip. With her heels ?   O, here's a sure pocket dag ! [2]
and my sister shoots him off, snip-snap, at her pleasure.
Sirrah Mephostophilis,[3] did not you bring letters from my
sister to the Frenchman ?

True. Signior, no.[4]   130

Cam. Did not you fetch him out of the tennis court ?

True. No, *point, par ma foi ;* you see I have many
tongues speak for me.

Hip. Did not he follow your crackship [5] at a beck
given ?

True. *Ita,* true, certes, he spied, and I spitting thus,
went thus.

Hip. But were stayed thus.

True. You hold a' my side, and therefore I must needs
stick to you ; 'tis true : I going, he followed, and following fingered me, just as your worship does now ; but I
struggled and straggled, and wriggled and wraggled, and
at last cried *vale, valete,* as I do now, with this fragment
of a rhyme,   144

---

[1] The word "burn" is frequently used *sensu obscœno.* See note on
Marlowe's Works, iii. 234.

[2] Pistol.   [3] The Fiend in Marlowe's *Faustus.*

[4] See note, p. 22.   [5] "*i.e.* boyship—little mastership."—*Dyce.*

My lady is grossly fall'n in love, and yet her waist is
    slender ;

Had I not slipt away, you would have made my buttocks
    tender.   [*Exit.*

Dandy. Shall Doyt and I play the bloodhounds, and
after him ?

Cam. No, let him run.

Hip. Not for this wager of my sister's love; run !
away, Dandyprat, catch Truepenny, and hold him ; thyself shall pass more current.[1]   152

Dandy. I fly, sir ; your Dandyprat is as light as a clipt
angel.[2]   [*Exit.*

Hip. Nay, God's lid, after him, Camillo ; reply not,
but away.

Cam. Content ; you know where to meet.   [*Exit.*

Hip. For I know that the only way to win a wench is
not to woo her ; the only way to have her fast is to have
her loose ; the only way to triumph over her is to make
her fall ; and the way to make her fall—   161

Doyt. Is to throw her down.

Hip. Are you so cunning, sir ?

Doyt. O Lord, sir, and have so perfect a master ?

Hip. Well, sir, you know the gentlewoman that dwells
in the midst of Saint Mark's Street ?

Doyt. Midst of Saint Mark's Street, sir ?

Hip. A pox on you ! the flea-bitten-faced lady.

---

[1] An allusion to the coin "Dandyprat."

[2] Old writers constantly joke irreverently about "angels." In the
Unfortunate Traveller Nashe has a pun about an "angel of light."
(The angel was a gold coin of the value of ten shillings.)

Doyt. O, sir, the freckle-cheeke[d] Madonna; I know
her, signior, as well—   170

Hip. Not as I do, I hope, sir.

Doyt. No, sir, I'd be loath to have such inward
acquaintance with her as you have.

Hip. Well, sir, slip, go presently to her, and from me
deliver to her own white hands Fontinelle's picture.

Doyt. Indeed, sir, she loves to have her chamber hung
with the pictures of men.

Hip. She does.   I'll keep my sister's eyes and his
painted face asunder.   Tell her, besides, the masque
holds, and this the night, and nine the hour: say we are
all for her: away.

Doyt. And she's for you all, were you an army.   182

[*Exeunt severally.*

SCENE II.

A Room in IMPERIA'S *House.*

Enter IMPERIA, *and* TRIVIA *and* SIMPERINA *with perfumes.*

Imp. Fie, fie, fie, fie, by the light oath of my fan, the
weather is exceeding tedious and faint. Trivia, Simperina, stir, stir, stir: one of you open the casements,
t'other take a ventoy[1] and gently cool my face.   Fie, I
ha' such an exceeding high colour, I so sweat! Simperina,
dost hear? prithee be more compendious; why, Simperina!

---

[1] Fan.

Simp. Here, madam.

Imp. Press down my ruff before. Away; fie, how thou blowest upon me! thy breath, (God's me!) thy breath, fie, fie, fie, fie, it takes off all the painting and colour from my cheek. In good faith, I care not if I go and be sick presently : heigho, my head so aches with carrying this bodkin! in troth I'll try if I can be sick. 　　14

Triv. Nay, good sweet lady.

Simp. You know a company of gallants will be here at night: be not out of temper, sweet mistress.

Imp. In good troth, if I be not sick, I must be melancholy then. This same gown never comes on but I am so melancholy and so heart-burnt! 'tis a strange garment : I warrant, Simperina, the foolish tailor that made it was troubled with the stitch when he composed it. 　　22

Simp. That's very likely, madam; but it makes you have, O, a most incony[1] body!

Imp. No, no, no, no, by Saint Mark, the waist is not long enough, for I love a long and tedious waist; besides, I have a most ungodly middle in it; and, fie, fie, fie, fie, it makes me bend i' th' back : O, let me have some music !

Simp. That's not the fault in your gown, madam, but of your bawdy. 　　[*Music.* 31

Imp. Fa, la, la, fa, la, la,—indeed, the bending of the back is the fault of the body,—la, la, la, la ! fa, la, la ! fa, la, la, la, la, la !

---

[1] Delicate. The word is of common occurrence, but its etymology is obscure.

Triv. O, rich!

Simp. O, rare!

Imp. No, no, no, no, no; 'tis slight and common all that I do. Prithee, Simperina, do not ingle[1] me; do not flatter me, Trivia: I ha' never a cast gown till the next week. Fa, la, la, la, la, la, fa, la, la, fa, la, la, &c. This stirring to and fro has done me much good. A song, I prithee. I love these French movings: O, they are so clean! if you tread them true, you shall hit them to a hair. Sing, sing, sing; some odd and fantastical thing, for I cannot abide these dull and lumpish tunes; the musician stands longer a-pricking them than I would do to hear them. No, no, no, give me your light ones, that go nimbly and quick, and are full of changes, and carry sweet division. Ho, prithee, sing! Stay, stay, stay; here's Hippolito's sonnet; first read it, and then sing it. 50

SONG.[2]

By TRIVIA *and* SIMPERINA.

First. *In a fair woman what thing is best?*

Second. *I think a coral lip.*

First. *No, no, you jest;*
        She has a better thing.

Second. *Then 'tis a pretty eye.*

First. *Yet 'tis a better thing,*
        Which more delight does bring.

Second. *Then 'tis a cherry cheek.*

---

[1] Wheedle.

[2] Old ed. "*Reades . Song.*"

First. *No, no, you lie ;*
   Were neither coral lip, nor cherry cheek, nor
     pretty eyes, [1]
   Were not her swelling breast stuck with straw-
     berries,
   Nor had smooth hand, soft skin, white neck,
     pure eye,   60
   Yet she at this alone your love can tie.
   It is, O, 'tis the only joy to men,
   The only praise to women !

[Second]   *What is't then ?*

First. *This it is, O, this it is, and in a woman's*
     middle it is plac'd,
   In a most beauteous body, a heart most chaste !
   This is the jewel kings may buy ;
   If women sell this jewel, women lie.

    [Doyt *knocks within ;* Frisco *answers within.*

Fris. [*within.*] Who, the pox, knocks?

Doyt [*within.*] One that will knock thy coxcomb, if he
do not enter.   70

Fris. [*within.*] If thou dost not enter, how canst thou
knock me ?

Doyt [*within.*] Why then I'll knock thee when I do
enter.

Fris. [*within.*] Why then thou shalt not enter, but instead of me knock thy heels.

Doyt [*within.*] Frisco, I am Doyt, Hippolito's page.

---

[1] Old ed. " *Were neither lip, nor cheekes currall, nor cherry eyes.*"

Fris. [*within.*] And I am Frisco, squire to a bawdy house.

Doyt [*within.*] I have a jewel to deliver to thy mistress.

Fris. [*within.*] Is't set with precious stones? 81

Doyt [*within.*] Thick, thick, thick.

Fris. [*within.*] Why, enter then, thick, thick, thick.

Imp. Fie, fie, fie, fie, fie, who makes that yawling at door?

Enter FRISCO, *and* DOYT *with* FONTINELLE'S *picture.*

Fris. Here's signior Hippolito's man (that shall be) come to hang you.

Imp. Trivia, strip that villain; Simperina, pinch him, slit his wide nose. Fie, fie, fie, I'll have you gelded for this lustiness. 90

Fris. And[1] she threatens to geld me unless I be lusty, what shall poor Frisco do?

Imp. Hang me?

Fris. Not I; hang me if you will, and set up my quarters too.

Imp. Hippolito's boy come to hang me?

Doyt. To hang you with jewels, sweet and gentle; that's Frisco's meaning, and that's my coming.

Imp. Keep the door.

Fris. That's my office: indeed I have been your door-keeper so long, that all the hinges, the spring-locks, and the ring, are worn to pieces. How if anybody knock at the door? 103

---

[1] If.

Imp. Let them enter. [*Exit* FRISCO.] Fie, fie, fie, fie, fie, his great tongue does so run through my little ears! 'tis more harsh than a younger brother's courting of a gentlewoman, when he has no crowns. Boy!

Doyt. At your service.

Imp. My service? alas, alas, thou canst do me small service! Did thy master send this painted gentleman to me?   111

Doyt. This painted gentleman to you.

Imp. Well, I will hang his picture up by the walls, till I see his face; and, when I see his face, I'll take his picture down. Hold it, Trivia.

Triv. It's most sweetly made.

Imp. Hang him up, Simperina.

Simp. It's a most sweet man.

Imp. And does the masque hold?—Let me see it again.   120

Doyt. If their vizards hold, here you shall see all their blind cheeks: this is the night, nine the hour, and I the jack [1] that gives warning.

Simp. He gives warning, mistress; shall I set him out?

Doyt. You shall not need; I can set out myself.

[*Exit.*

Imp. Flaxen hair, and short too; O, that's the French cut! but, fie, fie, fie, these [2] flaxen-haired men are such pulers, and such piddlers, and such chicken-hearts (and

---

[1] The figure that struck the bell on the outside of a clock.
[2] Old ed. "this."

yet great quarrellers), that when they court a lady they are
for the better part bound to the peace ! No, no, no, no;
your black-haired man (so he be fair) is your only sweet
man, and in any service the most active. A banquet,
Trivia ; quick, quick, quick. 134

Triv. In a twinkling.—'Slid, my mistress cries like the
rod-woman,—quick, quick, quick, buy any rosemary and
bays ? [*Aside and exit.*

Imp. A little face, but a lovely face : fie, fie, fie, no
matter what face he make, so the other parts be legitimate
and go upright. Stir, stir, Simperina ; be doing, be doing
quickly ; move, move, move. 141

Simp. Most incontinently.[1]—Move, move, move ? O
sweet ! [*Aside and exit.*

Imp. Heigho ! as I live, I must love thee and suck
kisses from thy lips. Alack, that women should fall thus
deeply in love with dumb things, that have no feeling !
but they are women's crosses, and the only way to take
them is to take them patiently.

Re-enter FRISCO, *and* TRIVIA *and* SIMPERINA *setting out
a banquet.*

Heigho ! set music, Frisco !

Fris. Music, if thou hast not a hard heart, speak to
my mistress. [*Music.* 151

Imp. Say he scorn to marry me, yet he shall stand me
in some stead by being my Ganymede. If he be the most
decayed gallant in all Venice, I will myself undo myself

---

[1] Immediately.

and my whole state to set him up again.   Though speaking truth would save my life, I will lie to do him pleasure. Yet to tell lies may hurt the soul : fie, no, no, no ; souls are things to be trodden under our feet when we dance after love's pipe.   Therefore here, hang this counterfeit [1] at my bed's feet.   160

Fris. If he be counterfeit, nail him up [2] upon one of your posts.   [*Exit with the picture.*

Imp. By the moist hand of love, I swear I will be his lottery, and he shall never draw but it shall be a prize !

CURVETTO *knocks within.*

Fris. [*within.*] Who knocks ?
Cur. [*within.*] Why, 'tis I, knave.
Fris. [*within.*] Then knave knock there still.
Cur. [*within.*] Wut [3] open door?
Fris. [*within.*] Yes, when I list I will.
Cur. [*within.*] Here's money.
Fris. [*within.*] Much ! [4]
Cur. [*within.*] Here's gold.
Fris. [*within.*] Away !
Cur. [*within.*] Knave, open.
Fris. [*within.*] Call to our maids ; good [5] night ; we
            are all aslopen.[6]   [*Entering.*
Mistress, if you have ever a pinnace to set out, you may

---

[1] Portrait.
[2] As a piece of counterfeit money is nailed up.
[3] Wilt.
[4] An ironical expression,—implying *little* or *none.*
[5] Old ed. "God."   [6] Asleep.

now have it manned and rigged ; for Signior Curvetto,—
he that cries, *I am an old courtier, but lie close, lie close,*
when our maids swear he lies as wide as any courtier in
Italy—   173
    Imp. Do we care how he lies ?

                   [CURVETTO *knocks again within.*

    Fris. Anon, anon, anon !—this old hoary red deer
serves himself in at your keyhole.

    Cur. [*within.*] What, Frisco !

    Fris. Hark ! shall he enter the breach ?

    Imp. Fie, fie, fie, I wonder what this gurnet's head
makes here ! Yet bring him in ; he will serve for picking
meat. [*Exit* FRISCO.] Let music play, for I will feign
myself to be asleep.   [*Music.* 182

        Re-enter FRISCO *with* CURVETTO.

    Cur. [*giving* FRISCO *money.*] Threepence, and here's a
        teston ;[1] yet take all ;
Coming to jump, we must be prodigal :
Hem !
I'm an old courtier, and I can lie close :
Put up, Frisco, put up, put up, put up.

    Fris. Anything at your hands, sir, I will put up,
because you seldom pull out anything.

    Simp. Softly, sweet signior Curvetto, for she's fast. 190

    Cur. Hah ! fast ? my roba[2] fast, and but young night ?
She's wearied, wearied :—ah, ha, hit I right ?

---

  [1] "Or *tester* (so called from the head, *teste,* stamped on it), *i.e.,* sixpence: it was originally of higher value."—*Dyce.*

  [2] Wanton.—*Bona roba* was a common term for a courtesan.

Simp. How, sir, wearied? marry, foh!

Fris. Wearied, sir? marry muff![1]

Cur. No words here, mouse?[2] no words, no words,
    sweet rose?

I'm an hoary courtier, and lie close, lie close.

Hem!

Fris. An old hoary courtier? why, so has a jowl of
ling and a musty whiting been, time out of mind.   Methinks, signior, you should not be so old by your face. 200

   Cur. I have a good heart, knave; and a good heart
Is a good face-maker; I'm young, quick, brisk.
I was a reveller in a long stock,[3]
(There's not a gallant now fills such a stock,)
Plump hose, pan'd,[4] stuft with hair (hair then was held
The lightest stuffing), a fair cod-piece,—ho!
An eel-skin sleeve lasht here and there with lace,
High collar lasht again, breech lasht also,
A little simpering ruff, a dapper cloak
With Spanish-button'd cape, my rapier here,   210
Gloves like a burgomaster here, hat here
(Stuck with some ten-groat brooch), and over all
A goodly long thick Abram-coloured[5] beard.

---

   [1] An expression of contempt.   Cf. First Pt. *Honest Whore*, ii. 1:—
" Marry muff, sir, are you grown so dainty?"
   [2] A common term of endearment.
   [3] Stocking.
   [4] With *panels* or stripes inserted.
   [5] Dyce quotes from *Soliman and Perseda*, 1599, sig. H. 3:—
            "Where is the eldest sonne of Pryam?
            That *abraham-couloured* Troion."
In tapestry Cain was represented with a sandy-coloured beard; Judas
with a red beard.   Steevens thought that " Abraham " might be a cor-

Ho God, ho God! thus did I revel it,
When Monsieur Motte lay here [1] ambassador.
But now those beards are gone, our chins are bare;
Our courtiers now do all against the hair. [2]
I can lie close and see this, but not see:
I'm hoary, but not hoary as some be.   219

    Imp. Heigho! who's that? Signior Curvetto! by my
virginity—

    Cur. Hem! no more.
Swear not so deep at these [3] years: men have eyes,
And though the most are fools, some fools are wise.

    Imp. Fie, fie, fie: and you meet me thus at half
weapon, one must down.

    Fris. She for my life.   [*Aside.*

    Imp. Somebody shall pay for't.

    Fris. He, for my head.   [*Aside.* 229

    Imp. Do not therefore come over me so with cross
blows: no, no, no, I shall be sick if my speech be stopt.
By my virginity I swear,—and why may not I swear by
that I have not, as well as poor musty soldiers do by
their honour, brides at four-and-twenty, ha, ha, ha! by
their maidenheads, citizens by their faith, and brokers as

---

ruption of "auburn:" in *Coriolanus*, ii. 3, where fol. 4 gives "our
heads are some brown, some black, some *auburn*," the three earlier
folios read "*Abram*."

  [1] *i.e.* England,—though the scene of the play is laid in Venice.
Monsieur Motte, or La Motte, was a prominent figure at the English
court in the early years of Elizabeth's reign.

  [2] "Against the hair" is equivalent to our expression "against the
grain."

  [3] Old ed. "this."

they hoped to be saved?—by my virginity I swear, I
dreamed that one brought me a goodly codshead, and in
one of the eyes there stuck, methought, the greatest precious stone, the most sparkling diamond : O, fie, fie, fie,
fie, fie, that diamonds should make women such fools ! 240

    Cur. A codshead and a diamond? ha, ha, ha !
'Tis common, common : you may dream as well
Of diamonds and of codsheads, where's not one,
As swear by your virginity, where's none.—
I am that codshead ; she has spied my stone,
My diamond : noble wench, but nobler stone ;[1]
I'm an old courtier, and lie close, lie close.

                     [*Aside, and puts it up.*
    [*The cornets sound a lavolta, which the masquers are
        to dance:* CAMILLO, HIPPOLITO, *and other gallants,
        every one, save* HIPPOLITO,[2] *with a lady masqued,
        and zanies*[3] *with torches,*[4] *enter suddenly :* CUR-
        VETTO *offers to depart.*

    Imp. No, no, no, if you shrink from me, I will not love
you : stay.

    Cur. I am conjured, and will keep my circle.   250
                          [*They dance.*

---

   [1] Dyce's correction for " no see " of the old ed.
   [2] " Because, probably, Imperia was to be his partner. The lavolta
was a dance for two persons, described by Sir J. Davies, in his *Orchestra,*
as 'a lofty jumping or a leaping round.' See also Douce's *Illust. of
Shakspeare,* vol. i. p. 489."—*Dyce.*
   [3] Here and in iii. 1 (where Frisco is described as " Imperia the
courtesan's *zany* "), the word *zany* must mean attendant. See the
quotation from Florio's *New World of Words* in Nares' *Glossary.*
   [4] Dyce's correction for " coaches " of the old ed.

Imp. Fie, fie, fie, by the neat tongue of eloquence, this measure is out of measure ; 'tis too hot, too hot. Gallants, be not ashamed to show your own faces. Ladies, un-apparel your dear beauties. So, so, so, so ; here is a banquet ; sit, sit, sit. Signior Curvetto, thrust in among them. Soft music, there ! do, do, do.

[*Music, while they seat themselves.*

Cur. I will first salute the men, close with the women, and last sit.

Hip. But not sit last : a banquet, and have these suckets[1] here ! O, I have a crew of angels[2] prisoners in my pocket, and none but a good bale[3] of dice can fetch them out.—Dice, ho!—Come, my little lecherous baboon ; by Saint Mark, you shall venture your twenty crowns. 263

Cur. And have but one.

Hip. I swore first.

Cur. Right, you swore ;
But oaths are now, like Blurt our constable,
Standing for nothing.—A mere plot, a trick :
The masque dogg'd me, I hit it in the nick ;
A fetch to get my diamond, my dear stone ;
I'm a hoary courtier, but lie close, close, close.—
I'll play, sir.   [*Aside.*

Hip. Come.

Cur. But in my t'other hose.[4]   [*Exit.* 270

---

[1] Sweetmeats.   [2] See note 2, p. 32.   [3] Pair.
[4] *Cf. Spanish Gipsy*, iii. 2 :—
        "But being asked, as I suppose,
        Your answer will be, *in your t'other hose.*"
The expression was proverbial, and was equivalent to " Not if I know it."

Omnes. Curvetto!

Hip. Let him go : I knew what hook would choke him, and therefore baited that for him to nibble upon. An old comb-pecked rascal, that was beaten out a' th' cock-pit, when I could not stand a' high lone[1] without I held a thing, to come crowing among us ! Hang him, lobster. Come, the same oath that your foreman took, take all, and sing.

SONG.

> *Love is like a lamb, and love is like a lion ;*
> *Fly from love, he fights, fight, then does he fly on ;* 280
> *Love is all in fire, and yet is ever freezing ;*
> *Love is much in winning, yet is more in leesing ;*[2]
> *Love is ever sick, and yet is never dying ;*
> *Love is ever true, and yet is ever lying ;*
> *Love does doat in liking, and is mad in loathing ;*
> *Love indeed is anything, yet indeed is nothing.*

During the song LAZARILLO *enters.*[3]

Laz. Mars armipotent with his court of guard, give sharpness to my toledo ! I am beleaguered. O Cupid, grant that my blushing prove not a linstock, and give

---

[1] Dyce mentions that in *Romeo and Juliet*, i. 3 (l. 35), the 1597 4to. reads "high lone" (1599 4to. "hylone ;" later eds. "alone"). He also compares W. Rowley's *A Shoemaker a Gentleman*, 1638 :—"The warres has lam'd many of my old customers, they cannot go *a hie* lone." Sig. B. 4. I have met the expression in Marston's 2d part of *Antonio and Mellida*, iv. 4 :—

> "As some weak-breasted dame
> Giveth her infant, puts it out to nurse ;
> And when it once goes *high-lone*, takes it back."

[2] *i.e.* losing.

[3] "His entrance is not marked in the old copy, and perhaps the poet intended that he should come in with the masquers."—*Dyce.*

fire too suddenly to the Roaring Meg[1] of my desires !—
Most sanguine-cheeked ladies— 291

Hip. 'S foot, how now, Don Dego?[2] sanguine-
cheeked? dost think their faces have been at cutler's?[3]
out, you roaring, tawney-faced rascal ! 'Twere a good
deed to beat my hilts about's coxcomb, and then make
him sanguine-cheeked too.

Cam. Nay, good Hippolito.

Imp. Fie, fie, fie, fie, fie ; though I hate his company,
I would not have my house to abuse his countenance ;
no, no, no, be not so contagious : I will send him hence
with a flea in's ear. 301

Hip. Do, or I'll turn him into a flea, and make him
skip under some of your petticoats.

Imp. Signior Lazarillo.

Laz. Most sweet face, you need not hang out your
silken tongue as a flag of truce, for I will drop at your
feet ere I draw blood in your chamber. Yet I shall
hardly drink up this wrong : for your sake I will wipe it

---

[1] "Roaring Meg" was the name of a cannon. See Nares' *Glossary*,
ed. Halliwell.

[2] "Don Diego" (or "Dego") was the name of a certain Spaniard,
who, as the dramatists are constantly reminding us, "made Paul's to
stink." Hence *Don Diego* was derisively used for Spaniard.

[3] "So Beaumont and Fletcher :—

'*Piso.* ——-—— O' my life, he looks
    Of a more rusty, swarth complexion
    Than an old armory doublet.
  Lod. I would send
    His *face to th' cutler's then, and have it sanguin'd.*'
                    —*Captain*, act. ii. sc. 2.

'*Sanguine.* The bloud-stone wherewith cutlers do sanguine their
hilts.'—*Cotgrave's Dict.*"—*Dyce.*

out for this time. I would deal with you in secret, so
you had a void room, about most deep and serious
matters.   311

Imp. I'll send these hence.—Fie, fie, fie, I am so
choked still with this man of gingerbread, and yet I can
never be rid of him! but hark, Hippolito.

[*Whispers* HIPPOLITO.

Hip. Good; draw the curtains, put out candles; and,
girls, to bed. [*Exeunt* [1] *all but* IMPERIA *and* LAZARILLO.

Laz. Venus, give me suck from thine own most white
and tender dugs, that I may batten in love. Dear instrument of many men's delight, are all these women? 319

Imp. No, no, no, they are half men and half women.

Laz. You apprehend too fast: I mean by women,
wives; for wives are no maids, nor are maids women.
If those unbearded gallants keep the doors of their wedlock, those ladies spend their hours of pastime but ill,
O most rich armful of beauty! But if you can bring all
those females into one ring, into one private place, I
will read a lecture of discipline to their most great and
honourable ears, wherein I will teach them so to carry
their white bodies, either before their husbands or before
their lovers, that they shall never fear to have milk thrown
in their faces, nor I wine in mine, when I come to sit
upon them in courtesy.   332

Imp. That were excellent: I'll have them all here at
your pleasure.

Laz. I will show them all the tricks and garbs of

---

[1] Not marked in the old ed.

Spanish dames; I will study for apt and [e]legant phrase to tickle them with; and when my devise is ready, I will come. Will you inspire into your most divine spirits the most divine soul of tobacco? 339

Imp. No, no, no; fie, fie, fie, I should be choked up, if your pipe should kiss my underlip.

Laz. Henceforth, most deep stamp of feminine perfection, my pipe shall not be drawn before you but in secret.

Re-enter HIPPOLITO *and the rest of the Masquers, as before, dancing :* HIPPOLITO *takes* IMPERIA *; and then exeunt all except* LAZARILLO.

Laz. Lament my case, since thou canst not provoke Her nose to smell, love fill thine own with smoke.[1]

[*Exit.*

---

[1] Dyce thought that part of this scene had been lost at the press. The conclusion is certainly very abrupt.

ACT III.

SCENE I.

A Street before HIPPOLITO'S *House.*

Enter HIPPOLITO *and* FRISCO.

Fris. The wooden picture you sent her hath set her on fire ; and she desires you, as you pity the case of a poor desperate gentlewoman, to serve that Monsieur in at supper to her.

Enter CAMILLO *with Musicians.*

Hip. The Frenchman ? Saint Denis, let her carve him up. Stay, here's Camillo. Now, my fool in fashion, my sage idiot, up with these brims,[1] down with this devil, Melancholy ! Are you decayed, concupiscentious ina-morato ? News, news ; Imperia doats on Fontinelle.   9

Cam. What comfort speaks her love to my sick heart ?

Hip. Marry, this, sir. Here's a yellow-hammer flew to me with thy water ; and I cast it, and find that his

---

[1] Camillo has his hat drawn over his eyes, as the Inamorato is repre-sented in the engraved frontispiece of Burton's *Anatomy of Melancholy.* Old ed. "this brimmes."

mistress being given to this new falling sickness, will cure
thee.   The Frenchman, you see, has a soft marmalady
heart, and shall no sooner feel Imperia's liquorish desire
to lick at him, but straight he'll stick the brooch of her
longing in it.   Then, sir, may you, sir, come upon my
sister, sir, with a fresh charge, sir ; sa, sa, sa, sa ! once
giving back, and thrice coming forward ; she yield, and
the town of Brest is taken.   20

 Cam. This hath some taste of hope.   Is that the
    Mercury
Who brings you notice of his mistress' love ?

 Fris. I may be her Mercury, for my running of errands ;
but troth is, sir, I am Cerberus, for I am porter to hell.

 Cam. Then, Cerberus, play thy part : here, search that
    hell ;   [*Gives him a key.*
There find and bring forth that false Fontinelle.
               [*Exit* FRISCO.
If I can win his stray'd thoughts to retire
From her encounter'd eyes, whom I have singled
In Hymen's holy battle, he shall pass
From hence to France, in company and guard   30
Of mine own heart :—he comes, Hippolito.

   Enter FONTINELLE *talking with* FRISCO.

Still looks he like a lover : poor gentleman,
Love is the mind's strong physic, and the pill
That leaves the heart sick and o'erturns the will.

 Font. O happy persecution, I embrace thee
With an unfetter'd soul !   So sweet a thing
Is it to sigh upon the rack of love,

Where each calamity is groaning witness
Of the poor martyr's faith.   I never heard
Of any true affection, but 'twas nipt   40
With care, that, like the caterpillar, eats
The leaves off the spring's sweetest book, the rose.
Love bred on earth, is often nurs'd in hell ;
By rote it reads woe, ere it learn to spell.

   Cam. Good morrow, French lord.

   Hip. Bon jour, Monsieur.

   Font. To your secure and more than happy self
I tender thanks, for you have honour'd me.
You are my jailor, and have penn'd me up,
Lest the poor fly, your prisoner, should alight
Upon your mistress' lip, and thence derive   50
The dimpled print of an infective touch.
Thou secure tyrant, yet unhappy lover,
Couldst thou chain mountains to my captive feet,
Yet Violetta's heart and mine should meet.

   Hip. Hark, swaggerer, there's a little dapple-coloured
rascal ; ho, a bona-roba ; her name's Imperia ; a gentlewoman, by my faith, of an ancient house, and has goodly
rents and comings in of her own ; and this ape would fain
have thee chained to her in the holy state.   Sirrah, she's
fallen in love with thy picture ; yes, faith.   To her, woo
her, and win her ; leave my sister, and thy ransom's paid ;
all's paid, gentlemen : by th' Lord, Imperia is as good a
girl as any is in Venice.   63

   Cam. Upon mine honour, Fontinelle, 'tis true ;
The lady doats on thy perfections :

Therefore resign my Violetta's heart
To me, the lord of it ; and I will send thee—
   Font. O, whither? to damnation, wilt thou not?
Think'st thou the purity of my true soul
Can taste your leperous counsel? no, I defy you.   70
Incestancy [1] dwell on his rivell'd [2] brow
That weds for dirt ; or on th' enforced heart
That lags in rearward of his father's charge,
When to some negro-guelderling he's clogg'd
By the injunction of a golden fee !
When I call back my vows to Violetta,
May I then slip into an obscure grave,
Whose mould, unprest with stony monument,
Dwelling in open air, may drink the tears
Of the inconstant clouds, to rot me soon   80
Out of my private linen sepulchre !
   Cam. Ay !
Is this your settled resolution ?
   Font. By my love's best divinity, it is.
   Cam. Then bear him to his prison back again.—
This tune must alter ere thy lodging mend :
To death, fond Frenchman, thy slight love doth tend.
   Font. Then, constant heart, thy fate with joy pursue ;
Draw wonder to thy death, expiring true.   [*Exit.* 89
   Hip. After him, Frisco ; enforce thy mistress's passion.
Thou shalt have access to him, to bring him love tokens :
if they prevail not, yet thou shalt still be in presence, be't
but to spite him. In, honest Frisco.

---

[1] A word coined by Middleton.   [2] Shrivell'd.

Fris. I'll vex him to the heart, sir; fear not me.
Yet here's a trick perchance may set him free.

[Aside and exit.

Hip. Come, wilt thou go laugh and lie down?[1] Now
sure there be some rebels in thy belly, for thine eyes do
nothing but watch and ward : thou'st not sleep these three
nights.

Cam. Alas, how can I? he that truly loves   100
Burns out the day in idle fantasies ;
And when the lamb bleating doth bid good night
Unto the closing day, then tears begin
To keep quick time unto the owl, whose voice
Shrieks like the belman[2] in the lover's ears :
Love's eye the jewel of sleep, O, seldom wears !
The early lark is waken'd from her bed,
Being only by love's plaints disquieted,
And, singing in the morning's ear, she weeps,
Being deep in love, at lovers' broken sleeps :   110
But say a golden slumber chance to tie,
With silken strings the cover of love's eye,
Then dreams, magician-like, mocking present
Pleasures, whose fading leaves more discontent.
Have you these golden charms?

Mus. We have, my lord.

Cam. Bestow them sweetly ; think a lover's heart
Dwells in each instrument, and let it melt

---

1 There was a game at cards called *laugh and lay down.*
2 " Here, perhaps, Middleton recollected *Macbeth :*—
   ' It was the owl that shriek'd, the fatal belman,
     Which gives the stern'st good night.'—Act ii. sc. 2."—*Dyce.*

In weeping strains.   Yonder direct your faces,
That the soft summons of a frightless parley
May creep into the casement.   So, begin :   120
Music, speak movingly ; assume my part ;
For thou must now plead to a stony heart.

SONG.

Pity, pity, pity !
Pity, pity, pity !
That word begins that ends a true-love ditty.
Your blessed eyes, like a pair of suns,
Shine in the sphere of smiling ;
Your pretty lips, like a pair of doves,
Are kisses still compiling.
Mercy hangs upon your brow, like a precious jewel : 130
O, let not then,
Most lovely maid, best to be lov'd of men,
Marble lie upon your heart, that will make you cruel !
Pity, pity, pity !
Pity, pity, pity !
That word begins that ends a true-love ditty.

                              [VIOLETTA *appears above.*

Viol. Who owes[1] this salutation?
Cam. Thy Camillo.
Viol. Is not your shadow there too, my sweet brother ?
Hip. Here, sweet sister.
Viol. I dreamt so.   O, I am much bound to you ! 140
For you, my lord, have us'd my love with honour.

---

[1] Owns.

Cam. Ever with honour.

Viol. Indeed, indeed, you have.

Hip. 'S light, she means her French *garçon*.

Viol. The same.   Good night; trust me, 'tis somewhat
   late,
And this bleak wind nips dead all idle prate.
I must to bed : good night.

  Cam. The god of rest
Play music to thine eyes ! whilst on my breast
The Furies sit and beat, and keep care waking.

  Hip. You will not leave my friend in this poor
   taking ?

  Viol. Yes, by the velvet brow of darkness !   150

  Hip. You scurvy tit—'s foot, scurvy anything !   Do
you hear, Susanna ? you punk, if I geld not your musk-
cat ! I'll do't, by Jesu. Let's go, Camillo.

  Viol. Nay but, pure swaggerer, ruffian, do you
   think
To fright me with your bugbear threats ? go by !
Hark, toss-pot, in your ear ; the Frenchman's mine,
And by these hands I'll have him !

  Hip. Rare rogue, fine !

  Viol. He is my prisoner, by a deed of gift ;
Therefore, Camillo, you have wrong'd me much
To wrong my prisoner.   By my troth, I love him   160
The rather for the baseness he endures
For my unworthy self.   I'll tell you what ;
Release him, let him plead your love for you ;
I love a' life [1] to hear a man speak French

---

[1] As my life.

Of his complexion ; I would undergo
The instruction of that language rather far
Than be two weeks unmarried.   By my life,
Because I'll speak true French, I'll be his wife.

    Cam. O, scorn to my chaste love ! burst, heart.
    Hip. 'S wounds, hold !   170
    Cam. Come, gentle friends, tie your most solemn tunes
By silver strings unto a leaden pace.
False fair, enjoy thy base belov'd : adieu :
He's far less noble, and shall prove less true.

             [*Exeunt* CAMILLO, HIPPOLITO, *and Musicians.*

      Enter TRUEPENNY *above with a letter.*

    True. Lady, Imperia the courtesan's zany[1] hath
brought you this letter from the poor gentleman in the
deep dungeon, but would not stay till he had an answer.

    Viol. Her groom employed by Fontinelle ?   O, strange !
I wonder how he got access to him.
I'll read, and reading my poor heart shall ache :   180
True love is jealous ; fears the best love shake.

                            [*Reads.*

    Meet me at the end of the old chapel, next Saint Lorenzo's
monastery.   Furnish your company with a friar, that there
he may consummate our holy vows.   Till midnight, farewell.
Thine,   FONTINELLE.
Hath he got opportunity to 'scape ?
O happy period of our separation !

---

[1] See note 3, p. 44.

Blest night, wrap Cynthia in a sable sheet,
That fearful lovers may securely meet?   [*Exeunt.*

SCENE II.

Before Saint Lorenzo's Monastery.

Enter FRISCO *in* FONTINELLE'S *apparel, and* FONTINELLE
making himself ready[1] *in* FRISCO'S : *they enter suddenly and in fear.*

Fris. Play you my part bravely; you must look like a
slave : and you shall see I'll counterfeit the Frenchman
most knavishly.   My mistress, for your sake, charged me
on her blessing to fall to these shifts.   I left her at cards :
she'll sit up till you come, because she'll have you play
a game at noddy.[2]   You'll to her presently?

Font. I will, upon mine honour.

Fris. I think she does not greatly care whether you
fall to her upon your honour or no.   So, all's fit.   Tell
my lady that I go in a suit of durance for her sake.
That's your way, and this pit-hole's mine.   If I can 'scape
hence, why so; if not, he that's hanged is nearer to
heaven by half a score steps than he that dies in a bed :
and so adieu, monsieur.   [*Exit.* 14

Font. Farewell, dear trusty slave.   Shall I profane
This temple with an idol of strange love?
When I do so, let me dissolve in fire.
Yet one day will I see this dame, whose heart

---

[1] "Make ready" = dress.   [2] A game at cards.

Takes off my misery : I'll not be so rude
To pay her kindness with ingratitude.   20

      Enter VIOLETTA *and a Friar apace.*

  Viol. My dearest Fontinelle !
  Font. My Violetta !
O God !
  Viol. O God !
  Font. Where is this reverend friar ?
  Friar. Here, overjoy'd young man.
  Viol. How didst thou 'scape ?
How came Imperia's man——
  Font. No more of that.
  Viol. When did Imperia——
  Font. Questions now are thieves,
And lies in ambush to surprise our joys.
[O] my most happy stars, shine still, shine on !
Away, come : love beset had need be gone.   28
                          [*Exeunt.*

SCENE III.

    A Room in IMPERIA'S *House.*

    Enter CURVETTO *and* SIMPERINA.

  Cur. I must not stay, thou sayst ?
  Sim. God's me, away !
  Cur. Buss, buss again :—here's sixpence ;—buss
        again,—
Farewell : I must not stay then ?
  Sim. Foh !
  Cur. Farewell .

At ten a' clock [1] thou sayst, and ring a bell,
Which thou wilt hang out at this window?
   Sim. Lord!
She'll hear this fiddling.
   Cur. No, close, on my word.
Farewell: just ten a' clock; I shall come in?
Remember to let down the cord,—just ten:
Thou'lt open, mouse? pray God thou dost. Amen!
    Amen! Amen!
I'm an old courtier, wench, but I can spy   10
A young duck: close, mum; ten; close, 'tis not I.
                                      [Exit.
   Sim. Mistress, sweet ladies!

      Enter IMPERIA *and Ladies with table-books.*[2]

   Imp. Is his old rotten aqua-vitæ bottle stopt up? is
he gone? Fie, fie, fie, fie, he so smells of ale and onions,
and rosa-solis, fie. Bolt the door, stop the keyhole, lest
his breath peep in. Burn some perfume. I do not love
to handle these dried stockfishes, that ask so much taw-
ing:[3] fie, fie, fie.
   First Lady. Nor I, trust me, lady; fie.   19
   Imp. No, no, no, no. Stools and cushions; low stools,
low stools; sit, sit, sit, round, ladies, round. [*They seat*

---

[1] In the preceding scene, Violetta meets Fontenelle at midnight.
[2] Note-books.
[3] " To *taw* is, properly, to dress leather with alum :—
    ' Yes, if they *taw* him, as they do whit-leather,
    Upon an iron, or beat him soft like stockfish.'
    —*Beaumont and Fletcher's Captain,* act iii. sc. 3."—*Dyce.*

themselves.] So, so, so, so; let your sweet beauties be
spread to the full and most moving advantage; for we
are fallen into his hands, who, they say, has an A B C for
the sticking in of the least white pin in any part of the
body.

Second Lady. Madam Imperia, what stuff is he like to
draw out before us?

Imp. Nay, nay, nay, 'tis Greek to me, 'tis Greek to
me: I never had remnant of his Spanish-leather learning.
Here he comes: your ears may now fit themselves out
of the whole piece.   32

Enter LAZARILLO.[1]

Laz. I do first deliver to your most skreet[2] and long-
fingered hands this head, or top of all the members, bare
and uncombed, to show how deeply I stand in reverence
of your naked female beauties. Bright and unclipt
angels,[3] if I were to make a discovery of any new-found
land, as Virginia or so, to ladies and courtiers, my speech
should hoist up sails fit to bear up such lofty and well-
rigged vessels: but because I am to deal only with the
civil chitty-matron, I will not lay upon your blushing
and delicate cheek[s] any other colours than such as will
give lustre to your chitty faces: in and to that purpose,
our thesis is taken out of that most plentiful, but most
precious book entitled the *Economical Cornucopia.*   45

First Lady. The what?

---

[1] Old ed. "Lazarino."   [2] Discreet.
[3] See note 2, p. 32.

Laz. The *Economical Cornucopia :* thus,
Wise is that wife, who with apt wit complains
That she's kept under, yet rules all the reins.

    Second Lady. O, again, sweet signior !—[*writing*]
           ——*complains*
That she's kept under——
What follows ?   53

    Laz. Yet *rules all the reins :*
Wise is that wife, who with apt wit complains
That she's kept under, yet rules all the reins.

Most pure and refined plants of nature, I will not, as this
distinction enticeth, take up the parts as they lie here in
order ; as first, to touch your *wisdom,* it were folly ; next,
your *complaining,* 'tis too common ; thirdly, your *keeping
under,* 'tis above my capachity ; and, lastly, *the reins in
your own hands,* that is the a-per-se [1] of all, the very cream
of all, and therefore how to skim off that only, only listen :
a wife wise, no matter ; apt wit, no matter ; complaining,
no matter ; kept under, no great matter ; but to rule the
roast is the matter.   66

    Third Lady. That ruling of the roast goes with me.
    Fourth Lady. And me.
    Fifth Lady. And me ; I'll have a cut of that roast.

    Laz. Since, then, a woman's only desire is to have the
reins in her own white hand, your chief practice, the
very same day that you are wived, must be to get hold
of these reins ; and being fully gotten, or wound about,
yet to complain, with apt wit, as though you had them not.

---

    [1] The chief excellence. See Nares' *Glossary.*

Imp. How shall we know, signior, when we have them all or not? 76

Laz. I will furnish your capable understandings out of my poor Spanish store with the chief implements, and their appurtenances. Observe; it shall be your first and finest praise to sing the note of every new fashion at first sight, and, if you can, to stretch that note above ela.[1]

Omnes. Good.

Laz. The more you pinch your servants' bellies for this, the smoother will the fashion sit on your back : but if your goodman like not this music, as being too full of crotchets, your only way is, to learn to play upon the virginals,[2] and so nail his ears to your sweet humours. If this be out of time too, yet your labour will quit the cost ; for by this means your secret friend may have free and open access to you, under the colour of pricking you lessons. Now, because you may tie your husband's love in most sweet knots, you shall never give over labouring till out of his purse you have digged *a garden ;*[3] and that garden must stand a pretty distance from the chitty ; for by repairing thither, much good fruit may be grafted.

First Lady. Mark that. 96

Laz. Then, in the afternoon, when you address your sweet perfumed body to walk to this garden, there to gather a nosegay,—sops-in-wine,[4] cowslips, columbines,

---

[1] The highest note in the scale.

[2] A rectangular musical instrument, of the spinnet kind.

[3] "As these words are given in italics, they are probably intended as a quotation from the *Economical Cornucopia.*"—*Dyce.*

[4] Supposed to be the flowers now called pinks.

heart's-ease, &c.,—the first principle to learn is, that you stick black patches for the rheum on your delicate blue temples, though there be no room for the rheum : black patches[1] are comely in most women, and being well fastened, draw men's eyes to shoot glances at you. Next, your ruff must stand in print ;[2] and for that purpose, get poking-sticks[3] with fair and long handles, lest they scorch your lily sweating hands. Then your hat with a little brim, if you have a little face ; if otherwise, otherwise. Besides, you must play the wag with your wanton fan ; have your dog,—called Pearl,[4] or Min, or Why ask you, or any other pretty name,—dance along by you ; your embroidered muff before you, on your ravishing hands ; but take heed who thrusts his fingers into your fur.   113

Second Lady. We'll watch for that.

Laz. Once a quarter take state upon you and be chick.[5] Being chick thus politicly, lie at your garden ; your, lip-sworn servant may there visit you as a physician ; where[6] otherwise, if you languish at home, be sure your husband will look to your water. This chickness may be increased, with giving out that you breed young bones ;

---

[1] It is hardly necessary to mention that black patches on the face were formerly considered ornamental.

[2] In a precise manner. Nicholas Breton describes an " effeminate fool " as one who loves " to have his ruffs set in print, to pick his teeth and play with a puppet."—*The Good and the Bad, &c.*, 1616.

[3] Sticks of steel for setting the plaits of the ruff.

[4] "Pearl" was a not uncommon name for a dog. It occurs in Day's *Isle of Gulls* (v. 4), Rowlands' *Letting of Humour's Blood in the Head Vein* (epigram 33), &c.

[5] Affected pronunciation of "sick." A few lines below we have " chickness."   [6] Whereas.

and to stick flesh upon those bones, it shall not be amiss
if you long for peascods at ten groats the cod, and for
cherries [1] at a crown the cherry. 123

First Lady. O dear tutor!

Second Lady. Interrupt him not.

Laz. If, while this pleasing fit of chickness hold you,
you be invited forth to supper, whimper and seem unwilling to go; but if your goodman, bestowing the sweet
duck and kiss upon your moist lip, entreat, go. Marry,
my counsel is, you eat little at table, because it may be
said of you, you are no cormorant; yet at your coming
home you may counterfeit a qualm, and so devour a posset.
Your husband need not have his nose in that posset; no,
trust your chambermaid only in this, and scarcely her;
for you cannot be too careful into whose hands you
commit your secrets. 136

Omnes. That's certain.

Laz. If you have daughters capable, marry them by no
means to chittizens, but choose for them some smooth-
chinned, curled-headed gentlemen; [2] for gentlemen will lift
up your daughters to their own content; and to make
these curled-pated gallants come off the more roundly,
make your husband go to the herald for arms; and let
it be your daily care that he have a fair and comely crest;
yea, go all the ways yourselves you can to be made ladies,
especially if, without danger to his person, or for love or
money, you can procure your husband to be dubbed.

---

[1] In *Eastward Ho* (i. 1) it is mentioned among the "humours of the
city-dames" that they "eat cherries only at an angel the pound."

[2] Old ed. "gentleman."

The goddess of memory lock up these jewels, which I have
bestowed upon you, in your sweet brains ! Let these be
the rules to square out your life by, though you ne'er go
level, but tread you[r] shoes awry. If you can get these
reins into your lily hand[s], you shall need no coaches,
but may drive your husbands. Put it down ; and, according to that wise saying of you, be saints in the church,
angels in the street, devils in the kitchen, and apes in
your bed : upon which leaving you tumbling, pardon me
that thus abruptly and openly I take you all up.   157

First Lady. You have got so far into our books, signior,
that you cannot 'scape without a pardon here, if you take
us up never so snappishly.

Imp. Music there, to close our stomachs ! How do you
like him, madonna ?   [*Music.*

Second Lady. O, trust me, I like him most profoundly !
why, he's able to put down twenty such as I am.

Third Lady. Let them build upon that ; nay, more,
we'll henceforth never go to a cunning woman, since men
can teach us our lerry.[1]

Fourth Lady. We are all fools to him ; and our husbands, if we can hold these reins fast, shall be fools to us.

Second Lady. If we can keep but this bias, wenches,
our goodmen may perchance once in a month get a fore-
game of us ; but, if they win a rubbers, let them throw
their caps at it.   173

Imp. No, no, no, dear features, hold their noses to the
grindstone, and they're gone. Thanks, worthy signior :
fie, fie, fie, you stand bare too long. Come, bright

---

[1] Learning.

mirrors, will you withdraw into a gallery and taste a slight banquet?

First Lady. We shall cloy ourselves with sweets, my sweet madonna.   180

Second Lady. Troth, I will not, madonna Imperia.

Imp. No, no, no. Fie, fie, fie, signior Lazarillo, either be you our foreman, or else put in these ladies, at your discretion, into the gallery, and cut off this striving.

Laz. It shall be my office; my fees being, as they pass, to take toll of their alablaster [1] hands. [*Exeunt Ladies: IMPERIA stays.*] Admired creature, I summon you to a parley: you remember this is the night?

Imp. So, so, so, I do remember: here is a key; that is your chamber.—Lights, Simperina.—About twelve a' clock you shall take my beauty prisoner:—fie, fie, fie, how I blush!—at twelve a' clock.   192

Laz. Rich argosy of all golden pleasure—

Imp. No, no, no, put up, put up your joys till anon: I will come, by my virginity. But I must tell you one thing, that all my chambers are many nights haunted, with what sprites none can see; but sometimes we hear birds singing, sometimes music playing, sometimes voices laughing: but stir not you, nor be frightened at anything.

Laz. By Hercules, if any spirits rise, I will conjure them in their own circles with toledo.   201

Imp. So, so, so; lights for his chamber.—Is the trap-door ready?   [*Aside.*

---

[1] A not uncommon form. William Alabaster, the well-known writer on Cabalistic divinity, sometimes spelt his name *Alablaster.*

Simp. 'Tis set sure.

Imp. So, so, so, I will be rid of this broiled red sprat, that stinks so in my stomach, fie ; I hate him worse than to have a tailor come a-wooing to me. [*Aside.*] God's me! the sweet ladies, the banquet,—I forget: fie, fie, fie, follow, dear signior.—The trap-door, Simperina. [*Aside, and exit.*

Simp. Signior, come away.

Laz. Cupid, I kiss the nock [1] of thy sweet bow :
A woman makes me yield ; Mars could not so.   212
[*Exit with* SIMPERINA.

---

[1] Notch (where the bowstring is tied).

ACT IV.

SCENE I.

A Street before IMPERIA'S *House ; a cord hanging from
the window.*

Enter CURVETTO, *with a lantern.*

Cur. Just ten? 'tis ten just : that's the fixed hour
For payment of my love's due fees ; that broke,
I forfeit a huge sum of joys : ho, love,
I will keep time just to a minute, I ;
A sweet guide's [1] loss is a deep penalty :
A night's so rich a venture [2] to taste wrack,
Would make a lover bankrupt, break his back.
No, if to sit up late, early to rise,
Or if this goldfinch, [3] that with sweet notes flies,
And wakes the dull eye even of a puritan,   10
Can work, then, wenches, Curvetto is the man.
I am not young, yet have I youthful tricks,

---

1 Probably a misprint, as Dyce suggested, for "girl's."
2 So the 4to. Dyce reads "adventure." He is not correct in saying
the 4to. reads "aventure."
3 Here the speaker chinks his purse.

Which peering day must not see ; no, close, close,
Old courtier, perilous [1] fellow, I can lie ;
Hug in your bosom, close, yet none shall spy.
Stay, here's the door, the window ; hah, this, this !
Cord ?—umph !—dear cord, thy blessed knot I kiss.
None peeps, I hope.   Night, clap thy velvet hand
Upon all eyes ! if now my friend thou stand,
I'll hang a jewel at thine ear, sweet night ;   20
And here it is, *lantern and candle-light.*[2]
A peal, a lusty peal, set, ring love's knell ;
I'll sweat, but thus I'll bear away the bell.

> [*Pulls the cord hanging from the window, and
> is drenched with water.*

Enter SIMPERINA *above.*

Sim. Signior,—who's there ? signior Curvetto ?
Cur. Umph, drown'd ! Noah's flood ! duck'd over
        head and ears !
O sconce, and O sconce ![3] an old [4] soaker, O !
I sweat now till I drop : what, villains, O !
Punks, punkateroes, nags, hags ! I will ban :
I've catch'd my bane.

---

[1] Shrewd.   The commoner form is *parlous.*

[2] "Lantern and candle-light" was the bellman's cry : see the song at the end of Heywood's *Rape of Lucrece.* One of Dekker's tracts is entitled *Lanthorne and Candlelight, or the Bellmans second Night Walke* (1609), and another *O per se O, Or a new Cryer of Lanthorne and Candlelight, being an Addition or Lengthening of the Bellman's second Night-walke* (1612).

[3] "*i.e.* (I suppose), O my head, and O my lantern ! "—*Dyce.*

[4] *i.e.* rare, fine.   In this sense the word "old" still keeps its place in the vocabulary of slang.

Sim. Who's there?

Cur. A water-man.

Sim. Who rings that scolding peal?

Cur. I am wringing wet,   30

I'm wash'd : foh, here's rose-water sold by th' ounce!

This sconce shall batter down those windows—bounce!

   Sim. What do you mean? why do you beat our

         doors?

What do you take us for?

   Cur. You're all damn'd whores.

   Sim. Signior Curvetto!

   Cur. Signior coxcomb, no.[1]

   Sim. What makes you be so hot?

   Cur. You lie, I'm cool;

I'm an old courtier, but stinking fool.

Foh!

   Sim. God's my life! what have you done? you are

in a sweet pickle if you pulled at this rope.   40

   Cur. Hang thyself, in't and I'll pull once again.

   Sim. Marry muff,[2] will you up and ride? you're

mine elder. By my pure maidenhead, here's a jest!

why, this was a water-work to drown a rat that uses to

creep in at this window.

   Cur. Fire on your water-works! catch a drown'd

         rat?

That's me, I have it, God a-mercy, head!

Rat? me; I smell a rat, I strike it dead.

   Sim. You smell a sodden sheep's-head: a rat? ay,

---

[1] See note 3, p. 22.   [2] See note 1, p. 42.

a rat : and you will not believe me, marry, foh! I have
been believed of your betters, marry, snick up!   51

Cur. Simp, nay, sweet Simp, open again; why, Simperina !

Sim. Go from my window,[1] go, go from, &c., away;
go by, old Jeronimo :[2] nay, and you shrink i' th' wetting,
walk, walk, walk.

Cur. I cry thee mercy ; if the bowl were set
To drown a rat, I shrink not, am not wet.

Sim. A rat by this hemp, and you could ha' smelt.
Hark you ; here's the bell, ting, ting, ting: would the
clapper were in my belly, if I am not mad at your
foppery ; I could scratch, fie, fie, fie, fie, fie, as my
mistress says. But go, hie you home, shift you, come
back presently : here you shall find a ladder of cords ;
climb up ; I'll receive you : my mistress lies alone ; she's
yours : away.   66

Cur. O Simp !

Sim. Nay, scud : you know what you promised me :
I shall have simple yawling for this : begone and mum.

                   [*Simperina claps-to the window.*[3]

Cur. Thanks, mum, dear girl; I'm gone : 'twas for a
       rat,
A rat upon my life : thou shalt have gifts ;

---

[1] These words are part of an old song, two stanzas of which are sung
by Merrythought in the *Knight of the Burning Pestle,* iii. 5. The whole
song is found, with some variations, at the end of Heywood's *Rape of
Lucrece.*

[2] The words "go by, old Jeronimo" are from Kyd's *Spanish Tragedy.*
They are constantly ridiculed by the dramatists.

[3] The stage direction in the old ed. is simply " *clap.*"

I love thee, though thou puts me to my shifts.
I knew[1] I could be over-reach'd by none ;
A parlous [2] head ! lie close, lie close : I'm gone.

[Exeunt severally.

SCENE II.

A Room in IMPERIA'S *House.*

Music suddenly plays and birds sing : enter LAZARILLO
*bareheaded, in his shirt, a pair of pantaples[3] on, a
rapier in his hand and a tobacco-pipe : he seems amazed,
and walks so up and down.[4]*

Laz. Saint Jacques and the Seven deadly Sins (that is,
the Seven Wise Masters of the world), pardon me, for
this night I will kill the devil !

[*Within.*] Ha, ha, ha !

Laz. Thou prince of blackamoors, thou shalt have
small cause to laugh, if I run thee through. This chamber is haunted : would I had not been brought a' bed in
it, or else were well delivered ! for my heart tells me 'tis
no good luck to have anything to do with the devil ; he's
a paltry merchant.[5]   10

[*Song within.*]
*Midnight's bell goes ting, ting, ting, ting, ting ;
Then dogs do howl ; and not a bird does sing*

---

[1] Old ed. " know."

[2] Dyce's correction for " Paulons " of the old ed.

[3] Slippers.—The commoner form is " pantables."

[4] In the old ed. is the further direction " A song presently within,"
—to instruct the singers to be in readiness.

[5] " Merchant " was (and is) sometimes used in a slang sense for
"fellow :" cf. " chap " (a contraction for " chapman ").

> *But the nightingale, and she cries twit, twit, twit,*
> *twit;*
> *Owls then on every bough do sit;*
> *Ravens croak on chimneys' tops;*
> *The cricket in the chamber hops;*
> *And the cats cry mew, mew, mew;*
> *The nibbling mouse is not asleep,*
> *But he goes peep, peep, peep, peep, peep;*
> *And the cats cries mew, mew, mew,*   20
> *And still the cats cries mew, mew, mew.*

Laz. I shall be moused by puss-cats, but I had rather
die a dog's death : they have nine lives a piece (like a
woman), and they will make it up ten lives, if they and I
fall a-scratching.   Bright Helena of this house, would
thy Troy were a-fire, for I am a-cold; or else would I
had the Greeks' wooden curtal[1] to ride away.   Most
ambrosian-lipped creature, come away quickly, for this
night's lodging lies cold at my heart.   [*The Spanish
pavin*[2] *played within.*]   The Spanish pavin?   I thought
the devil could not understand Spanish : but since thou
art my countryman, O thou tawny Satan,[3] I will dance
after thy pipe.   [*He dances the Spanish pavin.*]   Ho,[4]
sweet devil, ho ! thou wilt make any man weary of thee,
though he deal with thee in his shirt.   35
Sweet beauty ! she'll not come : I'll fall to sleep,
And dream of her ; love dreams are ne'er too deep.
        [*Lies down and falls through a trap-door.*

---

[1] Horse.   [2] A stately dance.
[3] "Old ed. ' Satin,'—a play on the words *Satan* and *satin.*"—*Dyce.*
[4] "The word here (as in our very earliest poets) is equivalent to
' stop.' "—*Dyce.*   There is, perhaps, also an allusion to the exclamation

Enter FRISCO *above, laughing.*

Fris. Ha, ha, ha!

Laz. Ho, ho, Frisco, madonna! I am in hell, but here
is no fire; hell-fire is all put out. What ho, so ho, ho!
I shall be drowned. I beseech thee, dear Frisco, raise
Blurt the constable, or some scavenger, to come and
make clean these kennels of hell : for they stink so, that
I shall cast [1] away my precious self.

Enter IMPERIA *above.*

Imp. Is he down, Frisco?

Fris. He's down : he cries out he's in hell; it's heaven
to me to have him cry so.

Imp. Fie, fie, fie, let him lie, and get all to bed. [*Exit.*

Fris. Not all ; I've fatting knavery in hand.
He cries he's damm'd in hell : the next shall cry   50
He's climbing up to heaven ; and here's the gin :
One woodcock's [2] ta'en ; I'll have his brother in. [*Exit.*

SCENE III.

A Street before IMPERIA'S *House ; a ladder of ropes
hanging from the window.*

Enter CURVETTO *with a lantern.*

Cur. Brisk as a capering tailor ! I was wash'd,
But did they shave me? no, I am too wise;

"Ho, ho!" with which the Devil in the Moralities greeted the audience
when he made his appearance on the stage.

1 Vomit.

2 "Woodcock" is a common term for "simpleton."

Lie close i' th' bosom of their knaveries ;
I'm an old hoary courtier, and strike dead ;
I hit my marks : ware, ware, a perilous [1] head !
Cast,[2]—I must find a ladder made of ropes ;

Enter BLURT, SLUBBER, WOODCOCK, *and the rest of
the Watch.*

Ladder and rope ; what follow ? hanging ; ay ;
But where ? ah ha, there does the riddle lie.
I have 'scap'd drowning ; but, but, but, I hope
I shall not 'scape the ladder and the rope.   10
    Wood. Yonder's a light, master constable.
    Blurt. Peace, Woodcock, the sconce [3] approaches.
    Cur. Whew !
    Blurt. Ay, whistling ?—Slubber, jog the watch, and
give the lantern a flap.
    Cur. Whew ! Simp, Simperina !

Enter FRISCO *above.*

    Fris. Who's there ?
    Cur. Who's there ?
    Fris. Signior Curvetto ? here's the ladder ; I watch to
do you a good turn : I am Frisco.   Is not Blurt abroad
and his bill-men ?   21
    Cur. No matter if they be ; I hear none nigh ;

---

[1] See note 1, p. 70.   [2] Plan, devise.
                [3] Lantern.

I will snug close ; out goes my candle's eye ;
My sconce takes this in snuff ;[1] all's one ; I care not.

 Fris. Why, when ?[2]

 Cur. I come ; close, close ; hold, rope, and spare
   not.   [*Begins to ascend the ladder.*

 Slub. Now the candle's out.

 Blurt. Peace !

 Cur. Frisco, light, light ! my foot is slipt ; call
   help.

 Fris. Help, help, help ! thieves, thieves ! help, thieves,
   &c.[3]   30

 Blurt. Thieves? where? Follow close. Slubber, the
lantern.—Hold, I charge you, in the duke's name, stand :
sirrah, you're like to hang for this.—Down with him.
       [*They take* CURVETTO *down.*

 Fris. Master Blurt, master constable, here's his ladder :
he comes to rob my mistress. I have been scared out
of my wits above seven times by him, and it's forty to
one if ever they come in again. I lay felony to his
charge.

 Cur. Felony? you cony-catching[4] slave.

 Fris. Cony-catching will bear an action. I'll cony-
catch you for this.—If I can find our key, I will aid you,
Master Blurt : if not, look to him, as you will answer it
upon your deathbed.   43

---

 [1] " A poor conceit : to *take in snuff* is to be angry, to take offence.
So Shakespeare :—'You'll mar the light, by taking it in snuff.'—*Love's
Labour's Lost,* act v. sc. 2."—*Dyce.*

 [2] A very common expression of impatience.

 [3] It was left, as frequently, to the actor to speak whatever he chose.

 [4] Cogging, cheating.

Blurt. What are you?

Cur. A Venetian gentleman.—Woodcock, how dost thou, Woodcock? [1]

Wood. Thank your worship.

Blurt. Woodcock, you are of our side [2] now, and therefore your acquaintance cannot serve. And you were a gentleman of velvet, I would commit you.   50

Cur. Why, what are you, sir?

Blurt. What am I, sir? do not you know this staff? I am, sir, the duke's own image: at this time the duke's tongue (for fault of a better) lies in my mouth; I am constable, sir.

Cur. Constable, and commit me? marry, Blurt, master-constable!

Blurt. Away with him!   [*He strives.*

Omnes. It's folly to strive.

Blurt. I say, away with him.—I'll Blurt you; I'll teach you to stand covered to authority: your hoary head shall be knocked when this staff is in place.   62

Cur. Ay, but, master-constable——

Blurt. No, pardon me, you abuse the duke in me, that am his cipher.—I say, away with him; Gulch, away with him; Woodcock, keep you with me. I will be known for more than Blurt.

        [*Exit, the rest of the Watch carrying off* CURVETTO.

---

[1] In the old ed. these words are given to Blurt.

[2] "Woodcock of our side" was a kind of proverbial expression, borrowed (as Dyce supposes) from some game.

Enter LAZARILLO.

Laz. Thou honest fellow, the man in the moon, I beseech thee set fire on thy bush of thorns, to light and warm me, for I am dung-wet. I fell like Lucifer, I think, into hell, and am crawled out, but in worse pickle than my lean Pilcher. Hereabout is the hothouse[1] of my love. Ho, ho ! why ho, there !   73

Fris. Who's that ? What devil stands hohing at my door so late?

Laz. I beseech thee, Frisco, take in Lazarillo's ghost.

Fris. Lazarillo's ghost? haunt me not, I charge thee ; I know thee not: I am in a dream of a dry summer, therefore appear not to me.

Laz. Is not this the mansion of the cherry-lipped madonna Imperia ?   81

Fris. Yes ; how then ? You fly-blown rascal, what art thou ?

Laz. Lazarillo de Tormes : sweet blood, I have a poor Spanish suit[2] depending in your house ; let me enter, most precious Frisco ; the mistress of this mansion is my beautiful hostess.

Fris. How, you turpentine pill, my wife your hostess ? away, you Spanish vermin !

Laz. I beseech thee, most pitiful Frisco, allow my lamentation.   91

Fris. And you lament here, I'll stone you with brick-bats : I am asleep.

---

[1] Euphemism for brothel.
[2] He had retreated in his shirt.

Laz. My slop[1] and mandillion[2] lie at thy mercy, fine
Frisco; I beseech thee, let not my case be thine: I must
and will lament.

Fris. Must you? I'll wash off your tears; away, you
hog's-face!   [*Drenches him with foul water, and exit.*

Laz. Thou hast soused my poor hog's-face. O Frisco,
thou art a scurvy doctor, to cast my water no better! it
is most rammish urine: Mars shall not save thee; I
will make a brown toast of thy heart, and drink it in a
pot of thy strong blood.   103

Re-enter BLURT *and all his Watch.*

Blurt. Such fellows must be taken down. Stand.
What white thing is yonder?

Slub. Who goes there? come before the constable.

Laz. My dear host Blurt!

Blurt. You have Blurted fair: I am by my office
to examine you, where you have spent these two
nights.   110

Laz. Most big Blurt, I answer thy great authority, that
I have been in hell, and am scratched to death with
puss-cats.

Blurt. Do you run a' th' score at an officer's house,
and then run above twelve score off?

Laz. I did not run, my sweet-faced Blurt: the Spanish
fleet is bringing gold enough to discharge all from the
Indies: lodge me, most pitiful bill-man.

---

[1] Loose breeches.
[2] A loose garment without sleeves.

Blurt. Marry, and will.   I am, in the duke's name, to charge you with despicions[1] of felony; and burglary is committed this night; and we are to reprehend any that we think to be faulty.   Were not you at madonna freckle-face's house?   123

Laz. Signior, si.

Blurt. Away with him, clap him up.

Laz. Most thundering Blurt, do not clap me; most thundering Blurt, do not clap me.

Blurt. Master Lazarus, I know you are a sore fellow where you take, and therefore I charge you, in the duke's name, to go without wrastling, though you be in your shirt.   131

Laz. Commendable Blurt——

Blurt. The end of my commendations is to commit you.

Laz. I am kin to Don Dego,[2] the Spanish adelantado.[3]

Blurt. If you be kin to Don Dego that was smelt out in Paul's, you pack; your lantedoes nor your lanteeroes cannot serve your turn.   I charge you, let me commit you to the tuition——

Laz. Worshipful Blurt, do not commit me into the hands of dogs.   141

Omnes. Dogs!

Blurt. Master Lazarus, there's not a dog shall bite you : these are true bill-men, that fight under the common-wealth's flag.

Laz. Blurt——

---

[1] Old ed. "despicious."   [2] See note 2, p. 47.   [3] See note 1, p. 21.
VOL. I.   F

Blurt. Blurt me no Blurts; I'll teach all Spaniards how to meddle with whores.

Laz. Most cunning constable, all Spaniards know that already; I have meddled with none.   150

Blurt. Your being in your shirt bewrays you.

Laz. I beseech thee, most honest Blurt, let not my shirt bewray [1] me.

Blurt. I say, away with him. [*Music.*] Music? that's in the courtesan's; they are about some ungodly act; but I'll play a part in't ere morning.   Away with Lazarus.

Omnes. Come, Spaniard.

Laz. Thy kites and thee for this shall watch in dirt, To feed on carrion.

Blurt. Hence, ptrooh!

Laz. O base Blurt!
O base Blurt! O base Blurt!   [*Exeunt.* 160

---

[1] A play on the words, *bewray* (betray) and *beray* (befoul).

ACT V.

SCENE I.

A Room in CAMILLO'S *House.*

Enter CAMILLO, HIPPOLITO, VIRGILIO, ASORINO, BAP-
TISTA, BENTIVOGLIO, DOYT, *and* DANDYPRAT, *all
weaponed, their rapiers' sheaths in their hands.*

Cam. Gentlemen and noble Italians, whom I love best,
who know best what wrongs I have stood under, being
laid on by him who is to thank me for his life; I did
bestow him, as the prize of mine honour, upon my love,
the most fair Violetta: my love's merit was basely sold
to him by the most false Violetta. Not content with this
felony, he hath dared to add the sweet theft of ignoble
marriage: she's now none's but his; and he, treacherous
villain, any one's but hers: he doats, my honoured friends,
on a painted courtesan; and, in scorn of our Italian
laws, our family, our revenge, loathes Violetta's bed, for
a harlot's bosom. I conjure you, therefore, by all the
bonds of gentility, that as you have solemnly sworn a
most sharp, so let the revenge be most sudden.   14

Vir. Be not yourself a bar to that suddenness by this
protraction.

Omnes. Away, gentlemen, away then!

Hip. As for that light hobbyhorse, my sister, whose foul name I will rase out with my poniard, by the honour of my family, which her lust hath profaned, I swear— and, gentlemen, be in this my sworn brothers—I swear, that as all Venice does admire her beauty, so all the world shall be amazed at her punishment.   Follow, therefore.   24

Vir. Stay, let our resolutions keep together : whither go we first?

Cam. To the strumpet Imperia's.

Omnes. Agreed : what then?

Cam. There to find Fontinelle : found, to kill him——

Vir. And killed, to hang out his reeking body at his harlot's window.   31

Cam. And by his body, the strumpet's——

Hip. And between both, my sister's.

Vir. The tragedy is just : on then, begin.

Cam. As you go, every hand pull in a friend, to strengthen us against all opposites.   He that has any drop of true Italian blood in him, thus vow, this morning, to shed others', or let out his own.   If you consent to this, follow me.   39

Omnes. *Via,*[1] away! the treacherous Frenchman dies.

Hip. Catso,[2] Saint Mark, my pistol! thus death flies.

[*Exeunt.*

---

[1] *i.e.* forward! go on!

[2] Dyce's correction for "At so" of the old ed.—"Catso," an obscene oath borrowed from the Italian, is of common occurrence.

SCENE II.

A Room in IMPERIA's *House.*

Enter FONTINELLE *and* IMPERIA, *arm in arm.*

Imp. Ah you little effeminate sweet chevalier, why dost thou not get a loose periwig of hair on thy chin, to set thy French face off? By the panting pulse of Venus, thou art welcome a thousand degrees beyond the reach of arithmetic. Good, good, good; your lip is moist and moving; it hath the truest French close, even like Mapew,[1] la, la, la, &c.

Font. Dear lady! O life of love, what sweetness dwells
In love's variety! The soul that plods
In one harsh book of beauty, but repeats   10
The stale and tedious learning, that hath oft
Faded the senses; when, in reading more,
We glide in new sweets, and are starv'd with store.
Now, by the heart of love, my Violet
Is a foul weed, (O pure Italian flower!)
She a black negro, to the white compare
Of this unequalled beauty? O most accurst,
That I have given her leave to challenge me!
But, lady, poison speaks Italian well,
And in her loath'd kiss I'll include her hell.   20

Imp. So, so, so; do, do, do. Come, come, come, will you condemn the mute rushes to be pressed to death

---

[1] "Qy. the beginning of some French song—*Mais peu?*"—*Dyce.*

by your sweet body? Down, down, down; here, here, here; lean your head upon the lap of my gown; good, good, good. O Saint Mark! here is a love-mark able to wear more ladies' eyes for jewels than—O, lie still, lie still! I will level a true Venetian kiss over your right shoulder.

Font. Shoot home, fair mistress, and as that kiss flies
From lip to lip, wound me with your sharp eyes.   30

Imp. No, no, no, I'll beat this cherry-tree thus, and thus, and thus, and you name wound.   [*Kisses him.*

Font. I will offend so, to be beaten still.

Imp. Do, do, do; and if you make any more such lips when I beat you, by my virginity, you shall buss this rod. Music, I pray thee be not a puritan; sister to the rest of the sciences, I knew the time when thou couldst abide handling. [*Loud music.*] O fie, fie, fie, forbear! thou art like a puny barber, new come to the trade; thou pickst [1] our ears too deep. So, so, so; will my sweet prisoner entertain a poor Italian song?   41

Font. O most willingly, my dear madonna!

Imp. I care not if I persuade my bad voice to wrestle

---

[1] It seems to have been the custom for barbers to pick their customers' ears. Stubbes, inveighing against barbers in his *Display of Corruptions*, says :—" And when they come to washing, oh how gingerly they behave themselves therein. For then shall your mouth be bossed with the lather or foam that riseth of the balls (for they have their sweet balls wherewith all they use to wash), your eyes closed must be anointed therewith also. Then snap go the fingers, full bravely, God wot. Thus, this tragedy ended, comes me warm cloths to wipe and dry him withall; next the *ears must be picked* and closed together again artificially forsooth " &c.

with this music, and catch a strain : so, so, so ; keep time,
keep time, keep time.   [*Sings.*

> *Love for such a cherry lip*
>> *Would be glad to pawn his arrows ;*
> *Venus here to take a sip*
>> *Would sell her doves and team of sparrows.*
>>> *But they shall not so ;*   50
>>>> *Hey nonny, nonny no !*
>>>> *None but I this lip must owe,*[1]
>>>> *Hey nonny, nonny no !*

Font. Your voice doth teach the music.
Imp. No, no, no.
Font. Again, dear love.
Imp. *Hey nonny, nonny no !*

> *Did Jove see this wanton eye,*
>> *Ganymede must wait no longer ;*
> *Phœbe*[2] *here one night did lie,*   60
>> *Would change her face and look much younger.*
>>> *But they shall not so ;*
>>>> *Hey nonny, nonny no !*
>>>> *None but I this lip must owe ;*
>>>> *Hey nonny, nonny no !*

Enter FRISCO, TRIVIA, *and* SIMPERINA, *running.*

Fris.[3] O madonna !
Triv. Mistress !
Sim. Madonna !

---

[1] Own.   [2] *i.e.* did Phœbe here &c.
[3] Old ed. " *Omnes.* O *Madona !* Mistris ! *Madona !*"

Fris. Case up this gentleman: there's rapping at door; and one, in a small voice, says there's Camillo and Hippolito.   71

Sim. And they will come in.

Font. Upon their deaths they shall, for they seek mine.

Imp. No, no, no: lock the doors fast; Trivia, Simperina, stir.

Triv. and Sim. Alas!

Font. Come they in shape of devils, this angel by, I'm arm'd; let them come in; ud's foot, they die.

Imp. Fie, fie, fie; I will not have thy white body——

Viol. [*within.*] What ho, madonna! [*Knocking within.*

Imp. O hark! Not hurt for the Rialto! go, go, go, put up; by my virginity, you shall put up.   82

Viol. [*within.*] Here are Camillo and Hippolito.

Imp. Into that little room; you are there as safe as in France or the Low Countries.

Font. O God!   [*Exit.*

Imp. So, so, so; let them enter. Trivia, Simperina, smooth my gown, tread down the rushes; let them enter; do, do, do. [*Exit* FRISCO.] No words, pretty darling. La, la, la, hey nonny, nonny no!   [*Singing.* 90

Re-enter FRISCO *with* VIOLETTA.

Fris. Are two men transformed into one woman?

Imp. How now? what motion's this?[1]

Viol. By your leave, sweet beauty, pardon my excuse,

---

[1] Motion = plot, device.

which, under the mask of Camillo's and my brother's names, sought entrance into this house. Good sweetness, have you not a property here improper to your house, my husband?

Imp. Hah! your husband here?

Viol. Nay, be as you seem to be, white dove, without gall. 100

Imp. Gall? your husband? ha, ha, ha! by my ventoy,[1] yellow [2] lady, you take your mark improper; no, no, no, my sugar-candy mistress, your goodman is not here, I assure you: here? ha, ha!

Triv. and Sim. Here!

Fris. Much [3] husbands here!

Viol. Do not mock me, fairest Venetian; come, I know he's here. Good faith, I do not blame him; for your beauty gilds [4] over his error. Troth, I am right glad that you, my countrywoman, have received the pawn of my affections: you cannot be hard-hearted, loving him; nor hate me, for I love him too. Since we both love him, let us not leave him, till we have called home the ill husbandry of a sweet straggler. Prithee, good wench, use him well. 115

Imp. So, so, so!

Viol. If he deserve not to be used well (as I'd be loath he should deserve it), I'll engage myself, dear beauty, to thine honest heart: give me leave to love him, and I'll

---

[1] Fan.
[2] Yellow was the colour of jealousy.
[3] See note 4, p. 40.
[4] Old ed. "glides."

give him a kind of leave to love thee. I know he hears me : I prithee, try mine eyes if they know him, that have almost drowned themselves in their own salt water, because they cannot see him. In troth, I'll not chide him : if I speak words rougher than soft kisses, my penance shall be to see him kiss thee, yet to hold my peace.

Fris. And that's torment enough : alas, poor wench !

Sim. She's an ass, by the crown of my maiden-head : I'd scratch her eyes out, if my man[1] stood in her tables.

Viol. Good partner, lodge me in thy private bed, 129
Where, in supposed folly, he may end
Determin'd sin. Thou smil'st : I know thou wilt.
What looseness may term dotage, truly read,
Is love ripe-gathered, not soon withered.

Imp. Good troth, pretty wedlock, thou makest my little eyes smart with washing themselves in brine. I keep your cock from his own roost, and mar such a sweet face, and wipe off that dainty red, and make Cupid toll the bell for your love-sick heart ? no, no, no ; if he were Jove's own ingle,[2] Ganymede ; fie, fie, fie, I'll none. Your chamber-fellow is within : thou shalt enjoy my bed and thine own pleasure this night.—Simperina, conduct in this lady.—Frisco, silence. Ha, ha, ha ! I am sorry to see a woman so tame a fool. Come, come, come. 143

Viol. Star of Venetian beauty, thanks.—O, who
Can bear this wrong, and be a woman too ? [*Exeunt.*

---

1 "A metaphor drawn from the game of tables."—*Dyce.*
2 Favourite.

SCENE III.

A Street before IMPERIA'S *House.*

Enter, on one side, CAMILLO, HIPPOLITO, VIRGILIO,
ASORINO, BAPTISTA, BENTIVOGLIO, DOYT, *and*
DANDYPRAT; *on the other, the* DUKE *and Gentlemen,*
and BLURT *and his Watch with torches.*

Omnes.[1] We are dishonoured ; give us way ; he dies,
He dies——

Duke. I charge you, by your duties to
The state, and love to gentry, sheathe your weapons.

Blurt. Stand : I charge you, put up your naked
weapons, and we'll put up our rusty bills.

Cam. Up to the hilts we will in his French body :
My lord, we charge you, by the ravish'd honour
Of an Italian lady, by our wrongs,
By that eternal blot, which, if this slave
Pass free without revenge, like leprosy   10
Will run o'er[2] all the body of our fames ;
Give open way to our just wrath, lest, barr'd——

Duke. Gentlemen——

Cam. Breaking the bonds of honour and of duty,
We cut a passage through you with our swords.

Omnes. He that withstands us, run him through.

Blurt. I charge you, i' th' duke's name, before his own
face, to keep the peace.

---

[1] " The speeches which in the present scene have this prefix may be
assigned to whatever individuals of Camillo's party the reader pleases
to select."—*Dyce.*   [2] Old ed. " over."

Cam. Keep thou the peace, that hast a peasant's heart.

Watch. Peasant? 20

Cam. Our peace must have her cheeks painted with
blood.

Omnes. Away through——

Blurt. Sweet gentlemen, though you have called the
duke's own ghost peasant, for I walk for him i' th' night—
Kilderkin and Piss-breech hold out—yet hear me, dear
bloods. The duke here, for fault of a better, and myself
—Cuckoo, fly not hence—for fault of a better, are to lay
you by the heels, if you go thus with fire and sword; for
the duke is the head, and I, Blurt, am the purtenance.—
Woodcock, keep by my side.—Now, sir[s]—— 30

Omnes. A plague upon this Woodcock! kill the watch.

Duke. Now, in the name of manhood, I conjure ye,
Appear in your true shapes, Italians;
You kill your honours more in this revenge
Than in his murder. Stay, stand; here's the house.

Blurt. Right, sir, this is the whore-house; here he
calls and sets in his staff.

Duke. Sheathe all your weapons, worthy gentlemen;
And by my life I swear, if Fontinelle
Have stain'd the honour of your sister's bed, 40
The fact being death, I'll pay you his proud head.

Cam. Arrest him then before our eyes; and see,
Our fury sleeps.

Duke. This honest officer——

Blurt. Blurt, sir——

Duke. Shall fetch him forth.—Go, sirrah, in our name
Attach the French lord.

Blurt. Garlic, and the rest, follow strongly.

                       [*Exit with Watch.*

  Duke. O what a scandal were it to a state,
To have a stranger, and a prisoner,
Murder'd by such a troop!   Besides, through Venice
Are numbers of his countrymen dispers'd,   51
Whose rage meeting with yours, none can prevent
The mischief of a bloody consequent.

   Re-enter BLURT *and Watch, holding* FONTINELLE *and
his weapons.*

  Blurt. The duke is within an inch of your nose, and
therefore I dare play with it, if you put not up; deliver,
I advise you.

  Font. Yield up my weapons, and my foe so nigh!
Myself and weapons shall together yield:
Come any one, come all.

    Omnes. Kill, kill the Frenchman! kill him!   60
  Duke. Be satisfied, my noble countrymen:
I'll trust you with his life, so you will pawn
The faiths of gentlemen, no desperate hand
Shall rob him of it; otherwise, he runs
Upon this dangerous point, that dares appose[1]
His rage 'gainst our authority.—French lord,
Yield up this strength; our word shall be your guard.

   Font. Who defies death, needs none; he's well prepar'd.

  Duke. My honest fellow, with a good defence,
Enter again; fetch out the courtesan,   70
And all that are within.

---

                [1] Oppose

Blurt. I'll tickle her: it shall ne'er be said that a brown bill[1] looked pale.   [*Exit with Watch.*

Cam. Frenchman, thou art indebted to our duke.

Font. For what?

Cam. Thy life; for, but for him, thy soul
Had long ere this hung trembling in the air,
Being frighted from thy bosom with our swords.

Font. I do not thank your duke; yet, if you will,
Turn bloody executioners: who dies
For so bright beauty 's a bright sacrifice.   80

Duke. The beauty you adore so is profane;
The breach of wedlock, by our law, is death.

Font. Law, give me law.

Duke. With all severity.

Font. In my love's eyes immortal joys do dwell;
She is my heaven; she from me, I'm in hell:
Therefore your law, your law.

Duke. Make way, she comes.

Re-enter BLURT *leading* IMPERIA, *the rest of the Watch
with* VIOLETTA *masqued.*

Imp. Fie, fie, fie.

Blurt. Your fie, fie, fie, nor your foh, foh, foh, canno:
serve your turn; you must now bear it off with head and
shoulders.   90

Duke. Now fetch Curvetto and the Spaniard hither;
Their punishments shall lie under one doom.
What is she masqu'd?

---

[1] See note 1, p. 17.

Blurt. A punk too.—Follow, fellows : Slubber, afore.
                          [*Exit with Watch.*
Viol. She that is masqu'd is leader of this masque.
What's here? bows, bills, and guns ! Noble Camillo,
                          [*Unmasquing.*
I'm sure you're lord of this misrule : [1] I pray,
For whose sake do you make this swaggering fray ?
    Cam. For yours, and for our [2] own ; we come resolv'd
To murder him that poisons your chaste bed,   100
To take revenge on you for your false heart ;
And, wanton dame, our wrath here must not sleep ;
Your sin being deep'st, your share shall be most deep.
    Viol. With pardon of your grace, myself to you all,
At your own weapons, thus do answer all.
For paying away my heart, that was my own ;
Fight not to win that, in good troth, 'tis gone.
For my dear love's abusing my chaste bed,
And her [3] sweet theft, alack, you are misled !
This was a plot of mine, only to try   110
Your love's strange temper ; sooth, I do not lie.
My Fontinelle ne'er dallied in her arms ;
She never bound his heart with amorous charms :
My Fontinelle ne'er loathed my sweet embrace ;
She never drew love's picture by his face :
When he from her white hand would strive to go,
She never cried, fie, fie, nor no, no, no.

---

1 Old ed. "I am sure you are lord of all this misrule." *Lord of Misrule* was the title of the person who presided over the Christmas revels in noblemen's houses.
  2 Old ed. "your."   3 Imperia's.

With prayers and bribes we hired her, both to lie
Under that roof : for this must my love die?
Who dare be so hard-hearted?   Look you, we kiss,
And if he loathe his Violet,[1] judge by this.   121
                                                            [*Kissing him.*

   Font. O sweetest Violet ! I blush——
   Viol. Good figure,
Wear still that maiden blush, but still be mine.
   Font. I seal myself thine own with both my hands,
In this true deed of gift.   Gallants, here stands
This lady's champion : at [t]his foot I'll lie [2]
That dares touch her : who taints my constancy,
I am no man for him ; fight he with her,
And yield, for she's a noble conqueror.
   Duke. This combat shall not need ; for see, ashamed
Of their rash vows, these gentlemen here break   131
This storm, and do with hands what tongues should speak.
   Omnes. All friends, all friends !
   Hip. Punk, you may laugh at this :
Here's tricks ! but, mouth, I'll stop you with a kiss.

   Enter CURVETTO *and* LAZARILLO, *led by* BLURT *and
the Watch.*

   Blurt. Room ; keep all the scabs back, for here comes
Lazarus.
   Duke. O, here's our other spirits that walk i' th' night !
Signior Curvetto, by complaint from her,
And by your writing here, I reach the depth

---

   [1] Old ed. "Violetta."   [2] Used transitively.

Of your offence.   They charge your climbing up
To be to rob her: if so, then by law   141
You are to die, unless she marry you.

    Imp. I? fie, fie, fie, I will be burnt to ashes first.

    Cur. How, die, or marry her? then call me daw:
Marry her—she's more common than the law—
For boys to call me ox? no, I'm not drunk;
I'll play with her, but, hang her! wed no punk.
I shall be a hoary courtier then indeed,
And have a perilous head; then I were best
Lie close, lie close, to hide my forked crest.   150
No, fie, fie, fie; hang me before the door
Where I was drown'd, ere I marry with a whore.

    Duke. Well, signior, for we rightly understand,
From your accusers, how you stood her guest,
We pardon you, and pass it as a jest:
And for the Spaniard sped so hardly too,
Discharge him, Blurt: signior, we pardon you.

    Blurt. Sir, he's not to be discharged, nor so to be shot
off: I have put him into a new suit, and have entered into
him with an action; he owes me two-and-thirty shillings.

    Laz. It is thy honour to have me die in thy debt. 161

    Blurt. It would be more honour to thee to pay me
before thou diest: twenty shillings of this debt came out
of his nose.

    Laz. Bear witness, great duke, he's paid twenty shil-
lings.

    Blurt. Signior, no, you cannot smoke me so.   He took
twenty shillings of it in a fume, and the rest I charge him
with for his lying.

    VOL. I.   G

Laz. My lying, most pitiful prince, was abominable.

Blurt. He did lie, for the time, as well as any knight
of the post[1] did ever lie.   172

Laz. I do here put off thy suit, and appeal: I warn
thee to the court of conscience, and will pay thee by
twopence a-week, which I will rake out of the hot embers
of tobacco-ashes, and then travel on foot to the Indies
for more gold, whose red cheeks I will kiss, and beat thee,
Blurt, if thou watch for me.

Hip. There be many of your countrymen in Ireland,[2]
signior ; travel to them.   180

Laz. No, I will fall no more into bogs.

Duke. Sirrah, his debt ourself will satisfy.

Blurt. Blurt, my lord, dare take your word for as much
more.

Duke. And since this heat of fury is all spent,
And tragic shapes meet comical event,
Let this bright morning merrily be crown'd
With dances, banquets, and choice music's sound.

                               [*Exeunt omnes.*

---

[1] " Knight of the post " was one who gained a living by giving false
evidence. Cf. *The Man in the Moon*, 1657 :—" How now, what art thou
whose head hangs down like a bulrush? O its a *knight of the post*, a
public and forsworn varlet. This fellow for 12 pence shall swear the
richest man in England out of his estate, and oaths goes down with
him as easy as a sow sucks a tub full of wash ; and hath as good an
appetite to forswear himself as a big-bellied woman longs for butter-
milk."

[2] This clearly refers to the 6000 Spaniards under Don Juan d'Aguilar,
who landed in Ireland to support Tyrone's rebellion. They landed in
September 1601 ; fortified themselves at Kinsale ; and were obliged
to capitulate in June 1602.

THE PHŒNIX.

The Phoenix, as it hath beene sundrye times Acted by the Children of Paules, And presented before his Maiestie.   London Printed by E. A. for A. I., and are to be solde at the signe of the white horse in Paules Churchyard.   1607.   4to.

A second edition—inaccurately printed—appeared in 1630.   *The Phœnix* was licensed by Sir George Buc, 9th May 1607.

DRAMATIS PERSONÆ.

DUKE OF FERRARA.
PHŒNIX, *his son.*
PRODITOR,
LUSSURIOSO, } *nobles.*
INFESTO,
FIDELIO, *son to* CASTIZA.
CAPTAIN, *married to* CASTIZA.
FALSO, a *justice of peace.*
LATRONELLO,
FUCATO, } *his servants.*
FURTIVO,[1]
KNIGHT.
TANGLE.
QUIETO.
Groom.
Constable.
Boy.
Drawer.
Soldiers.
Suitors.
Nobles, Gentlemen, Officers, &c.

CASTIZA, *mother to* FIDELIO, *and married to the*
    CAPTAIN.
Jeweller's wife, daughter to FALSO.
Niece to FALSO.
Maid to Jeweller's wife.

SCENE, FERRARA.

---

[1] He becomes Falso's servant at the death of Falso's brother. See i. 6.

THE PHŒNIX.

——o——

ACT I.[1]

SCENE I.

A Chamber in the Palace of the Duke of Ferrara.

Enter the DUKE, PRODITOR LUSSURIOSO, INFESTO, *and other Nobles, with Attendants.*

Duke. My lords,
Know that we, far from any natural pride,
Or touch of temporal sway, have seen our face
In our grave council's foreheads, where doth stand
Our truest glass, made by Time's wrinkled hand.
We know we're old; my days proclaim me so;
Forty-five years I've gently rul'd this dukedom;
Pray heaven it be no fault!
For there's as much disease, though not to th' eye,
In too much pity as in tyranny.   10
   Infes. Your grace hath spoke it right.
   Duke. I know that life
Has not long course in me; 'twill not be long
Before I show that kings have mortal bodies

---

[1] In the old eds. there is no division into acts and scenes.

As well as subjects : therefore to my comfort,
And your successful hopes, I have a son,
Whom I dare boast of——
    Lus. Whom we all do boast of ;
A prince elder in virtues than in years.
    Infes. His judgment is a father to his youth.
    Prod. Ay, ay, would he were from court !   [*Aside.*
    Infes. Our largest hopes grow in him.   20
    Prod. And 'tis the greatest pity, noble lord,
He is untravell'd.
    Lus. 'Tis indeed, my lord.
    Prod. Had he but travel to his time and virtue—
O, he should ne'er return again !   [*Aside.*
    Duke. It shall be so : what is in hope began,[1]
Experience quickens ; travel confirms the man,
Who [2] else lives doubtful, and his days oft sorry :
Who's rich in knowledge has the stock of glory.
    Prod. Most true, my royal lord.
    Duke. Some one attend our son.
    Infes. See, here he comes, my lord.

      Enter PHŒNIX, *attended by* FIDELIO.

    Duke. O, you come well.   30
    Phœ. 'Tis always my desire, my worthy father.
    Duke. Your serious studies, and those fruitful hours
That grow up into judgment, well become
Your birth, and all our loves : I weep that you are my son,

---

[1] Old eds. "begun,"—which destroys the rhyme.
[2] So ed. 2.—Ed. 1. "Who's."

But virtuously I weep, the more my gladness.
We have thought good and meet, by the consent
Of these our nobles, to move you toward travel,
The better to approve you to yourself,
And give your apter power foundation :
To see affections actually presented,   40
E'en by those men that owe [1] them, yield[s] more profit,
Ay, more content, than singly to read of them,
Since love or fear make writers partial.
The good and free example which you find
In other countries, match it with your own,
The ill to shame the ill ; which will in time
Fully instruct you how to set in frame
A kingdom all in pieces.
    Phœ. Honour'd father,
With care and duty I have listen'd to you.
What you desire, in me it is obedience :   50
I do obey in all, knowing for right,
Experience is a kingdom's better sight.
    Prod. O, 'tis the very lustre of a prince,
Travel ! 'tis sweet and generous.
    Duke. He that knows how to obey, knows how to
        reign ;
And that true knowledge have we found in you.
Make choice of your attendants.
    Phœ. They're soon chose ;
Only this man, my lord, a loving servant of mine.
    Duke. What ! none but he ?

---

[1] Own.

Phœ. I do intreat no more ;
For that's the benefit a private gentleman   60
Enjoys beyond our state, when he notes all,
Himself unnoted.
For, should I bear the fashion of a prince,
I should then win more flattery than profit,
And I should give 'em time and warning then
To hide their actions from me : if I appear a sun,
They'll run into the shade with their ill deeds,
And so prevent [1] me.

    Prod. A little too wise,[2] a little too wise to live
        long.   [*Aside.*
    Duke. You have answer'd us with wisdom : let it be ;
Things private are best known through privacy.   71

        [*Exeunt all but* PHŒNIX *and* FIDELIO.
    Phœ. Stay you, my elected servant.
    Fid. My kind lord.
    Phœ. The duke my father has a heavy burden
Of years upon him.
    Fid. My lord, it seems so, for they make him stoop.
    Phœ. Without dissemblance he is deep in age ;
He bows unto his grave.   I wonder much
Which of his wild nobility it should be
(For none of his sad [3] council has a voice in't),
Should so far travel into his consent,   80

---

  [1] Anticipate.
  [2] " So Shakespeare :
      ' So wise, so young, they say, do ne'er live long.'
                —*Richard III.*, act iii. sc. **1**."—*Dyce.*
  [3] Grave.

To set me over into other kingdoms,
Upon the stroke and minute of his death?

Fid. My lord, 'tis easier to suspect them all,
Than truly to name one.

Phœ. Since it is thus,
By absence I'll obey the duke my father,
And yet not wrong myself.

Fid. Therein, my lord,
You might be happy twice.

Phœ. So it shall be ;
I'll stay at home, and travel.

Fid. Would your grace
Could make that good !   89

Phœ. I can : and, indeed, a prince need no[t] travel
farther than his own kingdom, if he apply himself faith-
fully, worthy the glory of himself and expectation of others :
and it would appear far nobler industry in him to reform
those fashions that are already in his country, than to
bring new ones in, which have neither true form nor
fashion ; to make his court an owl, city an ape, and the
country a wolf preying upon the ridiculous pride of either :
and therefore I hold it a safer stern,[1] upon this lucky
advantage, since my father is near his setting, and I upon
the eastern hill to take my rise, to look into the heart
and bowels of this dukedom, and, in disguise, mark all
abuses ready for reformation or punishment.   102

Fid. Give me but leave unfeignedly to admire you,
Your wisdom is so spacious and so honest.

---

[1] "*i.e.* (I suppose) a safer course to steer. *Stern* is used by our early
writers in the sense of steerage, helm."—*Dyce.*

Phœ. So much have the complaints and suits of men, seven, nay, seventeen years neglected, still interposed by coin and great enemies, prevailed with my pity, that I cannot otherwise think but there are infectious dealings in most offices, and foul mysteries throughout all professions : and therefore I nothing doubt but to find travel enough within myself, and experience, I fear, too much : nor will I be curious[1] to fit my body to the humblest form and bearing, so the labour may be fruitful ; for how can abuses that keep low, come to the right view of a prince, unless his looks lie level with them, which else will be longest hid from him ?—he shall be the last man sees 'em. 117

For oft between kings' eyes and subjects' crimes
Stands there a bar of bribes : the under office
Flatters him next above it, he the next,
And so of most, or many.
Every abuse will choose a brother :
'Tis through the world, this hand will rub the other.

    Fid. You have set down the world briefly, my lord.

    Phœ. But how am I assur'd of faith in thee ?
Yet I durst trust thee.

    Fid. Let my soul be lost,
When it shall loose your secrets : nor will I
Only be a preserver of them, but,
If you so please, an assister.

    Phœ. It suffices :
That king stands sur'st who by his virtue rises 130

---

[1] *i.e.* nor will I scruple.

More than by birth or blood ; that prince is rare,
Who strives in youth to save his age from care.
Let's be prepar'd : away.
    Fid. I'll follow your grace.—   [*Exit* PHŒNIX.
Thou wonder of all princes, president, and glory,
True Phœnix, made of an unusual strain ![1]
Who labours to reform is fit to reign.
How can that king be safe that studies not
The profit of his people ?   See where comes
The best part of my heart, my love.   140

Enter NIECE.[2]

    Niece. Sir, I am bound to find you : I heard newly
Of sudden travel which his grace intends,
And only but yourself to accompany him.
    Fid. You heard in that little beside the truth ;
Yet not so sudden as to want those manners,
To leave you unregarded.
    Niece. I did not think so unfashionably of you.
How long is your return ?
    Fid. 'Tis not yet come to me, scarce to my lord,
Unless the duke refer it to his pleasure ;   150
But long I think it is not : the duke's age,
If not his apt experience, will forbid it.
    Niece. His grace commands, I must not think amiss :
Farewell.
    Fid. Nay, stay, and take this comfort ;

---

[1] Inborn disposition.
[2] Justice Falso's niece.   Her name nowhere appears.

You shall hear often from us; I'll direct
Where you shall surely know; and I desire you
Write me the truth, how my new father-in-law
The captain bears himself towards my mother;
For that marriage
Knew nothing of my mind, it never flourish'd 160
In any part of my affection.

    Niece. Methinks sh'as much disgrac'd herself.

    Fid. Nothing so,
If he be good, and will abide the touch;
A captain may marry a lady, if he can sail
Into her good will.

    Niece. Indeed that's all.

    Fid. 'Tis all
In all; commend me to thy breast; farewell.

                           [Exit NIECE.
So by my lord's firm policy we may see,
To present view, what absent forms would be.   *[Exit.*

SCENE II.

A Room in the CAPTAIN'S *House.*

Enter the CAPTAIN *with soldiering fellows.*

First Sol. There's noble purchase,[1] captain.
Second Sol. Nay, admirable purchase.
Third Sol. Enough to make us proud for ever.
Cap. Hah?

---

[1] Plunder.

First Sol. Never was opportunity so gallant.

Cap. Why, you make me mad.

Second Sol. Three ships, not a poop less.

Third Sol. And every one so wealthily burdened, upon my manhood.

Cap. Pox on't, and now am I tied e'en as the devil would ha't. 11

First Sol. Captain, of all men living, I would ha' sworn thou wouldst ne'er have married.

Cap. 'S foot, so would I myself, man; give me my due; you know I ha' sworn all heaven over and over?

First Sol. That you have, i'faith.

Cap. Why, go to then.

First Sol. Of a man that has tasted salt water to commit such a fresh trick!

Cap. Why, 'tis abominable! I grant you, now I see't.

First Sol. Had there been fewer women—— 21

Second Sol. And among those women fewer drabs——

Third Sol. And among those drabs fewer pleasing——

Cap. Then 't had been something——

First Sol. But when there are more women, more common, pretty sweethearts, than ever any age could boast of——

Cap. And I to play the artificer and marry! to have my wife dance at home, and my ship at sea, and both take in salt water together! O lieutenant, thou'rt happy! thou keepest a wench. 31

First Sol. I hope I am happier than so, captain, for a' my troth, she keeps me.

Cap. How? is there any such fortunate man breath-

ing ? and I so miserable to live honest ! I envy thee,
lieutenant, I envy thee, that thou art such a happy knave.
Here's my hand among you ; share it equally ; I'll to
sea with you.

Second Sol. There spoke a noble captain !

Cap. Let's hear from you ; there will be news
shortly.   41

First Sol. Doubt it not, captain.

[*Exeunt all but* CAPTAIN.

Cap. What lustful passion came aboard of me, that I
should marry ? was I drunk ? yet that cannot altogether
hold, for it was four a'clock i' th' morning ; had it been
five, I would ha' sworn it. That a man is in danger every
minute to be cast away, without he have an extraordinary
pilot that can perform more than a man can do ! and to
say truth too, when I'm abroad, what can I do at home ?
no man living can reach so far : and what a horrible thing
'twould be to have horns brought me at sea, to look as
if the devil were i' th' ship ! and all the great tempests
would be thought of my raising ! to be the general curse
of all merchants ! and yet they likely are as deep in as
myself ; and that's a comfort. O, that a captain should
live to be married ! nay, I that have been such a gallant
salt-thief, should yet live to be married ! What a fortunate elder brother is he, whose father being a rammish
ploughman, himself a perfumed gentleman spending the
labouring reek from his father's nostrils in tobacco, the
sweat of his father's body in monthly physic for his pretty
queasy harlot ! he sows apace i' th' country ; the tailor
o'ertakes him i' th' city, so that oftentimes before the corn

comes to earing,[1] 'tis up to the ears in high collars, and
so at every harvest the reapers take pains for the mercers :
ha! why, this is stirring happiness indeed.   Would my
father had held a plough so, and fed upon squeezed curds
and onions, that I might have bathed in sensuality! but
he was too ruttish himself to let me thrive under him;
consumed me before he got me; and that makes me so
wretched now to be shackled with a wife, and not greatly
rich neither.   72

Enter CASTIZA.[2]

Cas. Captain, my husband.
Cap. 'S life, call me husband again, and I'll play the
captain and beat you.
Cas. What has disturb'd you, sir, that you now look
So like an enemy upon me?
Cap. Go make a widower [of me], hang thyself!
How comes it that you are so opposite
To love and kindness?   I deserve more respect,   80
But that you please to be forgetful of it.
Cas. For love to you, did I neglect my state,
Chide better fortunes from me,
Gave the world talk, laid all my friends at waste!
Cap. The more fool you : could you like none but me?
Could none but I supply you?   I am sure
You were sued to by far worthier men,
Deeper in wealth and gentry.

---

[1] So ed. 2.—Ed. 1 "earning."
[2] Old eds. "his Lady."

What couldst thou see in me, to make thee doat
So on me ?   If I know I am a villain,   90
What a torment's this !   Why didst thou marry me ?
You think, as most of your insatiate widows,
That captains can do wonders ; when, alas,[1]
The name does often prove the better man !
   Cas. That which you urge should rather give me cause
To repent than yourself.
   Cap. Then to that end
I do it.
   Cas. What a miserable state
Am I led into !

Enter Servant.[2]

   Cap. How now, sir ?
   Serv. Count Proditor
Is now alighted.
   Cap. What ! my lord ?   I must
Make much of him ; he'll one day write me cuckold ; 100
It is good to make much of such a man :
E'en to my face he plies it hard,—I thank him.

Enter PRODITOR.

What, my worthy lord ?
   Prod. I'll come to you
In order, captain.   [*Kisses* CASTIZA.
   Cap. O that's in order !
A kiss is the gamut to pricksong.   [*Aside.*

---

[1] Old eds. "'lasse."   [2] Old eds. "seruus."

Prod. Let me salute you, captain.   [*Exit* CASTIZA.

Cap. My dear
Esteemed count, I have a life for you.

Prod. Hear you the news?

Cap. What may it be, my lord?

Prod. My lord, the duke's son, is upon his travel
To several kingdoms.

Cap.[1] May it be possible, my lord,   110
And yet so little rumour'd?

Prod. Take't of my truth;
Nay, 'twas well manag'd; things are as they are handl'd:
But all my care is still, pray heaven he return
Safe, without danger, captain.

Cap. Why, is there any doubt
To be had of that, my lord?

Prod. Ay, by my faith, captain:
Princes have private enemies, and great.
Put case a man should grudge him for his virtues,
Or envy him for his wisdom; why, you know,
This makes him lie bare-breasted to his foe.   120

Cap. That's full of certainty, my lord; but who
Be his attendants?

Prod. Thence, captain, comes the fear;
But singly[2] attended neither (my best gladness),
Only by your son-in-law, Fidelio.

----

[1] Perhaps a better metrical arrangement would be—
       "*Cap.* May it be possible, my lord, and yet
    So little rumour'd?
       Prod. Take it of my truth."
[2] Ed. 2, "simplie."

Cap. Is it to be believed? I promise you, my lord,
then I begin to fear him myself; that fellow will undo
him: I durst undertake to corrupt him with twelvepence
over and above, and that's a small matter; has a whorish
conscience; he's an inseparable knave,[1] and I could
ne'er speak well of that fellow.   130

Prod. All we of the younger house, I can tell you, do
doubt him much. The lady's removed: shall we have
your sweet society, captain?

Cap. Though it be in mine own house, I desire I may
follow your lordship.

Prod. I love to avoid strife.—
Not many months Phœnix shall keep his life.

                              [*Aside and exit.*

Cap. So; his way is in; he knows it.
We must not be uncourteous to a lord;
Warn him our house 'twere vild.[2]   140
His presence is an honour: if he lie with our wives, 'tis
for our credit; we shall be the better trusted; 'tis a sign
we shall live i' th' world. O, tempests and whirlwinds!
who but that man whom the forefinger[3] cannot daunt,
that makes his shame his living—who but that man, I
say, could endure to be thoroughly married? Nothing
but a divorce can relieve me: any way to be rid of her
would rid my torment; if all means fail, I'll kill or poison
her, and purge my fault at sea. But first I'll make gentle

---

[1] One whose knavery cannot be put away from him, an irredeemable
rogue.

[2] Old spelling of "vile."

[3] The forefinger pointed at him in scorn.

try of a divorce : but how shall I accuse her subtle
honesty ?   I'll attach this lord's coming to her, take hold
of that, ask counsel : and now I remember, I have
acquaintance with an old crafty client, who, by the
puzzle of suits and shifting of courts, has more tricks
and starting-holes than the dizzy pates of fifteen attorneys ; one that has been muzzled in law like a bear, and
led by the ring of his spectacles from office to office. 157
Him I'll seek out with haste ; all paths I'll tread,
All deaths I'll die, ere I die married.   *[Exit.*

SCENE III.

Another Room in the CAPTAIN'S *House.*

Enter PRODITOR *and* CASTIZA.

Prod. Pooh, you do resist me hardly.

Cas. I beseech your lordship, cease in this : 'tis never
to be granted.   If you come as a friend unto my honour,
and my husband, you shall be ever welcome ; if not, I
must entreat it——

Prod. Why, assure yourself, madam, 'tis not the fashion.

Cas. 'Tis more my grief, my lord ; such as myself
Are judg'd the worse for such.

Prod. Faith, you're too nice :
You'll see me kindly forth ?

Cas. And honourably welcome.   *[Exeunt.*

SCENE IV.

A Room in an Inn.

Enter Groom *lighting in* PHŒNIX *and* FIDELIO.

Groom. Gentlemen, your most neatly welcome.

Phœ. You're very cleanly, sir : prithee, have a care to our geldings.

Groom. Your geldings shall be well considered.

Fid. Considered ?

Phœ. Sirrah, what guess [1] does this inn hold now ?

Groom. Some five and twenty gentlemen, besides their beasts.

Phœ. Their beasts ?

Groom. Their wenches, I mean, sir ; for your worship knows those that are under men are beasts.   11

Phœ. How does your mother, sir ?

Groom. Very well in health, I thank you heartily, sir.

Phœ. And so is my mare, i'faith.

Groom. I'll do her commendations indeed, sir.

Fid. Well kept up, shuttlecock !

Phœ. But what old fellow was he that newly alighted before us ?

Groom. Who, he ? as arrant a crafty fellow as e'er made water on horseback. Some say, he's as good as a lawyer ; marry, I'm sure he's as bad as a knave : if you have any suits in law, he's the fittest man for your company ; has been so toused [2] and lugged himself, that he is

---

[1] Guests.

[2] Pulled violently about. Old eds. " toward ; " Dyce " towed."

able to afford you more knavish counsel for ten groats
than another for ten shillings.   25

Phœ. A fine fellow! but do you know him to be a
knave, and will lodge him?

Groom. Your worship begins to talk idly; your bed
shall be made presently: if we should not lodge knaves,
I wonder how we should be able to live honestly: are
there honest men enough, think you, in a term-time to
fill all the inns in the town? and, as far as I can see, a
knave's gelding eats no more hay than an honest man's;
nay, a [1] thief's gelding eats less, I'll stand to't; his master
allows him a better ordinary; yet I have my eightpence
day and night: 'twere more for our profit, I wus,[2] you
were all thieves, if you were so contented. I shall be
called for: give your worships good morrow. [*Exit.* 38

Phœ. A royal knave, i'faith: we have happened into a
godly inn.

Fid. Assure you, my lord, they belong all to one church.

Phœ. This should be some old, busy, turbulent fellow:
[a] villanous law-worm, that eats holes into poor men's
causes.

Entei TANGLE *with two Suitors, and* Groom.

First Suit. May it please your worship to give me leave?

Tan. I give you leave, sir; you have your *veniam.*
—Now fill me a brown toast, sirrah.

Groom. Will you have no drink to't, sir?

---

[1] So ed. 2.—Omitted in ed. 1.
[2] A vulgar form of "I wis" (the reading of ed. 2), which is a corruption of "i-wis," *i.e.* "certainly, assuredly."

Tan. Is that a question in law?

Groom. Yes, in the lowest court, i' th' cellar, sir.   50

Tan. Let me ha't removed presently, sir.

Groom. It shall be done, sir,   [*Exit.*

Tan. Now as you were saying, sir,—I'll come to you immediately too.

Phœ. O, very well, sir.

Tan. I'm a little busy, sir.

First Suit. But as how, sir?

Tan. I pray, sir?

First Suit. Has brought me into the court; marry, my adversary has not declared yet.   60

Tan. Non declaravit adversarius, sayest thou? what a villain's that! I have a trick to do thee good: I will get thee out a proxy, and make him declare, with a pox to him.

First Suit. That will make him declare to his sore grief; I thank your good worship: but put case he do declare?

Tan. Si declarasset, if he should declare there—

First Suit. I would be loath to stand out to the judgment of that court.

Tan. Non ad judicium, do you fear corruption? then I'll relieve you again; you shall get a *supersedeas non molestandum*, and remove it higher.   72

First Suit. Very good.

Tan. Now if it should ever come to a *testificandum*, what be his witnesses?

First Suit. I little fear his witnesses.

Tan. Non metuis testes? more valiant man than Orestes.

First Suit. Please you, sir, to dissolve this into wine,

ale, or beer. [*Giving money.*] I come a hundred mile to you, I protest, and leave all other counsel behind me.

Tan. Nay, you shall always find me a sound card : I stood not a' th' pillory for nothing in 88; all the world knows that.—Now let me dispatch you, sir.—I come to you *presenter.*	84

Second Suit. Faith, the party hath removed both body and cause with a *habeas corpus.*

Tan. Has he that knavery? but has he put in bail above, canst tell?

Second Suit. That I can assure your worship he has not.	90

Tan. Why, then, thy best course shall be, to lay out more money, take out a *procedendo,* and bring down the cause and him with a vengeance.

Second Suit. Then he will come indeed.

Tan. As for the other party, let the *audita querela* alone ; take me out a special *supplicavit,* which will cost you enough, and then you pepper him. For the first party after the *procedendo* you'll get costs ; the cause being found, you'll have a judgment ; *nunc pro tunc,* you'll get a *venire facias* to warn your jury, a *decem tales* to fill up the number, and a *capias utlagatum*[1] for your execution.

Second Suit. I thank you, my learned counsel.	102

Phœ. What a busy caterpillar's this ! let's accost him in that manner.

Fid. Content, my lord.

Phœ. O my old admirable fellow, how have I all this

---

[1] Writ of outlawry.

while thirsted to salute thee! I knew thee in *octavo* of
the duke——

   Tan. In *octavo* of the duke? I remember the year well.

   Phœ. By th' mass, a lusty, proper[1] man!   110

   Tan. O, was I?

   Phœ. But still in law.

   Tan. Still in law? I had not breathed else now; 'tis
very marrow, very manna to me to be in law; I'd been
dead ere this else. I have found such sweet pleasure in
the vexation of others, that I could wish my years over
and over again, to see that fellow a beggar, that bawling
knave a gentleman, a matter brought e'en to a judgment
to-day, as far as e'er 'twas to begin again to-morrow: O
raptures! here a writ of demur, there a *procedendo*, here
a *sursurrara*,[2] there a *capiendo*, tricks, delays, money-laws!

   Phœ. Is it possible, old lad?   122

   Tan. I have been a term-trotter[3] myself any time this
five and forty years; a goodly time and a gracious: in
which space I ha' been at least sixteen times beggared,
and got up again; and in the mire again, that I have
stunk again, and yet got up again.

   Phœ. And so clean and handsome now?

   Tan. You see it apparently; I cannot hide it from
you: nay, more, in *felici hora* be it spoken, you see I'm
old, yet have I at this present nine and twenty suits in law.

   Phœ. Deliver us, man!   132

---

[1] Handsome.

[2] A corruption of "certiorari." Cyril Tourneur uses the form
"sasarara" in the *Revenger's Tragedy*, iv. 1.

[3] One who frequented the capital in term-time.

Tan. And all not worth forty shillings.

Phœ. May it be believed?

Tan. The pleasure of a man is all.

Phœ. An old fellow, and such a stinger!

Tan. A stake pulled out of my hedge, there's one; I was well beaten, I remember, that's two; I took one a-bed with my wife again[1] her will, that's three; I was called cuckold for my labour, that's four; I took another a-bed again, that's five; then one called me wittol,[2] that's six; he killed my dog for barking, seven; my maid-servant was knocked at that time, eight; my wife miscarried with a push, nine; *et sic de cæteris.* I have so vexed and beggared the whole parish with process, subpœnas, and such-like molestations, they are not able to spare so much ready money from a term, as would set up a new weathercock; the churchwardens are fain to go to law with the poors' money.   149

Phœ. Fie, fie!

Tan. And I so fetch up all the men every term-time, that 'tis impossible to be at civil cuckoldry within ourselves, unless the whole country rise upon our wives.

Fid. A' my faith, a pretty policy!

Phœ. Nay, an excellent stratagem: but of all I most wonder at the continual substance of thy wit, that, having had so many suits in law from time to time, thou hast still money to relieve 'em.

Fid. Has the best fortune for that; I never knew him without.   160

---

[1] Against.
[2] A contented cuckold.

Tan. Why do you so much wonder at that? Why, this is my course : my mare and I come up some five days before a term.

Phœ. A good decorum!

Tan. Here I lodge, as you see, amongst inns and places of most receipt——

Phœ. Very wittily.

Tan. By which advantage I dive into countrymen's causes ; furnish 'em with knavish counsel, little to their profit ; buzzing into their ears this course, that writ, this office, that *ultimum refugium ;* as you know I have words enow for the purpose.   172

Phœ. Enow a' conscience, i'faith.

Tan. Enow a' law, no matter for conscience. For which busy and laborious sweating courtesy, they cannot choose but feed me with money, by which I maintain mine own suits : hoh, hoh, hoh !

Phœ. Why, let me hug thee : caper in mine arms.

Tan. Another special trick I have, nobody must know it, which is, to prefer most of those men to one attorney, whom I affect best : to answer which kindness of mine, he will sweat the better in my cause, and do them the less good : take 't of my word, I helped my attorney to more clients the last term than he will despatch all his lifetime ; I did it.   185

Phœ. What a noble, memorable deed was there !

Re-enter Groom.

Groom. Sir.

Tan. Now, sir?

Groom. There's a kind of captain very robustiously
inquires for you.   190
Tan. For me? a man of war?   A man of law is fit
for a man of war: we have no leisure to say prayers; we
both kill a' Sunday mornings.   I'll not be long from your
sweet company.
Phœ. O, no, I beseech you.
                              [*Exit* TANGLE *with* Groom.
Fid. What captain might this be?
Phœ. Thou angel sent amongst us, sober Law,
Made with meek eyes, persuading action,
No loud immodest tongue,
Voic'd like a virgin, and as chaste from sale,   200
Save only to be heard, but not to rail;
How has abuse deform'd thee to all eyes,
That where thy virtues sat, thy vices rise!
Yet why so rashly for one villain's fault
Do I arraign whole man?   Admired Law,
Thy upper parts must needs be sacred, pure,
And incorruptible; they're grave and wise:
'Tis but the dross beneath 'em, and the clouds
That get between thy glory and their praise,
That make the visible and foul eclipse;   210
For those that are near to thee are upright,
As noble in their conscience as their birth;
Know that damnation is in every bribe,
And rarely[1] put it from 'em; rate the presenters,
And scourge 'em with five years' imprisonment,

---

[1] Nobly.

For offering but to tempt 'em.
Thus is true justice exercis'd and us'd :
Woe to the giver when the bribe's refus'd !
'Tis not their will to have law worse than war,
Where still the poor'st die first ;   220
To send a man without a sheet to his grave,
Or bury him in his papers ;
'Tis not their mind it should be, nor to have
A suit hang longer than a man in chains,
Let him be ne'er so fasten'd.   They least know
That are above the tedious steps below :
I thank my time, I do.

    Fid. I long to know what captain this should be.
    Phœ. See where the bane of every cause returns.

Re-enter TANGLE *with* CAPTAIN.

    Fid. 'S foot, 'tis the captain my father-in-law, my lord.
    Phœ. Take heed.   231
    Cap. The divorce shall rest then, and the five hundred
crowns shall stand in full force and virtue.
    Tan. Then do you wisely, captain.
    Cap. Away sail I : fare thee well.
    Tan. A lusty crack of wind go with thee !
    Cap. But ah——
    Tan. Hah ?
    Cap. Remember, a scrivener.   239
    Tan. I'll have him for thee.   [*Exit* CAPTAIN.]—Why,
thus am I sought after by all professions.   Here's a
weather-beaten captain, who, not long since new married
to a lady widow, would now fain have sued a divorce

between her and him, but that her honesty is his only
hinderance : to be rid of which, he does determine to turn
her into white money ; and there's a lord, his chapman,
has bid five hundred crowns for her already.

Fid. How ?

Tan. Or for his part or whole in her.

Phœ. Why, does he mean to sell his wife ?　　　　250

Tan. His wife ?　Ay, by th' mass, he would sell his
soul if he knew what merchant would lay out money
upon't ; and some of 'em have need of one, they swear
so fast.

Phœ. Why, I never heard of the like.

Tan. Non audivisti, didst ne'er hear of that trick ?
Why, Pistor, a baker, sold his wife t'other day to a cheese-
monger, that made cake and cheese ; another to a cofferer ;
a third to a common player : why, you see 'tis common.
Ne'er fear the captain : he has not so much wit to be a
precedent himself.　I promised to furnish him with an
odd scrivener of mine own, to draw the bargain and sale
of his lady.　Your horses stand here, gentlemen ?[1]　263

Phœ. Ay, ay, ay.

Tan. I shall be busily plunged till towards bedtime
above the chin *in profundis*.　　　　　　　　　[*Exit.*

Phœ. What monstrous days are these !
Not only to be vicious most men study,
But in it to be ugly ; strive to exceed
Each other in the most deformed deed.　　　　270

Fid. Was this her private choice ? did she neglect

---

[1] So ed. 2.—Ed. 1 "Gentleman."

The presence and opinion of her friends
For this?
    Phœ. I wonder who that one should be,
Should so disgrace that reverend name of lord,
So loathsomely to buy adultery?
    Fid. We may make means to know.
    Phœ. Take courage, man; we'll beget some defence.
    Fid. I'm bound by nature.
    Phœ. I by conscience.
To sell his lady!   Indeed, she was a beast
To marry him; and so he makes of her.—   280
Come, I'll thorough now I'm enter'd.   [*Exeunt.*

SCENE V.

A Street.

Enter Jeweller's Wife and Boy.

    Jew. Wife. Is my sweet knight coming? are you certain
he's coming?
    Boy. Certain, forsooth; I am sure I saw him out of
the barber's shop, ere I would come away.
    Jew. Wife. A barber's shop?   O, he's a trim knight!
would he venture his body into a barber's shop, when he
knows 'tis as dangerous as a piece of Ireland?   O, yonder,
yonder he comes!   Get you back again, and look you
say as I advised you.
    Boy. You know me, mistress.   10
    Jew. Wife. My mask, my mask.   [*Exit Boy.*

Enter KNIGHT, *and Lackey following at some distance.*

Knight. My sweet Revenue!

Jew. Wife. My Pleasure, welcome! I have got single; none but you shall accompany me to the justice of peace, my father's.

Knight. Why, is thy father justice of peace, and I not know it?

Jew. Wife. My father? i'faith, sir, ay; simply though I stand here a citizen's wife, I am a justice of peace's daughter.   20

Knight. I love thee the better for thy birth.

Jew. Wife. Is that your lackey yonder, in the steaks [1] of velvet?

Knight. He's at thy service, my sweet Revenue, for thy money paid for 'em.

Jew. Wife. Why, then, let him run a little before, I beseech thee; for, a' my troth, he will discover us else.

Knight. He shall obey thee.—Before, sirrah, trudge. [*Exit Lackey.*]—But do you mean to lie at your father's all night?   30

Jew. Wife. Why should I desire your company else?

Knight. 'S foot, where shall I lie then?

Jew. Wife. What an idle question's that! why, do you think I cannot make room for you in my father's house as well as in my husband's? they're both good for nothing else.

---

[1] Dyce says:—"Some sort of dress ornamented with guards or facings, is meant, I suppose—if the reading be right." Perhaps we should read *stakes*, a jocular substitute for *pile* (the outer substance of velvet).

Knight. A man so resolute in valour as a woman in desire, were an absolute leader.   [*Exeunt.*

SCENE VI.

A Room in FALSO'S *House.*

Enter FALSO *and two Suitors.*

First Suit. May it please your good worship, master justice——

Fal. Please me and please yourself; that's my word.

First Suit. The party your worship sent for will by no means be brought to appear.

Fal. He will not? then what would you advise me to do therein?

First Suit. Only to grant your worship's warrant, which is of sufficient force to compel him.   9

Fal. No, by my faith, you shall not have me in that trap: am I sworn justice of peace, and shall I give my warrant to fetch a man against his will? why, there the peace is broken. We must do all quietly: if he come, he's welcome; and as far as I can see yet, he's a fool to be absent,—ay, by this gold is he—which he gave me this morning.   [*Aside.*

First Suit. Why, but may it please your good worship——

Fal. I say again, please me and please yourself; that's my word still.   20

First Suit. Sir, the world esteems it a common favour,

upon the contempt of the party, the justice to grant his warrant.

Fal. Ay, 'tis so common, 'tis the worse again; 'twere the better for me 'twere otherwise.

First Suit. I protest, sir, and this gentleman can say as much, it lies upon my half undoing.

Fal. I cannot see yet that it should be so,—I see not a cross [1] yet.   [*Aside.*

First Suit. I beseech your worship show me your immediate favour, and accept this small trifle but as a remembrance to my succeeding thankfulness.   32

Fal. Angels? I'll not meddle with them; you give 'em to my wife, not to me.

First Suit. Ay, ay, sir.

Fal. But I pray tell me now, did the party *viva voce*, with his own mouth, deliver that contempt, that he would not appear, or did you but jest in't?

First Suit. Jest? no, 'a my troth, sir; such was his insolent answer.   40

Fal. And do you think it stood with my credit to put up such an abuse? Will he not appear, says he? I'll make him appear with a vengeance.—Latronello!

Lat. Does your worship call?

Fal. Draw me a strong-limbed warrant for the gentleman speedily; he will be bountiful to thee.—Go and thank him within.

First Suit. I shall know your worship hereafter.

Fal. Ay, I prithee do. [*Exeunt Suitors with* LA-

---

[1] A piece of money.

TRONELLO.] Two angels one party, four another : and I think it a great spark of wisdom and policy, if a man come to me for justice, first to know his griefs by his fees, which be light, and which be heavy ; he may counterfeit else, and make me do justice for nothing : I like not that ; for when I mean to be just, let me be paid well for't : the deed so rare purges the bribe.   56

Enter FURTIVO.

How now ? what's the news, thou art come so hastily ? how fares my knightly brother ?

Fur. Troth, he ne'er fared worse in his life, sir ; he ne'er had less stomach tò his meat since I knew him.

Fal. Why, sir ?

Fur. Indeed he's dead, sir.

Fal. How, sir ?

Fur. Newly deceased, I can assure your worship : the tobacco-pipe new dropt out of his mouth before I took horse ; a shrewd sign ; I knew then there was no way but one [1] with him ; the poor pipe was the last man he took leave of in this world, who fell in three pieces before him, and seemed to mourn inwardly, for it looked as black i' th' mouth as my master.   70

Fal. Would he die so like a politician [2] and not once write his mind to me ?

---

[1] *i.e.* that he must die. The expression is proverbial : see Marlowe's Works (ed. Bullen), i. 92.

[2] Cf. Cyril Tourneur's *Revenger's Tragedy,* v. 1 :—"Show him the body of the Duke his father, and how quaintly he died like *a Politician in hugger-mugger, made no man acquainted with it.*" Mr. Churton

Fur. No, I'll say that for him, sir, he died in the perfect state of memory; made your worship his full and
whole executor, bequeathing his daughter, and with her
all his wealth, only to your disposition.

Fal. Did he make such a godly end, sayest thou? did
he die so comfortably, and bequeath all to me?

Fur. Your niece is at hand, sir, the will, and the
witnesses.   80

Fal. What a precious joy and comfort's this, that a
justice's brother can die so well, nay, in such a good and
happy memory, to make me full executor! Well, he
was too honest to live, and that made him die so soon.
Now I beshrew my heart, I am glad he's in heaven, has
left all his cares and troubles with me, and that great
vexation of telling of money: yet I hope he had so much
grace before he died to turn his white money [1] into gold,
a great ease to his executor.   89

Fur. See, here comes your niece, my young mistress, sir.

Enter NIECE *and two Gentlemen.*

Fal. Ah, my sweet niece, let me kiss thee, and drop a
tear between thy lips! one tear from an old man is a
great matter; the cocks of age are dry. Thou hast lost
a virtuous father, to gain a notable uncle.

Niece. My hopes now rest in you next under heaven.

Collins, the accomplished editor of Tourneur, wished to read " Politian "
for " Politician;" but the present passage of Middleton shows that
there is no need to make any change.

   [1] " White money" was a cant term for silver.   Cf. *Philaster*, ii. 2 :—
" She's coming, sir, behind, will take *white money*."

Fal. Let 'em rest, let 'em rest.

First Gent. Sir——

Fal. You're most welcome ere ye begin, sir.

First Gent. We are both led by oath and dreadful
           promise,

Made to the dying man at his last sense,   100

First to deliver these into your hands,

The sureties and revealers of his state—   [*Giving papers.*

Fal. Good.

First Gent. With this his only daughter, and your niece,

Whose fortunes are at your disposing set ;

Uncle and father are in you both met.

Fal. Good, i'faith ; a well-spoken gentleman !

You're not an esquire, sir ?

First Gent. Not, sir.   109

Fal. Not, sir ? more's the pity ; by my faith, better
men than you are, but a great many worse : you see I
have been a scholar in my time, though I'm a justice
now.—Niece, you're most happily welcome : the charge
of you is wholly and solely mine own ; and since you are
so fortunately come, niece, I'll rest a perpetual widower.

Niece. I take the meaning chaster than the words :

Yet I hope well of both, since it is thus,

His phrase offends least that's known humorous.

Fal. [*reading the will.*] *I make my brother,* says he,
full and whole executor : honestly done of him, i'faith !
seldom can a man get such a brother : and here again
says he, very virtuously, *I bequeath all to him and his disposing.* An excellent fellow, a' my troth ! Would you
might all die no worse, gentlemen !   124

Enter KNIGHT *and* Jeweller's Wife.

First Gent. But as much better as might be.

Knight. Bless your uprightness, master justice!

Fal. You're most soberly welcome, sir.—Daughter, you've that ye kneel for: rise, salute your weeping cousin.

Jew. Wife. Weeping, cousin?

Niece. Ay, cousin.   130

Knight. Eye to weeping is very proper, and so is the party that spake it; believe me, a pretty, fine, slender, straight, delicate-knit body:

O, how it moves a pleasure through our senses!

How small are women's waists to their expenses!

I cannot see her face, that's under water yet.

Jew. Wife. News as cold to the heart as an old man's kindness; my uncle dead!

Niece. I have lost the dearest father!

Fal. [*reading the will.*] *If she marry by your consent, choice, and liking, make her dowry five thousand crowns:* hum, five thousand crowns? therefore by my consent she shall ne'er marry; I will neither choose for her, like of it, nor consent to't.   [*Aside.* 144

Knight. Now, by the pleasure of my blood, a pretty cousin! I would not care if I were as near kin to her as I have been to her kinswoman.   [*Aside.*

Fal. Daughter, what gentleman might this be?

Jew. Wife. No gentleman, sir; he's a knight.

Fal. Is he but a knight?[1] troth, I would a' sworn had been a gentleman; to see, to see, to see.   151

---

[1] Cf. *Hans Beer Pot,* 1618:—
   " 'Twas strange to see what knighthood once would do,

Jew. Wife. He's my husband's own brother, I can tell you, sir.

Fal. Thy husband's brother? speak certainly, prithee.

Jew. Wife. I can assure you, father, my husband and he has lain both in one belly.

Fal. I'll swear then he is his brother indeed, and by the surer side.—I crave hearty pardon, sweet kinsman, that thou hast stood so long unsaluted in the way of kindred: 160
Welcome[1] to my board: I have a bed for thee:
My daughter's husband's brother shall command
Keys of my chests and chambers:
I have stable for thy horse, chamber for thyself, and a
loft above for thy lousy lackey, all fit.
Away with handkerchers, [and] dry up eyes:
At funeral we must cry; now let's be wise.
        [*Exeunt all but* KNIGHT *and* Jeweller's Wife.
Jew. Wife. I told you his affection.
Knight.[2] It falls sweetly.

        Stir great men up to lead a martial life,
        Such as were nobly born of great estates,
        To gain this honour and this dignity,
        So noble a mark to their posterity.
        But now, alas! it's grown ridiculous,
        Since bought with money, sold for basest prize,
        That some refuse it which are counted wise." (G. 3, verso.)
The dramatists constantly sneer at those who bought the honour of knighthood from King James.
  [1] "One of those snatches of blank verse (and printed as such in the old eds.) which sometimes occur in the midst of prose speeches."—*Dyce.* It is frequently very difficult to decide whether a passage should be arranged as verse or prose.
  [2] Old ed. "*Fal.*"

Jew. Wife. But here I bar you from all plots to-night,
The time is yet too heavy to be light.   170

 Knight. Why, I'm content ; I'll sleep as chaste as you,
And wager night by night who keeps most true.

 Jew. Wife. Well, we shall see your temper. [*Exeunt.*

ACT II.

SCENE I.

A Room in an Inn.

Enter PHŒNIX *and* FIDELIO.

Phœ. Fear not me, Fidelio ; become you that invisible ropemaker the scrivener, that binds a man as he walks, yet all his joints at liberty, as well as I'll fit that common folly of gentry, the easy-affecting venturer ; and no doubt our purpose will arrive most happily.

Fid. Chaste duty, my lord, works powerfully in me ; and rather than the poor lady my mother should fall upon the common side of rumour to beggar her name, I would not only undergo all habits, offices, disguised professions, though e'en opposite to the temper my blood holds ; but in the stainless quarrel of her reputation, alter my shape for ever.   12

Phœ. I love thee wealthier ; thou hast a noble touch :[1]

---

[1] " So Shakespeare :—
    ' Come, my sweet wife, my dearest mother, and
      My friends of *noble touch.*'—*Coriol.* act iv. sc. 1.
Which Warburton rightly explains,—of true metal unalloyed : a metaphor from trying gold on the touchstone."—*Dyce.*

and by this means, which is the only safe means to preserve thy mother from such an ugly land and sea monster
as a counterfeit captain is, he resigning and basely selling
all his estate, title, right, and interest in his lady, as the
form of the writing shall testify,
What otherwise can follow but to have
A lady safe deliver'd of a knave?　　　　　　　　　　20

　　Fid. I am in debt my life to the free goodness of your
inventions.

　　Phœ. O, they must ever strive to be so good !
Who sells his vow is stamp'd the slave of blood.

　　　　　　　　　　　　　　　　　　　　　[Exeunt.

SCENE II.

A Room in the CAPTAIN'S *House.*

Enter CAPTAIN, *and* CASTIZA *following him.*

　　Cap. Away !
　　Cas. Captain, my husband——
　　Cap. Hence ! we're at a price for thee, at a price ;
Wants but the telling and the sealing ; then——
　　Cas. Have you no sense, neither of my good name
Or your own credit ?
　　Cap. Credit ? pox of credit,
That makes me owe so much ! it had been
Better for me by a thousand royals [1]
I had lost my credit seven year ago.

-----

[1] Gold coins worth fifteen shillings.

'T has undone me : that's it that makes me fly :   10
What need I to sea else, in the spring-time,
When woods have leaves, to look upon bald oak ?
Happier that man, say I, whom no man trusts !
It makes him valiant, dares outface the prisons ;
Upon whose carcass no gown'd raven jets :
O, he that has no credit owes no debts !
'Tis time I were rid on't.

    Cas. O, why do you
So wilfully cherish your own poison,
And breathe against the best of life, chaste credit ?
Well may I call it chaste ; for, like a maid,   20
Once falsely broke, it ever lives decay'd.
O captain, husband ! you name that dishonest,
By whose good power all that are honest live :
What madness is it to speak ill of that,
Which makes all men speak well !   Take away credit,
By which men amongst men are well reputed,
That man may live, but still lives executed.
O, then, show pity to that noble title,
Which else you do usurp ! you're no true captain,
To let your enemies lead you : foul disdain   30
And everlasting scandal, O, believe it !
The money you receive for my good name
Will not be half enough to pay your shame.

    Cap. No ? I'll sell thee then to the smock : see, here
        comes
My honourable chapman.

Enter PRODITOR *and Lackey.*

Cas. O my poison!
Him whom mine honour and mine eye abhors.   [*Exit.*
    Prod. Lady,—what, so unjovially departed?
    Cap. Fine she-policy! she makes my back her bolster;
but before my face she not endures him: tricks! [*Aside.*
    Prod. Captain, how haps it she remov'd so strangely?[1]
    Cap. O, for modesty's cause, awhile, my lord,   41
She must restrain herself; she's not yours yet.
Beside, it were not wisdom to appear
Easy before my sight.
Faugh! wherefore serves modesty but to pleasure a lady
now and then, and help her from suspect? that's the best
use 'tis put to.
    Prod. Well observed of a captain!
    Cap. No doubt you'll be soon friends, my lord.
    Prod. I think no less.   50
    Cap. And make what haste I can to my ship, I durst
wager you'll be under sail before me.
    Prod. A pleasant voyage, captain!
    Cap. Ay, a very pleasant voyage as can be.   I see the
hour is ripe:
Here comes the prison's bawd, the bond-maker,
One that binds heirs before they are begot.
    Prod. And here are the crowns, captain.
                                    [*Giving him money.*

---

1 Coyly. Cf. *Changeling*, iii. 4 :—
        "What makes your lip so *strange?*"

Enter PHŒNIX *and* FIDELIO, *both disguised.*

Go, attend : let our bay-courser wait.

   Lackey. It shall be obeyed.   [*Exit.* 60

   Cap. A farmer's son, is't true ?

   Fid. Has crowns to scatter.

   Cap. I give you your salute, sir.

   Phœ. I take it not unthankfully, sir.

   Cap. I hear a good report of you, sir; you've money.

   Phœ. I have so, true.

   Cap. An excellent virtue.

   Phœ. Ay, to keep from you.   [*Aside.*

Hear you me, captain ?   I have a certain generous itch,
sir, to lose a few angels in the way of profit : 'tis but a
game at tennis, where, if   71
The ship keep above line, 'tis three to one ;
If not, there's but three hundred angels gone.

   Cap. Is your venture three hundred ? you're very
preciously welcome : here's a voyage toward will make
us all——

   Phœ. Beggarly fools and swarming knaves.   [*Aside.*

   Prod. Captain, what's he ?

   Cap. Fear him not, my lord ; he's a gull : he ventures
with me ; some filthy farmer's son ; the father's a Jew
and the son a gentleman : faugh !   81

   Prod. Yet he should be a Jew too, for he is new come
from giving over swine.

   Cap. Why, that in our country makes him a gentleman.

   Prod. Go to ; tell your money, captain.

Cap. Read aloft, scrivener.—One, two.

                                         [*Counting the money.*

Fid. [*reads.*] *To all good and honest Christian people,
to whom this present writing shall come : know you for a
certain, that I captain, for and in the consideration of the
sum of five hundred crowns, have clearly bargained, sold,
given, granted, assigned, and set over, and by these presents
do clearly bargain, sell, give, grant, assign, and set over,
all the right, estate, title, interest, demand, possession, and
term of years to come, which I the said captain have, or
ought to have——*   96

Phœ. If I were as good as I should be.   [*Aside.*

*Fid. In and to Madonna Castiza, my most virtuous,
modest, loving, and obedient wife——*

Cap. By my troth, my lord, and so she is.—
Three, four, five, six, seven.   [*Counting the money.*

Phœ. The more slave he that says it, and not sees it.
                                                  [*Aside.*

*Fid. Together with all and singular those admirable
qualities with which her noble breast is furnished.*

Cap. Well said, scrivener ; hast put 'em all in ?—
You shall hear now, my lord.

*Fid. In primis, the beauties of her mind, chastity, tem-
perance, and, above all, patience——*

Cap. You have bought a jewel, i'faith, my lord.—
Nine and thirty, forty.   [*Counting the money.* 110

*Fid. Excellent in the best of music, in voice delicious, in
conference wise and pleasing, of age contentful, neither too
young to be apish, nor too old to be sottish——*

Cap. You have bought as lovely a pennyworth, my lord, as e'er you bought in your life.

Prod. Why should I buy her else, captain?

Fid. And which is the best of a wife, a most comfortable sweet companion.

Cap. I could not afford her so, i'faith, but that I am going to sea, and have need of money.   120

Fid. A most comfortable sweet companion.

Prod. What, again? the scrivener reads in passion.[1]

Fid. I read as the words move me; yet if that be a fault, it shall be seen no more:—*which said Madonna Castiza lying and yet being in the occupation of the said captain*——

Cap. Nineteen—[*counting the money*]—occupation? Pox on't, out with occupation; a captain is of no occupation, man.

Phœ. Nor thou of no religion.   [*Aside.*   130

Fid. Now I come to the *habendum,—to have and to hold, use, and*——

Cap. Use? put out use too, for shame, till we are all gone, I prithee.

Fid. And to be acquitted of and from all former bargains, former sales——

Cap. Former sales?—nine and twenty, thirty—[*counting the money*]—by my troth, my lord, this is the first time that ever I sold her.

Prod. Yet the writing must run so, captain.   140

---

[1] In a sorrowful tone.

Cap. Let it run on then,—nine and forty, fifty.

[*Counting the money.*

*Fid. Former sales, gifts, grants, surrenders, re-en-
tries——*

Cap. For re-entries I will not swear for her.

*Fid. And furthermore, I the said, of and for the con-
sideration of the sum of five hundred crowns to set me aboard,
before these presents, utterly disclaim for ever any title, estate,
right, interest, demand, or possession, in or to the said Madonna Castiza, my late virtuous and unfortunate wife——*

Phœ. Unfortunate indeed! that was well plac'd. [*Aside.*

*Fid. As also neither to touch, attempt, molest, or incumber
any part or parts whatsoever, either to be named or not to
be named, either hidden or unhidden, either those that boldly
look abroad, or those that dare not show their face[s]——*

Cap. Faces? I know what you mean by faces:
scrivener, there's a great figure in faces.   156

*Fid. In witness whereof, I the said captain have inter-
changeably set to my hand and seal, in presence of all these,
the day and date above written.*

Cap. Very good, sir; I'll be ready for you presently—
four hundred and twenty, one, two, three, four, five.

[*Counting the money.*

Phœ. Of all deeds yet this strikes the deepest wound
Into my apprehension.

Reverend and honourable Matrimony,[1]

---

[1] " In a note on [*sic*] the Aldine edition of Milton I have pointed out
the resemblance between the present passage and that in *Par. Lost*, b.
iv. 750 :—

'Hail, wedded love, mysterious law.'"—*Dyce.*

Mother of lawful sweets, unshamed mornings,
Dangerless pleasures ! thou that mak'st the bed
Both pleasant and legitimately fruitful !
Without thee,
All the whole world were soiled bastardy.
Thou art the only and the greatest form   170
That put'st a difference between our desires
And the disorder'd appetites of beasts,
Making their mates those that stand next their lusts.
Then,—
With what base injury is thy goodness paid !
First, rare to have a bride commence a maid,
But does beguile joy of the purity,
And is made strict by power of drugs and art,[1]
An artificial maid, a doctor'd virgin,
And so deceives the glory of his bed ;   180
A foul contempt against the spotless power
Of sacred wedlock !   But if chaste and honest,
There is another devil haunts marriage—
None fondly loves but knows it—jealousy,
That wedlock's yellow sickness,
That whispering separation every minute,
And thus the curse takes his effect or progress.
The most of men in their sudden furies
Rail at the narrow bounds of marriage,
And call't a prison ; then it is most just,   190
That the disease a' th' prison, jealousy,

---

[1] See Burton s *Anatomy of Melancholy*, Part iii. Sect. 3, Memb. 2, Subs. 1.

Should still affect 'em.[1] But O ! here I am fix'd,
To make sale of a wife, monstrous and foul,
An act abhorr'd in nature, cold in soul :
Who that has man in him could so resign
To make his shame the posy to the coin ?

    Cap. Right, i'faith, my lord ; fully five hundred.

    Prod. I said how you should find it, captain ; and with this competent sum you rest amply contented ?

    Cap. Amply contented.   200

    Fid. Here's the pen, captain : your name to the sale.

    Cap. 'S foot, dost take me to be a penman ? I protest I could ne'er write more than A B C, those three letters, in my life.

    Fid. Why, those will serve, captain.

    Cap. I could ne'er get further.

    Phœ. Would you have got further than A B C ?— (Ah, base captain !)—that's far enough, i'faith.

    Fid. Take the seal off, captain.

    Cap. It goes on hardly, and comes off easily.   210

    Phœ. Ay, just like a coward.

    Fid. Will you write witness, gentleman ?

    Cap. He ? he shall. Prithee, come and set thy hand for witness, rogue : thou shalt venture with me ?

    Phœ. Nay, then I ha' reason, captain, that commands me.   [*Writes.*

    Cap. What a fair fist the pretty whorson writes, as if he had had manners and bringing up ! A farmer's son ! his father damns himself to sell musty corn, while he

---

[1] Old eds. "a'm" (which Dyce retains).

ventures the money : 'twill prosper well at sea, no doubt ;
he shall ne'er see't again.   221

   Fid. So, captain, you deliver this as your deed ?

   Cap. As my deed ; what else, sir ?

   Phœ. The ugliest deed that e'er mine eye did witness.
                                              [Aside.

   Cap. So, my lord, you have her ; clip [1] her, enjoy her ;
she's your own : and let me be proud to tell you now, my
lord, she's as good a soul if a man had a mind to live
honest and keep a wench, the kindest, sweetest, com-
fortablest rogue——

   Prod. Hark in thine ear,—   230
The baser slave art thou ; and so I'll tell her :
I love the pearl thou sold'st, hate thee the seller.
Go to sea ; the end of thee—is lousy.

   Cap. This [is] fine work ! a very brave end, hum——

   Prod. Well thought upon, this scrivener may furnish
         me.   *[Whispers* FIDELIO.

   Phœ. Why should this fellow be a lord by birth,
Being by blood a knave, one that would sell
His lordship if he lik'd her ladyship ?   *[Aside.*

   Fid. Yes, my lord.

   Phœ. What's here now ?   240

   Prod. I have employment for a trusty fellow,
Bold, sure,—

   Fid. What if he be a knave, my lord ?

   Prod. There thou com'st to me : why, he should be so ;
And men of your quill are not unacquainted.

---

                  [1] Embrace.

Fid. Indeed all our chief living, my lord, is by fools and knaves; we could not keep open shop else; fools that enter into bonds, and knaves that bind 'em.

Prod. Why, now we meet.

Fid. And, as my memory happily leads me, I know a fellow of a standing estate, never flowing:	250
I durst convey treason into his bosom,
And keep it safe nine years.

Prod. A goodly time.

Fid. And if need were, would press to an attempt,
And cleave to desperate action.

Prod. That last fits me;
Thou hast the measure right : look I hear from thee.

Fid. With duteous speed.

Prod. Expect a large reward.—
I will find time of her to find regard.	[*Exit.*

Cap. The end of me is lousy!

Fid. O my lord, I have strange words to tell you!

Phœ. Stranger yet?	260
I'll choose some other hour to listen to thee;
I am yet sick of this.   Discover [1] quickly.

Fid. Why, will you make yourself known, my lord?

Phœ. Ay:
Who scourgeth sin let him do't dreadfully.

Cap. Pox of his dissemblance! I will to sea.

Phœ. Nay, you shall to sea, thou wouldst poison the whole land else.   [*Aside.*]—Why, how now, captain?

Cap. In health.

---

[1] Let us put off our disguise.

Fid. What, drooping?   270

Phœ. Or ashamed of the sale of thine own wife?

Cap. You might count me an ass then, i'faith.

Phœ. If not ashamed of that, what can you be ashamed of then?

Cap. Prithee ha' done; I am ashamed of nothing.

Phœ. I easily believe that.   [*Aside.*

Cap. This lord sticks in my stomach.

Phœ. How? take one of thy feathers down, and fetch him up.

Fid. I'd make him come.   280

Phœ. But what if the duke should hear of this?

Fid. Ay, or your son-in-law Fidelio knows of the sale of his mother?

Cap. What and they did? I sell none but mine own. As for the duke, he's abroad by this time; and for Fidelio, he's in labour.

Phœ. He in labour?

Cap. What call you travelling?

Phœ. That's true: but let me tell you, captain, whether the duke hear on't, or Fidelio know on't, or both, or neither, 'twas a most filthy, loathsome part——   291

Fid. A base, unnatural deed——

      [*They discover themselves, and lay hands on him.*

Cap. Slave, and fool—— Ha, who? O!——

Phœ. Thou hateful villain! thou shouldst choose to sink,

To keep thy baseness shrouded.

Enter CASTIZA.

Fid. Ugly wretch!

Cas. Who hath laid violence upon my husband,
My dear sweet captain?   Help!

Phœ. Lady, you wrong your value:
Call you him dear that has sold you so cheap?   300

  Cas. I do beseech your pardon, good my lord.

             [*Kneels.*

 Phœ. Rise.

 Fid. My abused mother!

 Cas. My kind son!
Whose liking I neglected in this match.

  Fid. Not that alone, but your far happier fortunes.

  Cap. Is this the scrivener and the farmer's son?
Fire on his lordship! he told me they travell'd.

  Phœ. And see the sum told out to buy that jewel,
More precious in a woman than her eye,
Her honour.—
Nay, take it to you, lady; and I judge it   310
Too slight a recompense for your great wrong,
But that his riddance helps it.

  Cap. 'S foot, he undoes me! I'm a rogue and a beggar:
The Egyptian plague creeps over me already;
I begin to be lousy.

  Phœ. Thus happily prevented, you're set free,
Or else made over to adultery.

  Cas. To heaven and to you my modest thanks.

  Phœ. Monster, to sea! spit thy abhorred foam
Where it may do least harm; there's air and room;   320

Thou'rt dangerous in a chamber, virulent venom
Unto a lady's name and her chaste breath.
If past this evening's verge the dukedom hold thee,
Thou art reserv'd for abject punishment.

Cap. I do beseech your good lordship, consider the
state of a poor downcast captain.

Phœ. Captain? off with that noble title! thou becomest
it vildly; I ne'er saw the name fit worse: I'll sooner
allow a pander a captain than thee.

Cap. More's the pity.   330

Phœ. Sue to thy lady for pardon.

Cas. I give it without suit.

Cap. I do beseech your ladyship not so much for
pardon, as to bestow a few of those crowns upon a poor
unfeathered rover, that will as truly pray for you,—and
wish you hanged [*aside*]—as any man breathing.

Cas. I give it freely all.

Phœ. Nay, by your favour;
I will contain [1] you, lady.—Here, be gone:
Use slaves like slaves: wealth keeps their faults unknown.

Cap. Well, I'm yet glad I've liberty and these: 341
The land has plagu'd me, and I'll plague the seas. [*Exit.*

Phœ. The scene is clear'd, the bane of brightness fled;
Who sought the death of honour is struck dead.—
Come, modest lady.

Fid. My most honest mother!

Phœ. Thy virtue shall live safe from reach of shames:
That act ends nobly preserves ladies' fames.   [*Exeunt.*

---

[1] Check, restrain.

SCENE III.

A Room in FALSO'S *House.*

Enter FALSO, *Knight, and Jeweller's Wife.*

Fal. Why, this is but the second time of your coming, kinsman; visit me oftener.—Daughter, I charge you bring this gentleman along with you :—gentleman ! I cry ye mercy, sir; I call you gentleman still; I forget you're but a knight;[1] you must pardon me, sir.

Knight. For your worship's kindness—worship ! I cry you mercy, sir; I call you worshipful still; I forget you're but a justice.

Fal. I am no more, i'faith.

Knight. You must pardon me, sir.   10

Fal. 'Tis quickly done, sir : you see I make bold with you, kinsman, thrust my daughter and you into one chamber.

Knight. Best of all, sir : kindred you know may lie anywhere.

Fal. True, true, sir.—Daughter, receive your blessing: take heed the coach jopper not too much ; have a care to the fruits of your body.—Look to her, kinsman.

Knight. Fear it not, sir.

Jew. Wife. Nay, father, though I say it, that should not say it, he looks to me more like a husband than a kinsman.   22

---

[1] See note 1, p. 135.

Fal. I hear good commendations of you, sir.

Knight. You hear the worst of me, I hope, sir : I salute my leave, sir.

Fal. You're welcome all over your body, sir. [*Exeunt* Knight *and* Jeweller's Wife.]—Nay, I can behave myself courtly, though I keep house i' th' country. What, does my niece hide herself? not present, ha?—Latronello.

Enter LATRONELLO.

Lat. Sir.   30

Fal. Call my niece to me.

Lat. Yes, sir.   [*Exit.*

Fal. A foolish, coy, bashful thing it is ; she's afraid to lie with her own uncle : I'd do her no harm, i'faith. I keep myself a widower a' purpose, yet the foolish girl will not look into't : she should have all, i'faith ; she knows I have but a time, cannot hold long.   See, where she comes.

Enter Niece.

Pray, who [1] am I, niece ?

Niece. I hope you're yourself,
Uncle to me, and brother to my father.   40

Fal. O, am I so ? it does not appear so, for surely you would love your father's brother for your father's sake, your uncle for your own sake.

Niece. I do so.

Fal. Nay, you do nothing, niece.

---

[1] So ed. 2.—Ed. 1 "whome."

Niece. In that love which becomes you best I love
          you.

Fal. How should I know that love becomes me best?

Niece. Because 'tis chaste and honourable.

Fal. Honourable? it cannot become me then, niece,
For I'm scarce worshipful.   Is this an age   50
To entertain bare love without the fruits?
When I receiv'd thee first, I look'd
Thou should'st have been a wife unto my house,
And sav'd me from the charge of marriage.
Do you think your father's five thousand pound would
ha' made me take you else? no, you should ne'er ha'[1]
been a charge to me.   As far as I can perceive yet by
you, I've as much need to marry as e'er I had: would
not this be a great grief to your friends, think you, if
they were alive again?   60

Niece. 'Twould be a grief indeed.

Fal. You have[2] confess'd,
All about house, that young Fidelio,
Who in his travels does attend the prince,
Is your vow'd love.

Niece. Most true, he's my vow'd husband.

Fal. And what's a husband?   Is not a husband a
stranger at first? and will you lie with a stranger before
you lie with your own uncle?   Take heed what ye do,
niece: I counsel you for the best.   Strangers are
drunken fellows, I can tell you; they will come home
late a' nights, beat their wives, and get nothing but

---

[1] Old eds. "a ha."   [2] Old eds. "Y'aue."

girls : look to't ; if you marry, your stubbornness is your
dowry ; five thousand crowns were bequeathed to you,
true, if you marry with my consent ; but if e'er you go
to marrying by my consent, I'll go to hanging by yours :
go to, be wise, and love your uncle.   75

Niece. I should have cause then to repent indeed.
Do you so far forget the offices
Of blushing modesty ?   Uncles are half fathers ;
Why, they come so near our bloods, they're e'en part
        of it.

Fal. Why, now you come to me, niece : if your uncle
be part of your own flesh and blood, is it not then fit
your own flesh and blood should come nearest to you ?
answer me to that, niece.   83

Niece. You do allude all to incestuous will,
Nothing to modest purpose.   Turn me forth ;
Be like an uncle of these latter days,
Perjur'd enough, enough unnatural ;
Play your executorship in tyranny,
Restrain my fortunes, keep me poor,—I care not.
In this alone most women I'll excel,   90
I'll rather yield to beggary than to hell.   [*Exit.*

Fal. Very good ; a' my troth, my niece is valiant : sh'as
made me richer by five thousand crowns, the price of her
dowry.   Are you so honest?   I do not fear but I shall
have the conscience to keep you poor enough, niece, or
else I am quite altered a' late.

Enter LATRONELLO.

The news, may it please you, sir ?

Lat. Sir, there's an old fellow, a kind of law-driver, entreats conference with your worship.

Fal. A law-driver? prithee, drive him hither. 100

[*Exit* LATRONELLO.

Enter TANGLE.

Tan. No, no, I say; if it be for defect of apparance,[1] take me out a special *significavit*.

Suitor[2] [*within*]. Very good, sir.

Tan. Then if he purchase an *alias* or *capias*, which are writs of custom, only to delay time, your *procedendo* does you knight's service—that's nothing at all; get your *distringas* out as soon as you can for a jury.

Suit. [*within*]. I'll attend your good[3] worship's coming out.

Tan. Do, I prithee, attend me; I'll take it kindly, *a voluntate*. 111

Fal. What, old signior Tangle!

Tan. I am in debt to your worship's remembrance.

Fal. My old master of fence! come, come, come, I have not exercised this twelve moons; I have almost forgot all my law-weapons.

Tan. They are under fine and recovery; your worship shall easily recover them.

Fal. I hope so.—When,[4] there?

---

[1] Appearance.

[2] " This word I have substituted for the ' *Whin* ' of the first ed. and the ' *Whi.*' of the second.—Perhaps Tangle ought not to enter till Falso says, ' What, old signior,' &c."—*Dyce.*

[3] So ed. 2.—Ed. 1 " gour."

[4] An impatient call addressed to the servant (ed. 1 " Wheu ").

Enter LATRONELLO.

Lat. Sir?   120

Fal. The rapier and dagger foils instantly.—[*Exit* LATRONELLO.]—And what's thy suit to me, old Tangle? I'll grant it presently.

Tan. Nothing but this, sir ; to set your worship's hand to the commendation of a knave whom nobody speaks well on.

Fal. The more shame for 'em : what was his offence, I pray?

Tan. Vestras deducite culpas ; nothing but robbing a vestry.   130

Fal. What, what? alas, poor knave! Give me the paper. He did but save the churchwardens a labour : come, come, he has done a better deed in't than the parish is aware of, to prevent [1] the knaves ; he robs but seldom, they once a quarter : methinks 'twere a part of good justice to hang 'em at year's end, when they come out of their office, to the true terrifying of all collectors and sidemen.[2]

Tan. Your worship would make a fruitful common-wealth's man : the constable lets 'em alone, looks on, and says nothing.   141

Fal. Alas, good man! he lets 'em alone for quietness' sake, and takes half a share with 'em : they know well enough too he has an impediment in his tongue ; he's always drunk when he should speak.

---

[1] Anticipate.
[2] Assistants to the churchwarden.

Tan. Indeed, your worship speaks true in that, sir: they blind him with beer, and make him so narrow-eyed, that he winks naturally at all their knaveries.

Fal. So, so ; here's my hand to his commendations.

[*Signs the paper.*

Tan. A *caritate,* you do a charitable deed in't, sir. 151

Fal. Nay, if it be but a vestry matter, visit me at any time, old Signior Law-thistle.

Re-enter LATRONELLO *with rapier and dagger foils, and then exit.*

O well done ! here are the foils : come, come, sir ; I'll try a law-bout with you.

Tan. I am afraid I shall overthrow you, sir, i'faith.

Fal. 'Tis but for want of use then, sir.

Tan. Indeed, that same odd word, use, makes a man a good lawyer, and a woman an arrant——tuh, tuh, tuh, tuh, tuh ! Now am I for you, sir: but first to bring you into form ; can your worship name all your weapons ? 162

Fal. That I can, I hope. Let me see : Longsword, what's Longsword ? I am so dulled with doing justice, that I have forgot all, i'faith.

Tan. Your Longsword, that's *a writ of delay.*

Fal. Mass, that sword's long enough, indeed ; I ha' known it reach the length of fifteen terms.

Tan. Fifteen terms ? that's but a short sword.

Fal. Methinks 'tis long enough : proceed, sir. 170

Tan. A *writ of delay*, Longsword; *scandala magnatum*,[1] Backsword.

Fal. Scandals are backswords indeed.

Tan. *Capias cominus*, Case of Rapiers.

Fal. O desperate!

Tan. A[2] *latitat*, Sword and Dagger; *a writ of execution*, Rapier and Dagger.

Fal. Thou art come to our present weapon: but what call you Sword and Buckler, then?   179

Tan. O, that's out of use now! Sword and Buckler was called *a good conscience*, but that weapon's left long ago: that was too manly a fight, too sound a weapon for these our days. 'Slid, we are scarce able to lift up a buckler now, our arms are so bound to the pox; one good bang upon a buckler would make most of our gentlemen fly a' pieces: 'tis not for these linty times: our lawyers are good rapier and dagger men; they'll quickly despatch your—money.

Fal. Indeed, since sword and buckler time,[3] I have

---

[1] "This form seems to have been common; so Taylor, the water-poet:

'From *scandala magnatum* I am cleare,

Farewell to the Tower-bottles, p. 126.—*Workes*, ed. 1630.
See also *The Sculler*, p. 29, *ibid.*"—*Dyce.*

[2] The old eds. give these words to Falso.

[3] A good illustration of this passage is to be found in Howe's Stow, 1631, p. 1023:—"This manner of fight [with sword and buckler] was frequent with all men until the fight of rapier and dagger took place, and then suddenly the general quarrel of fighting abated, which began about the 20 year of Queen Elizabeth; for until then it was usual to have frays, fights and quarrels upon the Sundays and holidays, sometimes twenty, thirty, and forty swords and bucklers, half against half as

observed there has been nothing so much fighting : where be all our gallant swaggerers ? there are no good frays a' late.   192

Tan. O, sir, the property's altered ; you shall see less fighting every day than other ; for every one gets him a mistress, and she gives him wounds enow ; and you know the surgeons cannot be here and there too : if there were red wounds too, what would become of the Reinish [1] wounds ?

Fal. Thou sayst true, i'faith ; they would be but ill-favouredly looked to then.   200

Tan. Very well, sir.

Fal. I expect you, sir.

Tan. I lie in this court for you, sir ; my Rapier is my attorney, and my Dagger his clerk.

Fal. Your attorney wants a little oiling, methinks ; he looks very rustily.

Tan. 'Tis but his proper colour, sir ; his father was an ironmonger : he will ne'er look brighter, the rust has so eat into him ; has never any leisure to be made clean.

Fal. Not in the vacation ?   210

Tan. *Non vacat exiguis rebus adesse Jovi.* [2]

---

well by quarrels of appointment as by chance. . . . And although they made great show of much fury and fought often, yet seldom any man hurt, for thrusting was not then in use ; neither would one of twenty strike beneath the waist, by reason they held it cowardly and beastly. But the ensuing deadly fight of rapier and dagger suddenly suppressed the fighting with sworld and buckler."

[1] " A wretched pun—*Rhenish.*"—*Dyce.* Wretched indeed.

[2] Ovid, *Trist.* ii. 216.

Fal. Then Jove will not be at leisure to scour him, because he ne'er came to him before.

Tan. You're excellent at it, sir: and now you least think on't, I arrest you, sir.

Fal. Very good, sir.

Tan. Nay, very bad, sir, by my faith: I follow you still, as the officers will follow you, as long as you have a penny.

Fal. You speak sentences, sir: by this time have I tried my friends, and now I thrust in bail.   221

Tan. This bail will not be taken, sir; they must be two citizens that are no cuckolds.

Fal. Byrlady,[1] then I'm like to lie by it; I had rather 'twere a hundred that were.

Tan. Take heed I bring you not to a *nisi prius*, sir.

Fal. I must ward myself as well as I may, sir.

Tan. 'Tis court-day now; *declarat atturnatus*, my attorney gapes for money.

Fal. You shall have no advantage yet; I put in my answer.   231

Tan.[2] I follow the suit still, sir.

Fal. I like not this court, byrlady; I take me out a writ of remove; a writ of remove, do you see, sir?

Tan. Very well, sir.

Fal. And place my cause higher.

Tan. There you started me, sir: yet for all your demurs, *pluries*, and *sursurraras*,[3] which are all Long-

---

[1] A common contraction of "By our Lady."
[2] So ed. 2.—Ed. 1 "*Fals.*"
[3] See note 2, p. 122.

swords,[1] that's delays, all the comfort is, in nine years
a man may overthrow you.   240

Fal. You must thank your good friends then, sir.

Tan. Let nine years pass, five hundred crowns cast
away a' both sides, and the suit not twenty, my counsellor's wife must have another hood, you know, and my
attorney's wife will have a new forepart ; yet see at length
law, I shall have law : now, beware, I bring you to a
narrow exigent, and by no means can you avoid the pro-
clamation.

Fal. O !

Tan. Now follows a writ of execution ; a *capias utlagatum* gives you a wound mortal, trips up your heels, and
lays you i' th' counter.   [*Overthrows him.*

Fal. O villain !   253

Tan. I cry your worship heartily mercy, sir ; I thought
we had been in law together, *adversarius contra adver-
sarium*, by my troth.

Fal. O, reach me thy hand ! I ne'er had such an
overthrow in my life.

Tan. 'Twas 'long of your attorney there ; he might a'
stayed the execution of *capias utlagatum*, and removed
you, with a *supersedeas non molestandum*, into the court of
equity.   262

Fal. Pox on him, he fell out of my hand when I had
most need of him.

Tan. I was bound to follow the suit, sir.

---

[1] So ed. 2.—Ed. 1 " Longsword."

Fal. Thou couldst do no less than overthrow me, I must needs say so.

Tan. You had recovered cost else, sir.

Fal. And now, by th'[1] mass, I think I shall hardly recover without cost.   270

Tan. Nay, that's *certo scio ;* an execution is very chargeable.

Fal. Well, it shall teach me wit as long as I am a justice.   I perceive by this trial, if a man have a sound fall in law, he'll feel it in his bones all his life after.

Tan. Nay, that's *recto* upon record ; for I myself was overthrown in 88 by a tailor, and I have had a stitch in my side ever since,—O !   [*Exeunt.*[2]

---

[1] So ed. 2.—Ed. 1 " by th' the."

[2] In the old eds. follows a further stage-direction :—" *Towards the close of the musick* " [played between the acts] " *the Justices three men prepare for a robberie.* " Stage-directions of this kind show that the piece was printed from a play-house transcript.

ACT III.

SCENE I.

A Hall in FALSO'S *House.*

Enter FALSO *untrussed.*

Fal. Why, Latronello! Furtivo! Fucato! Where be
these lazy knaves that should truss me?[1] not one stirring
yet?

[*A Cry within.*] Follow, follow, follow!

Fal. What news there?

[*A Cry within.*] This way, this way; follow, follow!

Fal. Hark, you sluggish soporiferous villains! there's
knaves abroad when you are a-bed: are ye not ashamed
on't? a justice's men should be up first, and give example
to[2] all knaves.   10

Enter LATRONELLO *and* FUCATO, *tumbling in, in false
beards.*

Lat. O, I beseech your good worship!

Fuc. Your worshipful worship!

---

[1] Tie the points that joined the breeches to the doublet.
[2] So ed. 2.—Not in ed. 1.

Fal. Thieves ! my two-hand sword ! I'm robbed i' th' hall.   Latronello, knaves, come down ! my two-hand sword, I say !

Lat. I am Latronello, I beseech your worship.

Fal. Thou Latronello? thou liest ; my men scorn to have beards.

Lat. We forget our beards.   [*They take off their false beards.*]—Now, I beseech your worship quickly remember us.   21

Fal. How now?

Fuc. Nay, there's no time to talk of *how now ;* 'tis done.

[*A Cry within.*] Follow, follow, follow !

Lat. Four mark and a livery is not able to keep life and soul together : we must fly out once a quarter ; 'tis for your worship's credit to have money in our purse. Our fellow Furtivo is taken in the action.

Fal. A pox on him for a lazy knave ! would he be taken ?   31

Fuc. They bring him along to your worship ; you're the next justice.   Now or never show yourself a good master, an upright magistrate, and deliver him out of their hands.

Fal. Nay, he shall find me—apt enough to do him good, I warrant him.

Lat. He comes in a false beard, sir.

Fal. 'S foot, what should he do here else? there's no coming to me in a true one, if he had one.   The slave to be taken ! do not I keep geldings swift enough ?   41

Lat. The goodliest geldings of any gentleman in the shire.

Fal. Which did the whorson knave ride upon?

Lat. Upon one of your best, sir.

Fuc. Stand-and-deliver.

Fal. Upon Stand-and-deliver? the very gelding I choose for mine own riding; as nimble as Pegasus the flying horse yonder. Go shift yourselves into your coats; bring hither a great chair and a little table.   50

Fuc. With all present speed, sir.

Fal. And, Latronello——

Lat. Ay, sir.

Fal. Sit you down, and very soberly take the examination.

Lat. I'll draw a few horse-heads in a paper; make a show. I hope I shall keep my countenance.   57

                    [*Exeunt* LATRONELLO *and* FUCATO.

Fal. Pox on him again! would he be taken? he frets me. I have been a youth myself: I ha' seen the day I could have told money out of other men's purses,—mass, so I can do now,—nor will I keep that fellow about me that dares not bid a man stand; for as long as drunkenness is a vice, stand is a virtue: but I would not have 'em taken. I remember now betimes in a morning, I would have peeped through the green boughs, and have had the party presently, and then to ride away finely in fear: 'twas e'en venery to me, i'faith, the pleasantest course of life! one would think every woodcock a constable, and every owl an officer. But those days are past with me; and, a' my troth, I think I am a greater thief now, and in no danger. I can take my ease, sit in my chair, look in your faces now, and rob you; make you bring your money by authority, put off your hat, and thank me for robbing of you. O, there is nothing to a thief under covert barn![1]   75

Enter Phœnix *and* Fidelio; *Constable and Officers with* Furtivo; *and* Latronello *and* Fucato *bringing in a chair and table.*

Con. Come, officers, bring him away.

Fal. Nay, I see thee through thy false beard, thou midwind-chined rascal. [*Aside.*]—How now, my masters, what's he? ha?

Con. Your worship knows I never come but I bring a thief with me.   81

Fal. Thou hast left thy wont else, constable.

Phœ. Sir, we understand you to be the only uprightness of this place.

Fal. But I scarce understand you, sir.

Phœ. Why, then, you understand not yourself, sir.

Fal. Such another word, and you shall change places with the thief.

Phœ. A maintainer of equal causes, I mean.

Fal. Now I have you; proceed, sir.   90

Phœ. This gentleman and myself, being led hither by

---

[1] A corruption of *covert baron.*—"Coverture is particularly applied in our common law to the estate and condition of a married woman, who by the laws of our realm is *in potestate viri*, and therefore disabled to contract with any to the prejudice of herself or her husband without his consent and privity, or at the least without his allowance and confirmation."—*Cowell's Interpreter.*

occasion of business, have been offered the discourtesy of the country, set upon by three thieves, and robbed.

Fal. What are become of the other two ?—Latronello.[1]

Lat. Here, sir.

Phœ. They both made away from us ; the cry pursues 'em, but as yet none but this taken.

Fal. Latronello.

Lat. Sir ?

Fal. Take his examination.   100

Lat. Yes, sir.

Fal. Let the knave stand single.

Fur. Thank your good worship.

Fal. Has been a suitor at court, sure ; he thanks me for nothing.

Phœ. He's a thief now, sure.

Fal. That we must know of him.—What are ye, sir ?

Fur. A piece next to the tail, sir, a servingman.

Fal. By my troth, a pretty phrase, and very cleanly handled ! Put it down, Latronello ; thou mayst make use on't.—Is he of honour or worship whom thou servest ?   113

Fur. Of both, dear sir ; honourable in mind, and worshipful in body.

Fal. Why, would one wish a man to speak better ?

Phœ. O, sir, they most commonly speak best that do worst.

Fal. Say you so, sir ? then we'll try him farther.—

---

[1] Old ed. " Latronello and Fuca."

Does your right worshipful master go before you as an
ensample of vice, and so encourage you to this slinking [1]
iniquity?   He is not a lawyer, is he?   122

Fur. Has the more wrong, sir; both for his conscience
and honesty he deserves to be one.

Fal. Pity he's a thief, i' faith; I should entertain him
else.

Phœ. Ay, if he were not as he is, he would be better
than himself.

Fur. No, 'tis well known, sir, I have a master the very
picture of wisdom——   130

Lat. For indeed he speaks not one wise word.[*Aside.*

Fur. And no man but will admire to hear of his
virtues——

Lat. Because he ne'er had any in all his life. [*Aside.*

Fal. You write all down, Latronello?

Lat. I warrant you, sir.

Fur. So sober, so discreet, so judicious——

Fal. Hum.

Fur. And above all, of most reverend gravity.

Fal. I like him for one quality; he speaks well of his
master; he will fare the better.—Now, sir, let me touch
you.   142

Fur. Ay, sir.

Fal. Why, serving a gentleman of such worship and
wisdom, such sobriety and virtue, such discretion and
judgment, as your master is, do you take such a beastly
course, to stop horses, hinder gentlewomen from their

----

[1] Ed. 2 "stinking."

meetings, and make citizens never ride but a' Sundays, only to avoid morning prayer and you? Is it because your worshipful master feeds you with lean spits, pays you with Irish money, or clothes you in northern dozens?[1]   152

Fur. Far be it from his mind, or my report. 'Tis well known he kept worshipful cheer the day of his wife's burial; pays our four marks a-year as duly by twelve pence a-quarter as can be——

Phœ. His wisdom swallows it.   [*Aside.*

Fur. And for northern dozens—fie, fie, we were ne'er troubled with so many.

Fal. Receiving then such plenteous blessings from your virtuous and bountiful master, what cause have you to be thief now? answer me to that gear.[2]   162

Fur. 'Tis e'en as a man gives his mind to't, sir.

Fal. How, sir?

Fur. For, alas, if the whole world were but of one trade, traffic were nothing! if we were all true[3] men, we

---

[1] "In *The Rates of the Custome House*, &c., 1582, among the cloths enumerated we find

> ' Kerseyes of all sorts
> *Northen dosens*
> Bridge Waters ' &c. &c.
>
> Sig. G 2.

"Strutt cites the following act : ' Every *Northern cloth* shall be seven quarters of a yard in width, from twenty-three to twenty-five yards in length, and weigh sixty-six pounds each piece; the half piece of each cloth, called *dozens*, shall run from twelve to thirteen yards in length, the breadth being the same, and shall weigh thirty-six pounds.'—*Dress and Habits*, &c., vol. ii. p. 197."—*Dyce.*

[2] Business.   [3] Honest.

should be of no trade : what a pitiful world would here
be ! heaven forbid we should be all true men ! Then
how should your worship's next suit be made? not a
tailor left in the land : of what stuff would you have it
made ? not a merchant left to deliver it : would your
worship go in that suit still ? You would ha' more thieves
about you than those you have banished, and be glad
to call the great ones home again, to destroy the little.

Phœ. A notable rogue !   175

Fal. A' my troth, a fine knave, and has answered me
gloriously.—What wages wilt thou take after thou art
hanged ?

Fur. More than your worship's able to give : I would
think foul scorn to be a justice then.   180

Fal. He says true too, i'faith ; for we are all full of
corruption here. [*Aside.*]—Hark you, my friends.

Phœ. Sir ?

Fal. By my troth, if you were no crueller than I, I
could find in my heart to let him go.

Phœ. Could you so, sir ? the more pitiful justice you.

Fal. Nay, I did but to try you ; if you have no pity,
I'll ha' none.—Away ! he's a thief; to prison with him !

Fur. I am content, sir.

Fal. Are you content ?—Bring him back.—Nay, then,
you shall not go.—I'll be as cruel as you can wish.—
You're content ? belike you have a trick to break prison,
or a bribe for the officers.   193

Con. For us, sir.

Fal. For you, sir ! what colour's silver, I pray ? you
ne'er saw money in your life : I'll not trust you with

him.—Latronello and Fucato, lay hold upon him; to
your charge I commit him.

Fur. O, I beseech you, sir!

Fal. Nay, if I must be cruel, I will be cruel.   200

Fur. Good sir, let me rather go to prison.

Fal. You desire that? I'll trust no prison with you:
I'll make you lie in mine own house, or I'll know why I
shall not.

Fur. Merciful sir!

Fal. Since you have no pity, I will be cruel.

Phœ. Very good, sir; you please us well.

Fal. You shall appear to-morrow, sirs,

Fur. Upon my knees, sir!

Fal. You shall be hanged out a' th' way.—Away with
him, Latronello and Fucato!—Officers, I discharge you
my house; I like not your company.   212
Report me as you see me, fire and fuel;
If men be Jews, justices must be cruel.

     [Exeunt all but PHŒNIX *and* FIDELIO.

Phœ. So, sir, extremes set off all actions thus,
Either too tame, or else too tyrannous:
He being bent to fury, I doubt now
We shall not gain access unto your love,
Or she to us.

Fid. Most wishfully here she comes.

    Enter NIECE.

Phœ. Is that she?   220

Fid. This is she, my lord.

Phœ. A modest presence.

Fid. Virtue bless you, lady!

Niece. You wish me well, sir.

Fid. I'd first in charge this kiss, and next this paper;
You'll know the language; tis Fidelio's.

Niece. My ever-vowed love! how is his health?

Fid. As fair as is his favour with the prince.

Niece. I'm sick with joy: does the prince love him so?

Fid. His life cannot requite it. 230
Not to wrong the remembrance of his love,
I had a token for you, kept it safe,
Till by misfortune of the way this morning,
Thieves set upon this gentleman and myself,
And with the rest robb'd that.

Niece. Was it your loss?[1]
O me, I'm dearly sorry for your chance!
They boldly look you in the face that robb'd you;
No farther villains than my uncle's men.

Phœ. What, lady?

Niece. 'Tis my grief I speak so true.

Fid. Why, my lord[2]—— 240

Phœ. But give me pausing, lady; was he one
That took th' examination?

Niece. One, and the chief.

Phœ. Henceforth hang him that is no way a thief;
Then I hope few will suffer.
Nay, all the jest was, he committed him
To the charge of his fellows, and the rogue

---

[1] Old eds. "O me, I'm dearly sorry for your chance, was it your loss?"

[2] Ed. 2 " lady."

Made it lamentable, cried to leave 'em :
None live so wise, but fools may once deceive 'em.

 Fid. An uncle so insatiate !

 Phœ. Ay, is't not strange too,
That all should be by nature vicious,   250
And he bad against nature ?

 Niece. Then you have heard the sum of all my wrongs ?

 Phœ. Lady, we have, and desire rather now
To heal 'em than to hear 'em :
For by a letter from Fidelio
Direct to us, we are intreated jointly
To hasten your remove from this foul den
Of theft and purpos'd incest.

 Niece. I rejoice
In his chaste care of me : I'll soon be furnish'd.

 Fid. He writes that his return cannot be long.   260

 Niece. I'm chiefly glad,—but whither is the place ?

 Phœ. To the safe seat of his late wronged mother.

 Niece. I desire it ;
Her conference will fit mine : well you prevail.

 Phœ. At next grove we'll expect you.

 Niece. I'll not fail.   [*Exeunt.*

SCENE II.

A Street.

Enter Knight and Jeweller's Wife.

 Knight. It stands upon the frame of my reputation,
I protest, lady.

 Jew. Wife. Lady ? that word is worth an hundred

angels at all times, for it cost more ; if I live till to-morrow night, my sweet Pleasure, thou shalt have them.

Knight. Could you not make 'em a hundred and fifty, think you ?

Jew. Wife. I'll do my best endeavour to multiply, I assure you.

Knight. Could you not make 'em two hundred ?   10

Jew. Wife. No, by my faith——

Knight. Peace ; I'll rather be confined in the hundred and fifty.

Jew. Wife. Come e'en much about this time, when taverns give up their ghosts, and gentlemen are in their first cast [1]——

Knight. I'll observe the season.

Jew. Wife. And do but whirl the ring a' th' door once about ; my maid-servant shall be taught to understand the language.   20

Knight. Enough, my sweet Revenue.

Jew Wife. Good rest, my effectual Pleasure. [*Exeunt.*

---

[1] Vomit.

ACT IV.

SCENE I.

A Street before the Jeweller's House, and the Court of Law.

Enter PRODITOR *and* PHŒNIX.

Prod. Come hither, Phœnix.[1]

Phœ. What makes your honour break so early?

Prod. A toy, I have a toy.[2]

Phœ. A toy, my lord?

Prod. Before thou lay'st thy wrath upon the duke,
Be advis'd.

Phœ. Ay, ay, I warrant you, my lord.

Prod. Nay, give my words honour; hear me.
I'll strive to bring this act into such form
And credit amongst men, they shall suppose,
Nay, verily believe, the prince, his son,
To be the plotter of his father's murder.

---

[1] It is curious that the prince did not assume a new name with his disguise. From i. 2 (" Not many months *Phœnix* shall keep his life ") it is clear that Proditor knew the prince by the name of Phœnix. But the oversight is trifling.

[2] Conceit, whim.

Phœ. O that were infinitely admirable!   10
Prod. Were't not? it pleaseth me beyond my bliss.
Then if his son meet death as he returns,
Or by my hired instruments turn up,
The general voice will cry, O happy vengeance!
Phœ. O blessed vengeance!
Prod. Ay, I'll turn my brain
Into a thousand uses, tire my inventions,
Make my blood sick with study, and mine eye
More hollow than my heart, but I will fashion,
Nay, I will fashion it.   Canst counterfeit?
Phœ. The prince's hand most [1] truly, most direct;   20
You shall admire it.
Prod. Necessary mischief,
Next to a woman, but more close in secrets!
Thou'rt all the kindred that my breast vouchsafes.
Look into me anon: I must frame, and muse,
And fashion.   [*Exit.*
Phœ. 'Twas time to look into thee, in whose heart
Treason grows ripe, and therefore fit to fall:
That slave first sinks whose envy threatens all.
Now is his venom at full height.
                        [*Voices within.*
First Voice [*within*]. Lying or being in the said county,
in the tenure and occupation aforesaid.   31
Second Voice [*within*]. No more then; a writ of course
upon the matter of——

---

[1] Old eds. "more."

Third Voice [*within*]. Silence!

Fourth Voice [*within*]. O-o-o-o-yes! Carlo Turbulenzo, appear, or lose twenty mark in the suits.

Phœ. Hah, whither have my thoughts conveyed me? I am now
Within the dizzy murmur of the law.

First Voice [*within*]. So that then, the cause being found clear, upon the last citation—— 41

Fourth Voice [*within*]. Carlo Turbulenzo, come into the court.

Enter TANGLE *and two Suitors after him.*

Tan. Now, now, now, now, now, upon my knees I praise Mercury, the god of law! I have two suits at issue, two suits at issue.

First Suit. Do you hear, sir?

Tan. I will not hear; I've other business.

First Suit. I beseech you, my learned counsel——

Tan. Beseech not me, beseech not me; I am a mortal man, a client as you are; beseech not me. 51

First Suit. I would do all by your worship's direction.

Tan. Then hang thyself.

Second Suit. Shall I take out a special *supplicavit?*

Tan. Mad me not, torment me not, tear me not; you'll give me leave to hear mine own cause, mine own cause.

First Voice [*within*]. Nay, moreover and farther——

Tan. Well said, my lawyer, well said, well said! 60

First Voice [*within*]. All the opprobrious speeches that

man could invent, all malicious invectives, called wittol [1]
to his face.

Tan. That's I, that's I : thank you, my learned counsel,
for your good remembrance. I hope I shall overthrow
him horse and foot.[2]

First Suit. Nay, but good sir——

Tan. No more, sir : he that brings me happy news
first I'll relieve first.

Both Suit. Sound executions rot thy cause and thee !
[*Exeunt.*

Tan. Ay, ay, ay, pray so still, pray so still; they'll
thrive the better.   72

Phœ. I wonder how this fellow keeps out madness ;
What stuff his brains are made on.

Tan. I suffer, I suffer, till I hear a judgment !

Phœ. What, old signior?

Tan. Prithee, I will not know thee now; 'tis a busy
time, a busy time with me.

Phœ. What, not me, signior?

Tan. O, cry thee mercy ! give me thy hand—fare thee
well.—Has no relief again [3] me then ; his demurs will not
help him ; his sursurraras [4] will but play the knaves with
him.   83

Enter FALSO.

Phœ. The justice? 'tis he.

Fal. Have I found thee, i'faith ? I thought where I
should smell thee out, old Tangle.

---

[1] See note 2, p. 123.

[2] So in Day's *Law Tricks*, iv. 1 :—" I am undone, *horse and foot.*"

[3] Against.   [4] See note 2, p. 122.

Tan. What, old signior justicer ? embrace me another time and you can possible :—how does all thy wife's children,—well ? that's well said, i'faith ?

Fal. Hear me, old Tangle.   90

Tan. Prithee, do not ravish me ; let me go.

Fal. I must use some of thy counsel first.

Tan. Sirrah, I ha' brought him to an exigent : hark ! that's my cause, that's my cause yonder : I twinged him, I twinged him.

Fal. My niece is stolen away.

Tan. Ah, get me a *ne exeat regno* quickly ! nay, you must not stay upon't ; I'd fain have you gone.

Fal. A *ne exeat regno ?* I'll about it presently : adieu.
                                                          [*Exit.*

Phœ. You seek to catch her, justice ; she'll catch you.

Re-enter First Suitor.

First Suit. A judgment, a judgment !   101

Tan. What, what, what ?

First Suit. Overthrown, overthrown, overthrown !

Tan. Ha ?—ah, ah !——

Re-enter Second Suitor.

Second Suit. News, news, news !

Tan. The devil, the devil, the devil !

Second Suit. Twice Tangle's overthrown, twice Tangle's overthrown !

Tan. Hold !

Phœ. Now, old cheater of the law——   110

Tan. Pray, give me leave to be mad.

Phœ. Thou that hast found such sweet pleasure [1] in the vexation of others——

Tan. May I not be mad in quiet?

Phœ. Very marrow, very manna to thee to be in law——

Tan. Very syrup of toads and preserved adders!

Phœ. Thou that hast vexed and beggared the whole parish, and made the honest churchwardens go to law with the poor's money——   120

Tan. Hear me, do but hear me! I pronounce a terrible, horrible curse upon you all, and wish you to my attorney. See where a *præmunire* comes, a *dedimus potestatem*, and that most dreadful execution, *excommunicato capiendo!* There's no bail to be taken; I shall rot in fifteen jails: make dice of my bones, and let my counsellor's son play away his father's money with 'em; may my bones revenge my quarrel! A *capias cominus?* here, here, here, here; quickly dip your quills in my blood, off with my skin, and write fourteen lines of a side. There's an honest conscionable fellow; he takes but ten shillings of a bellows-mender: here's another deals all with charity; you shall give him nothing, only his wife an embroidered petticoat, a gold fringe for her tail, or a border for her head. Ah, sirrah, you shall catch me no more in the springe of your knaveries!   [*Exit.* 136

First Suit. Follow, follow him still; a little thing now sets him forward.   [*Exeunt* Suitors.

Phœ. None can except against him; the man's mad,

---

[1] Phœnix is repeating what Tangle had said in the inn. See p. 122.

And privileg'd by the moon, if he say true :   140
Less madness 'tis to speak sin than to do.
This wretch, that lov'd before his food his strife,
This punishment falls even with his life.
His pleasure was vexation, all his bliss
The torment of another ;
Their hurt[1] his health, their starved hopes his store :
Who so loves law dies either mad or poor.

Enter FIDELIO.

Fid. A miracle, a miracle !
Phœ. How now, Fidelio ?
Fid. My lord, a miracle !
Phœ. What is't ?
Fid. I have found
One quiet, suffering, and unlawyer'd man ;   150
An opposite, a very contrary
To the old turbulent fellow.
Phœ. Why, he's mad.
Fid. Mad ? why, he is in his right wits : could he be
madder than he was ? if he be any way altered from what
he was, 'tis for the better, my lord.
Phœ. Well, but where's this wonder ?
Fid. 'Tis coming, my lord : a man so truly a man, so
indifferently a creature, using the world in his right nature
but to tread upon ; one that would not bruise the coward-
liest enemy to man, the worm, that dares not show his
malice till we are dead : nay, my lord, you will admire
his temper : see where he comes.   162

---

[1] Old eds. " heart."

Enter QUIETO.

I promis'd your acquaintance, sir : yon is
The gentleman I did commend for temper.

    Qui. Let me embrace you simply,
That's perfectly, and more in heart than hand :
Let affectation keep at court.

    Phœ. Ay, let it.

    Qui. 'Tis told me you love quiet.

    Phœ. Above wealth.

    Qui. I above life : I have been wild and rash,
Committed many and unnatural crimes,   170
Which I have since repented.

    Phœ. 'Twas well spent.

    Qui. I was mad, stark mad, nine years together.

    Phœ. I pray, as how ?

    Qui. Going to law, i'faith, it made me mad.

    Phœ. With the like frenzy, not an hour since,
An aged man was struck.

    Qui. Alas, I pity him !

    Phœ. He's not worth pitying, for 'twas still his glad-
           ness
To be at variance.

    Qui. Yet a man's worth pity :
My quiet blood has blest me with this gift :
I have cur'd some ; and if his wits be not   180
Too deeply cut, I will assay to help 'em.

    Phœ. Sufferance does teach you pity.

Enter Boy.

Boy. O master, master! your abominable next neighbour came into the house, being half in drink, and took
away your best carpet.[1]

Qui. Has he it?

Boy. Alas, sir!

Qui. Let him go; trouble him not: lock the door
quietly after him, and have a safer care who comes in
next.   190

Phœ. But, sir, might I advise you, in such a cause as
this a man might boldly, nay, with conscience, go to law.

Qui. O, I'll give him the table too first! Better
endure a fist than a sharp sword: I had rather they
should pull off my clothes than flay off my skin, and
hang that on mine enemy's hedge.

Phœ. Why,
For such good causes was the law ordain'd.

Qui. True,
And in itself 'tis glorious and divine;   200
Law is the very masterpiece of heaven:
But see yonder,
There's many clouds between the sun and us;
There's too much cloth before we see the law.

Phœ. I'm content with that answer; be mild still:
'Tis honour to forgive those you could kill.

Qui. There do I keep.

---

[1] Table-cover. Cf. *Taming of the Shrew*, iv. 1 :—" Be the jacks fair
within, the jills fair without, the *carpets laid* and everything in order?"

Phœ. Reach me your hand : I love you,
And you shall know me better.

Qui. 'Tis my suit.

Phœ. The night grows deep, and——

Enter two Officers.

First Off. Come away, this way, this way.   210

Phœ. Who be those? stand close a little.

[*As they retire,* PHŒNIX *happens to jar the ring of the
Jeweller's door ; the Maid enters from the house and
catches hold of him.*

Maid. O, you're come as well as e'er you came in your
life! my master's new gone to bed. Give me your
knightly hand : I must lead you into the blind parlour ;
my mistress will be down to you presently.

[*Takes in* PHŒNIX.

First Off. I tell you our safest course will be to arrest
him when he comes out a' th' tavern, for then he will be
half drunk, and will not stand upon his weapon.

Second Off. Our safest course indeed, for he will draw.

First Off. That he will, though he put it up again,
which is more of his courtesy than of our deserving.   221

[*Exeunt* Officers.

Qui. The world is nothing but vexation,
Spite, and uncharitable action.

Fid. Did you see the gentleman?

Qui. Not I.

Fid. Where should he be? it may be he's past by :
Good sir, let's overtake him.   [*Exeunt.*

SCENE II.

A Room in the Jeweller's House.

Enter PHŒNIX *and Maid.*

Maid. Here, sir: now you are there, sir, she'll come down to you instantly. I must not stay with you; my mistress would be jealous: you must do nothing to me; my mistress would find it quickly. [*Exit.*

Phœ. 'S foot, whither am I led? brought in by th' hand? I hope it can be no harm to stay for a woman, though indeed they were never more dangerous: I have ventured hitherto and safe, and I must venture to stay now. This should be a fair room, but I see it not: the blind parlour calls she it? 10

Enter Jeweller's Wife.

Jew. Wife. Where art thou, O my knight?

Phœ. Your knight? I am the duke's knight.

Jew. Wife. I say you're my knight, for I'm sure I paid for you.

Phœ. Paid for you?—hum.—'S foot, a light!
  [*Snatches in a light, and then extinguishes it.*

Jew. Wife. Now out upon the marmoset! Hast thou served me so long, and offer to bring in a candle?

Phœ. Fair room, villanous face, and worse woman! I ha' learnt something by a glimpse a' th' candle. [*Aside.*

Jew. Wife. How happened it you came so soon? I looked not for you these two hours; yet, as the sweet

chance is, you came as well as a thing could come, for
my husband's newly brought a-bed.   23

Phœ. And what has Jove sent him?

Jew. Wife. He ne'er sent him anything since I knew
him : he's a man of a bad nature to his wife ; none but his
maids can thrive under him.

Phœ. Out upon him.

Jew. Wife. Ay, judge whether I have a cause to be a
courtesan or no? to do as I do?   An elderly fellow as
he is, if he were married to a young virgin, he were able
to break her heart, though he could break nothing else.
Here, here ; there's just a hundred and fifty [*giving money*] ;
but I stole 'em so hardly from him, 'twould e'en have
grieved you to have seen it.   35

Phœ. So 'twould, i'faith.

Jew. Wife. Therefore, prithee, my sweet Pleasure, do
not keep company so much.   How do you think I am
able to maintain you?   Though I be a jeweller's wife,
jewels are like women, they rise and fall ; we must be
content to lose sometimes, to gain often ; but you're
content always to lose, and never to gain.   What need
you ride with a footman before you?   43

Phœ. O, that's the grace !

Jew. Wife. The grace? 'tis sufficient grace that you've
a horse to ride upon.   You should think thus with yourself
every time you go to bed,—if my head were laid, what
would become of that horse? he would run a bad race
then, as well as his master.

Phœ. Nay, and you give me money to chide me—— 50

Jew. Wife. No, if it were as much more, I would think it

foul scorn to chide you. I advise you to be thrifty, to take the time now, while you have it : you shall seldom get such another fool as I am, I warrant you. Why, there's Metreza[1] Auriola keeps her love with half the cost that I am at : her friend can go a' foot like a good husband, walk in worsted stockings, and inquire for the sixpenny ordinary.[2]

Phœ. Pox on't, and would you have me so base ?

Jew. Wife. No, I would not have you so base neither : but now and then, when you keep your chamber, you might let your footman out for eighteenpence a-day ; a great relief at year's end, I can tell you.   62

Phœ. The age must needs be foul when vice reforms it.   [*Aside.*

Jew. Wife. Nay, I've a greater quarrel to you yet.

Phœ. I'faith, what is't ?

Jew. Wife. You made me believe at first the prince had you in great estimation, and would not offer to travel without you, nay, that he could not travel without your direction and intelligence.   70

Phœ. I'm sorry I said so, i'faith ; but sure I was overflown[3] when I spoke it, I could ne'er ha' said it else.

---

[1] Mistress.   " Probably meant as Italian ; but only Frenchified Italian, made from *maitresse.*"—*Nares.*

[2] " There were ordinaries of all prices. Our author notices, in *Father Hubburd's Tales*, a three-halfpenny ordinary ; in *No Wit, no Help like a Woman's*, a twelve-penny ordinary, act ii. sc. 3 ; in *The Black Book*, an eighteen-penny ordinary ; in *A Trick to catch the Old One*, a two-shilling ordinary, act i. sc. 1 ; Fletcher, in *The Wild-Goose Chase*, a ten-crown ordinary, act i. sc. 1 ; and our author, in *Father Hubburd's Tales*, mentions a person who had spent five pounds at a sitting in an ordinary."—*Dyce.*

[3] " *i.e.* drunk.—' The young Gentleman is come in, Madam, and as

Jew. Wife. Nay more; you swore to me that you were the first that taught him to ride a great horse, and tread the ring[1] with agility.

Phœ. By my troth, I must needs confess I swore a great lie in that, and I was a villain to do it, for I could ne'er ride great horse in my life.

Jew. Wife. Why, lo, who would love you now but a citizen's wife? so inconstant, so forsworn! You say women are false creatures; but, take away men, and they'd be honester than you. Nay, last of all, which offends me most of all, you told me you could countenance me at court; and you know we esteem a friend there more worth than a husband here. 85

Phœ. What I spake of that, lady, I'll maintain.

Jew. Wife. You maintain? you seen at court?

Phœ. Why, by this diamond——

Jew. Wife. O, take heed! you cannot have that; 'tis always in the eye of my husband. 90

Phœ. I protest I will not keep it, but only use it for this virtue, as a token to fetch you, and approve[2] my power, where you shall not only be received, but made known to the best and chiefest.

---

you foresaw very high *flowne*, but not so drunke as to forget your promise.' —BROME'S *Mad Couple well Match'd*, act iv. sc. 2. *Five New Playes,* 1653."—*Dyce.*

[1] The circular piece of ground in which the horse went through his feats of agility. In Christopher Clifford's *School of Horsemanship*, 1585, directions are given for "trotting the great *ring*, and what order is to be observed therein;" also "How and at what time you shall learn your horse to gallop the great ring."

[2] Prove.

Jew. Wife. O, are you true?

Phœ. Let me lose my revenue [1] else.

Jew. Wife. That's your word, indeed! and upon that condition take it, this kiss, and my love for ever.

[*Giving the diamond.*

Phœ. Enough.

Jew. Wife. Give me thy hand, I'll lead thee forth. 100

Phœ. I'm sick of all professions; my thoughts burn:
He travels best that knows when to return.   [*Aside.*

[*Exeunt.*

SCENE III.

A Street before the Jeweller's House.

Enter Knight, two Officers watching for him.

Knight. Adieu, farewell; [2] to bed you; I to my sweet city-bird, my precious Revenue: the very thought of a hundred and fifty angels increases oil and spirit, ho!

First Off. I arrest you, sir.

Knight. O!

First Off. You have made us wait a goodly time for you, have you not, think you? You are in your rouses and mullwines,[3] a pox on you! and have no care of poor officers staying for you.

Knight. I drunk but one health, I protest; but I could void it now.   At whose suit, I pray?   11

---

[1] A word continually in the Knight's mouth. See the beginning of the next scene.

[2] Addressed to his tavern-companions.

[3] A corruption of *mulled wines.*

First Off. At the suit of him that makes suits, your tailor.

Knight. Why, he made me the last; this, this that I wear.

First Off. Argo,[1]—nay, we have been scholars, I can tell you,—we could not have been knaves so soon else; for as in that notable city called London stand two most famous universities Poultry and Wood-street,[2] where some are of twenty years' standing, and have took all their degrees, from the Master's side[3] down to the Mistress' side, the Hole, so in like manner——   22

Knight. Come, come, come, I had quite forgot the hundred and fifty angels.

Second Off. 'Slid, where be they?

Knight. I'll bring you to the sight of 'em presently.

First Off. A notable lad, and worthy to be arrested! We'll have but ten for waiting; and then thou shalt choose whether thou shalt run away from us, or we from thee.   30

Knight. A match at running! come, come, follow me.

Second Off. Nay, fear not that.

---

[1] A corruption of "ergo." The reader will remember the grave-digger's "argal" in *Hamlet*.

[2] Sir Thomas Overbury concludes his character of "A Prison" with these words:—"But (not so much to dishonour it) it is an *university of poor scholars*, in which three arts are chiefly studied; to pray, to curse, and to write letters." Cf. Middleton's *Michaelmas Term*, iii. 4.

[3] The governor of a prison was allowed to let certain rooms for his own profit; hence "to lie of the Master's side" meant to have the best lodging in the prison. The "Hole" was where the poorest prisoners were confined.

Knight. Peace; you may happen to see toys,[1] but do not see 'em.

First Off. Pah!

Knight. That's the door.

First Off. This?   [*Knocks.*

Knight. 'S foot, officer, you have spoiled all already.

First Off. Why?

Knight. Why? you shall see: you should have but whirled the ring once about, and there's a maid-servant brought up to understand it.   42

Maid [*opening the door*]. Who's at door?

Knight. All's well again.—Phist, 'tis I, 'tis I.

Maid. You? what are you?

Knight. Pooh! where's thy mistress?

Maid. What of her?

Knight. Tell her one—she knows who—her Pleasure's here, say.

Maid. Her pleasure? my mistress scorns to be without her pleasure at this time of night. Is she so void of friends, think you? take that for thinking so.   52

   [*Gives him a box on the ear, and shuts the door.*

First Off. The hundred and fifty angels are locked up in a box; we shall not see 'em to-night.

Knight. How's this? am I used like a hundred-pound gentleman? does my Revenue forsake me? Damn me, if ever I be her Pleasure again!—Well, I must to prison.

---

[1] Whimsical proceedings.

First Off. Go prepare his room; there's no remedy:
I'll bring him along; he's tame enough now.   60
                                        [*Exit* Second Officer.
   Knight. Dare my tailor presume to use me in this
       sort?
He steals, and I must lie in prison for't.
   First Off. Come, come away, sir!

       Enter a Gentleman *and a* Drawer.

   Gent. Art sure thou sawest him arrested, drawer?
   Dra. If mine eyes be sober.
   Gent. And that's a question. Mass, here he goes! he
shall not go to prison; I have a trick shall bail him:
away!   [*Exit* Drawer.
       [*Blinds the* First Officer, *while the* Knight
          escapes.
   First Off. O!
   Gent. Guess, guess! who am I? who am I?   70
   First Off. Who the devil are you? let go: a pox on
you! who are you? I have lost my prisoner.
   Gent. Prisoner? I've mistook; I cry you heartily
mercy; I have done you infinite injury; a' my troth, I
took you to be an honest man.
   First Off. Where were your eyes? could you not see
I was an officer?—Stop, stop, stop, stop!
   Gent. Ha, ha, ha, ha!   [*Exeunt severally.*

ACT V.

SCENE I.

The Presence-Chamber in the DUKE OF FERRARA'S
Palace.

Enter PRODITOR *and* PHŒNIX.

Prod. Now, Phœnix.[1]
Phœ. Now, my lord.
Prod. Let princely blood
Nourish our hopes; we bring confusion now.
Phœ. A terrible sudden blow.
Prod. Ay: what day
Is this hangs over us?
Phœ. By th' mass, Monday.
Prod. As I could wish; my purpose will thrive best:
'Twas first my birthday, now my fortune's day.
I see whom fate will raise needs never pray.
Phœ. Never.
Prod. How is the air?
Phœ. O, full of trouble!

[1] See note 1, p. 177.

Prod. Does not the sky look piteously black?

Phœ. As if 'twere hung with rich men's consciences.

Prod. Ah, stuck not a comet, like a carbuncle,　　11
Upon the dreadful brow of twelve last night?

Phœ. Twelve? no, 'twas about one.

Prod. About one? most proper,
For that's the duke.

Phœ. Well shifted from thyself!　　　　[*Aside.*

Prod. I could have wish'd it between one and two,
His son and him.

Phœ. I'll give you comfort then.

Prod. Prithee.

Phœ. There was a villanous raven seen last night
Over the presence-chamber, in hard justle
With a young eaglet.　　　　　　　　　　20

Prod. A raven? that was I: what did the raven?

Phœ. Marry, my lord, the raven—to say truth,
I left the combat doubtful.

Prod. So 'tis still,
For all is doubt till the deed crown the will.
Now bless thy loins with freedom, wealth, and honour;
Think all thy seed young lords, and by this act
Make a foot-cloth'd[1] posterity; now imagine
Thou see'st thy daughters with their trains borne up,
Whom else despisèd want may curse to whoredom,
And public shames which our state never threat:　　30
She's never lewd that is accounted great.

---

1 "*i.e.* make your descendants persons of great consequence, riding
with *foot-cloths* (long housings) on their horses."—*Dyce.*

Phœ. I'll alter that court axiom, thus renew'd,
She's never great that is accounted lewd.   [*Aside.*

Enter several Nobles.

Prod. Stand close; the presence fills. Here, here
          the place;
And at the rising, let his fall be base,
Beneath thy foot.
     Phœ. How for his guard, my lord?
     Prod. My gold and fear keeps with the chief of them.
     Phœ. That's rarely well.
     Prod. Bold, heedless slave, that dares attempt a deed
Which shall in pieces rend him!   [*Aside.*

Enter LUSSURIOSO *and* INFESTO.

My lords both!   40
     Lus. The happiness of the day!
     Phœ. Time my returning;
Treasons have still the worst, yet still are spurning.
                                                   [*Aside.*

Enter the DUKE *attended.*

     Prod. The duke!
     Phœ. I ne'er was gladder to behold him.
     All. Long live your grace!
     Duke. I do not like that strain:
You know my age affords not to live long.
     Prod. Spoke truer than you think for.   [*Aside.*
     Duke. Bestow that wish upon the prince our son.
     Phœ. Nay, he's not to live long neither.   [*Aside.*

Prod. Him as the wealthy treasure of our hopes,
You as possession of our present comfort,   50
Both in one heart we reverence in one.

    Phœ. O treason of a good complexion!   [*Aside.*
                         [*Horn winded within.*

    Duke. How now? what fresher news fills the court's
        ear?

Enter FIDELIO.

Prod. Fidelio!

Fid. Glad tidings to your grace!
The prince is safe return'd, and in your court.

    Duke. Our joy breaks at our eyes;[1] the prince is
        come!

    Prod. Soul-quicking[2] news!—pale vengeance to my
        blood!   [*Aside.*

Fid. By me presenting to your serious view
A brief of all his travels.   [*Delivers a paper.*

    Duke. 'Tis most welcome;
It shall be dear and precious to our eye.   60

    Prod. He reads; I'm glad he reads.—
Now take thy opportunity, leave that place.

    Phœ. At his first rising let his fall be base.[3]

    Prod. That must be alter'd now.

    Phœ. Which? his rising or his fall?

---

[1] Cf. *Changeling*, iii. 4 :—
            "Our sweet'st delights
      Are evermore born weeping."
[2] So ed. 2.—Ed. 1 "qucking."
[3] Phœnix is repeating the words that Proditor had used. See p. 197.

Prod. Art thou dull now?
Thou hear'st the prince is come.

Duke. What's here? [1]

Prod. My lord?

Duke [*reads*]. *I have got such a large portion of knowledge, most worthy father, by the benefit of my travel——* 70

Prod. And so he has, no doubt, my lord.

Duke [*reads*]. *That I am bold now to warn you of Lord Proditor's insolent treason, who has irreligiously seduced a fellow, and closely conveyed him e'en in the presence-chair to murder you.*

Phœ. O guilty, guilty!

Duke. What was that fell? what's he?

Phœ. I am the man.

Prod. O slave!

Phœ. I have no power to strike.

Prod. I'm gone, I'm gone!

Duke. Let me admire heaven's wisdom in my son. 80

Phœ. I confess it, he hir'd me——

Prod. This is a slave:
'Tis forg'd against mine honour and my life;
For in what part of reason can't appear,
The prince being travell'd should know treasons here?
Plain counterfeit.

Duke. Dost thou make false our son?

Prod. I know the prince will not affirm't.

Fid. He can
And will, my lord.

---

[1] Old eds. "What's heere my Lord."

Phœ. Most just, he may.

Duke. A guard!

Lus. We cannot but in loyal zeal ourselves
Lay hands on such a villain.

　　　　　　　　　　[*Attendants secure* PRODITOR.

Duke. Stay you; I find you here too.

Lus. Us, my lord?　　　　　　　　　　　　　90

Duke [*reads*]. *Against Lussurioso and Infesto, who not only most riotously consume their houses in vicious gaming, mortgaging their livings to the merchant, whereby he with his heirs enter upon their lands; from whence this abuse comes, that in short time the son of the merchant has more lordships than the son of the nobleman, which else was never born to inheritance: but that which is more impious, they most adulterously train out young ladies to midnight banquets, to the utter defamation of their own honours, and ridiculous abuse of their husbands.*　　　　　　100

Lus. How could the prince hear that?

Phœ. Most true, my lord:
My conscience is a witness 'gainst itself;
For to that execution of chaste honour
I was both hir'd and led.

Lus. I hope the prince, out of his plenteous wisdom,
Will not give wrong to us: as for this fellow,
He's poor, and cares not to be desperate.

Enter FALSO.

Fal. Justice, my lord! I have my niece stol'n from
　　me:
Sh'as left her dowry with me, but she's gone:

I'd rather have had her love than her money, I. 110
This, this is one of them.   Justice, my lord !
I know him by his face ; this is the thief.

 Prod. Your grace may now in milder sense perceive
The wrong done to us by this impudent wretch,
Who has his hand fix'd at the throat of law,
And therefore durst be desperate of his life

 Duke. Peace, you're too foul ; your crime is in excess:
One spot of him makes not your ulcers less.

 Prod. O !

 Duke. Did your violence force away his niece ?

 Phœ. No, my good lord ; I'll still confess what's truth ;
I did remove her from her many wrongs, 121
Which she was pleas'd to leave, they were so vild.

 Duke. What are you nam'd ?

 Fal. Falso, my lord, Justice Falso ;
I'm known by that name.

 Duke. Falso ? you came fitly ;
You are the very next that follows here.

 Fal. I hope so, my lord ; my name is in all the records,
I can assure your good grace.

Enter Niece *and* CASTIZA *behind.*

 Duke [*reads*]. *Against Justice Falso——*
 Fal. Ah !
 Duke [*reads*]. *Who, having had the honest charge of his
niece committed to his trust by the last will and testament of
her deceased father, and with her all the power of his wealth,
not only against faith and conscience detains her dowry, but
against nature and humanity assays to abuse her body.* 134

Niece [*coming forward*]. I'm present to affirm it, my
        lov'd lord.

Fal. How? what make I here?[1]

Niece. Either I must agree
To loathed lust, or despis'd beggary.

Duke Are you the plaintiff here?

Fal. Ay, my good lord,
For fault of a better.

Duke. Seldom comes a worse.—[*Reads*] *And moreover,
not contained in this vice only, which is odious too much,
but, against the sacred use of justice, maintains three thieves
to his men.*   143

Fal. Cuds me!

Duke [*reads*]. *Who only take purses in their master's
liberty, where if any one chance to be taken, he appears
before him in a false beard, and one of his own fellows takes
his examination.*

Fal. By my troth, as true as can be; but he shall not
know on't.   [*Aside.* 150

Duke [*reads*]. *And in the end will execute justice so
cruelly upon him, that he will not trust him in a prison,
but commit him to his fellows' chamber.*

Fal. Can a man do nothing i' the country but 'tis told
at court? there's some busy informing knave abroad, a'
my life.   [*Aside.*

Phœ. That this is true, and these, and more, my lord,

---

[1] What is my business here?—Cf. mad Hieronimo's exclamation when
the servants approach with the torches in the garden,—" What make
you with your torches in the dark?"

Be it, under pardon, spoken for mine own ;
He the disease of justice, these of honour,
And this of loyalty and reverence,   160
The unswept venom of the palace.
   Prod. Slave !
   Phœ. Behold the prince to approve it !
                       [*Discovers himself.*[1]
   Prod. O, where ?
   Phœ. Your eyes keep with your actions, both look
       wrong.
   Prod. An infernal to my spirit !
   All. My lord, the prince !
   Prod. Tread me to dust, thou in whom wonder keeps ![2]
Behold the serpent on his belly creeps.
   Phœ. Rankle not my foot ; away !
Treason, we laugh at thy vain-labouring stings,[3]
Above the foot thou hast no power o'er kings !
   Duke. I cannot with sufficient joy receive thee.   170
And yet my joy's too much.
   Phœ. My royal father,
To whose unnatural murder I was hir'd,
I thought it a more natural course of travel,
And answering future expectation,
To leave far countries, and inquire mine own.
   Duke. To thee let reverence all her powers engage,
That art in youth a miracle to age !

---

  [1] In ed. 1 there is no stage-direction.—Ed. 2 gives " to approoue it
discouers himselfe."
  [2] Dwells.
  [3] Ed. 1 " strings."—Ed. 2 " string."

State is but blindness; thou hadst piercing art:
We only saw the knee, but thou the heart.
To thee, then, power and dukedom we resign: 180
He's fit to reign whose knowledge can refine.

Phœ. Forbid it my obedience!

Duke. Our word's not vain:
I know thee wise, canst both obey and reign.
The rest of life we dedicate to heaven.

All. A happy and safe reign to our new duke!

Phœ. Without your prayers safer and happier.—
Fidelio.

Fid. My royal lord.

Phœ. Here, take this diamond:[1]
You know the virtue on't; it can fetch vice.
Madam Castiza——

Fid. She attends, my lord.   [*Exit.*

Phœ. Place a guard near us.—   190
Know you yon fellow, lady?

Cas. [*coming forward*]. My honour's evil!

Prod. Torment again![2]

Phœ. So ugly are thy crimes,
Thine eye cannot endure 'em:
And that thy face may stand perpetually
Turn'd so from ours, and thy abhorred self
Neither to threaten wrack of state or credit,
An everlasting banishment seize on thee!

Prod. O fiend!

---

[1] The diamond which he had received from the jeweller's wife.
[2] Ed. 2 "Tormentagent" (which Dyce thought to be a corruption of "Torment's agent").

Phœ. Thy life is such it is too bad to end.

Prod. May thy rule, life, and all that's in thee glad,
Have as short time as thy begetting had !   201

Phœ. Away ! thy curse is idle.   [*Exit* PRODITOR.
The rest are under reformation,
And therefore under pardon.

Lus. &c. Our duties shall turn edge upon our crimes.

Fal. 'Slid, I was afraid of nothing, but that for my
thievery and bawdery I should have been turned to an
innkeeper.   [*Aside.*

    Re-enter FIDELIO *with* Jeweller's Wife.

My daughter !   I am ashamed her worship should see me.

Jew. Wife. Who would not love a friend at court?
what fine galleries and rooms am I brought through !   I
had thought my Knight durst not have shown his face
here, I.   213

Phœ. Now, mother of pride and daughter of lust, which
is your friend now?

Jew. Wife. Ah me !

Phœ. I'm sure you are not so unprovided to be without
a friend here : you'll pay enough for him first.

Jew. Wife. This is the worst room that ever I came in.

Phœ. I am your servant,[1] mistress ;[2] know you not me ?

Jew. Wife. Your worship is too great for me to know :
I'm but a small-timbered woman, when I'm out of my
apparel, and dare not venture upon greatness.   223

Phœ. Do you deny me then? know you this purse ?

---

[1] Often used in the sense of lover or paramour.
[2] So ed. 2.—Ed. 1 " Master."

Jew. Wife. That purse? O death, has the Knight
    serv'd me so?
Given away my favours?

    Phœ. Stand forth, thou one of those
For whose close lusts the plague ne'er leaves the city.
Thou worse than common! private, subtle harlot!
That dost deceive three with one feigned lip,   230
Thy husband, the world's eye, and the law's whip.
Thy zeal is hot, for 'tis to lust and fraud,
And dost not dread to make thy book thy bawd.
Thou'rt curse enough to husband's ill-got gains,
For whom the court rejects his gold maintains.
How dear and rare was freedom wont to be!
Now few but are by their wives' copies free,
And brought to such a head, that now we see
City and suburbs wear one livery!

    Jew. Wife. 'Tis 'long of those,[1] an't like your grace
that come in upon us, and will never leave marrying of
our widows till they make 'em all as free as their first
husbands.   243

    Phœ. I perceive you can shift a point well.

    Jew. Wife. Let me have pardon, I beseech your grace,
and I'll peach 'em all, all the close women that are; and,
upon my knowledge, there's above five thousand within
the walls and the liberties.

    Phœ. A band! they shall be sent against the Turk;[2]
Infidels against infidels.   250

---

[1] So ed. 2.—Ed. 1 "these."
[2] Ed. 2 "Turks."

Jew. Wife. I will hereafter live so modestly, I will not lie with mine own husband, nor come near a man in the way of honesty.

Fal. I'll be her warrant, my lord.

Phœ. You are deceiv'd ; you think you're still a justice.

Fal. 'S foot, worse than I was before I kneeled ! I am no justice now ; I know I shall be some innkeeper at last.

Jew. Wife. My father? 'tis mine own father.   259

Phœ. I should have wonder'd else, lust being so like.

Niece. Her birth was kin to mine; she may prove
   modest :
For my sake I beseech you pardon her.

Phœ. For thy sake I'll do more.—Fidelio, hand her.
My favours on you both ; next, all that wealth
Which was committed to that perjur'd's trust.

Fal. I'm a beggar now ; worse than an innkeeper.

Enter TANGLE *mad.*

Tan. Your *mittimus* shall not serve : I'll set myself free with a *deliberandum ;* with a *deliberandum,* mark you.

Duke. What's he? a guard !

Phœ. Under your sufferance,
Worthy father, his harm is to himself;   270
One that has lov'd vexation so much,
He cannot now be rid on't :
Has been so long in suits, that he's law-mad.

Tan. A judgment, I crave a judgment, yea ! *nunc pro tunc, corruptione alicujus.* I peeped me a raven in the

face, and I thought it had been my solicitor : O, the pens
prick me !

Enter QUIETO.

Phœ. And here comes he (wonder for temperance)
Will take the cure upon him.

Qui. A blessing to this fair assembly !   280

Tan. Away ! I'll have none on't : give me an *audita
querela*, or a *testificandum*, or a despatch in twelve terms :
there's a blessing, there's a blessing !

Phœ. You see the unbounded rage of his disease.

Qui. 'Tis the foul fiend, my lord, has got within him.
The rest are fair to this : this breeds in ink,
And to that colour turns the blood possess'd :
For instance, now your grace shall see him dress'd.

Tan. Ah ha ! I rejoice then he's puzzled, and muzzled
   too :
It's come to a *cepi corpus ?*

Qui. Ah, good sir,   290
This is for want of patience !

Tan. That's a fool :
She never saw the dogs and the bears fight ;[1]
A country thing.

Qui. This is for lack of grace.

---

[1] The bull-baiting at Paris Garden, in Southwark, was a great attrac-
tion to visitors from the country.   Dyce quotes appositely from Brath-
wait's *Barnabees Journall :*—

> " Seven Hils there were in Rome, and so there be
> Seven Sights in New-Troy crave our memorie :
> 1 Tombes, 2 Guild-Hall Giants, 3 Stage-plaies, 4 Bedlam poore,
> 5 Ostrich, 6 *Beare-garden*, 7 Lyons in the Towre."

Tan. I've other business, not so much idle time.

Qui. You never say your prayers.

Tan. I'm advised by my learned counsel.

  Qui. The power of my charm come o'er thee,
Place by degrees thy wits before thee!
With silken patience here I bind thee,
Not to move till I unwind thee.   300

    Tan. Yea! is my cause so muddy? do I stick, do I
          stick fast?
Advocate, here's my hand, pull; art made of flint?
Wilt not help out? alas, there's nothing in't!

  Phœ. O, do you sluice the vein now?

  Qui. Yes, my honour'd lord.

  Phœ. Pray, let me see the issue.

  Qui. I therefore seek to keep it.—Now burst out,
Thou filthy stream of trouble, spite, and doubt!

    Tan. O, an extent, a proclamation, a summons, a recog-
nisance, a tachment, and injunction! a writ, a seizure, a
writ of 'praisement, an absolution, a *quietus est!*

  Qui. You're quieter, I hope, by so much dregs.   312
—Behold, my lord!

  Phœ. This! why, it outfrowns ink.

  Qui. 'Tis the disease's nature, the fiend's drink.

    Tan. O sick, sick, signior Ply-fee, sick! lend me thy
nightcap, O!

  Qui. The balsam of a temperate brain
I pour into this thirsty vein,
And with this blessed oil of quiet,
Which is so cheap, that few men buy it,   320
Thy stormy temples I allay:

Thou shalt give up the devil, and pray ;
Forsake his works, they're foul and black,
And keep thee bare in purse and back.
No more shalt thou in paper quarrel,
To dress up apes in good apparel.
He throws his stock and all his flock
   Into a swallowing gulf,
That sends his goose unto his fox,
   His lamb unto his wolf.   330
Keep thy increase,
And live at peace,
For war's[1] not equal to this battle :
That eats but men ; this men and cattle :
Therefore no more this combat choose,
Where he that wins does always lose ;
And those that gain all, with this curse receive it,
From fools they get it, to their sons they leave it.
   Tan. Hail, sacred patience ! I begin to feel
I have a conscience now ; truth in my words,   340
Compassion in my heart, and, above all,
In my blood peace's music. Use me how you can,
You shall find me an honest, quiet man.
O, pardon, that I dare behold that face !
Now I've least[2] law I hope I have most grace.
   Phœ. We both admire the workman and his piece.
Thus when all hearts are tun'd to honour's strings,
There is no music to the quire of kings. [*Exeunt omnes.*

---

[1] So ed. 2.—Ed. 1 " war."
[2] So ed. 2.—Ed. 1 " left."

MICHAELMAS TERM.

Michaelmas Terme.   As it hath been svndry times acted by the Children of Paules.   At London, Printed for A. I. and are to be sould at the signe of the white horse in Paules Churchyard.   An. 1607.   4to.   Another edition, *newly corrected,* appeared in 1630. *Michaelmas Term* was licensed by Sir George Buc, 15th May 1607.

DRAMATIS PERSONÆ.

EASY,
REARAGE, } *gentlemen.*
SALEWOOD,
COCKSTONE,
QUOMODO, *a woollen-draper.*
SHORTYARD, } *his attendants ; familiar spirits.*[1]
FALSELIGHT,
SIM, *son to* QUOMODO.
ANDREW LETHE, *an adventurer, son to* MOTHER GRUEL.
HELLGILL, *a pander.*
Father to the Country Wench.
Judge.
DUSTBOX, *a scrivener.*
Tailor.
Drawer.
Boy.
Beadle.
Liverymen, Officers, &c.

THOMASINE, *wife to* QUOMODO, *afterwards married to* EASY.
SUSAN, *her daughter.*
THOMASINE'S *mother.*
MOTHER GRUEL.
Country Wench, seduced by LETHE.
MISTRESS COMINGS, *a tire-woman.*
WINEFRED, *maid to* THOMASINE.

INDUCTION.

Michaelmas Term.
The other Three Terms.
Boy, &c.

SCENE, LONDON.

---

1 Though Shortyard and Falselight are several times throughout the play termed "spirits," they exercise no supernatural power, and are knaves of the ordinary type.

MICHAELMAS TERM.

—o—

INDUCTION.

Enter MICHAELMAS TERM *in a whitish cloak, new come up out of the country, a* Boy *bringing his gown after him.*

Mich. T. Boy.
Boy. Here, sir.
Mich. T. Lay by my conscience ;
Give me my gown ; that weed is for the country :
We must be civil now, and match our evil :
Who first made civil black, he pleas'd the devil.
So :
Now know I where I am : methinks already
I grasp best part of the autumnian blessing
In my contentious fathom ;[1] my hand's free :   10
From wronger and from wronged I have fee ;
And what by sweat from the rough earth they draw
Is to enrich this silver harvest, law ;
And so through wealthy variance and fat brawl,

---

[1] Comprehension.—Old eds. "fadome."

The barn is made but steward to the hall.
Come they up thick enough?

    Boy. O, like hops and harlots, sir.

    Mich. T. Why dost thou couple them?

    Boy. O very aptly; for as the hop well boiled will
make a man not stand upon his legs, so the harlot in
time will leave a man no legs to stand upon.   21

    Mich. T. Such another, and be my heir! I have no
            child,
Yet have I wealth would redeem beggary.
I think it be a curse both here and foreign,
Where bags are fruitful'st there the womb's most barren:
The poor has all our children, we their wealth.
Shall I be prodigal when my life cools,
Make those my heirs whom I have beggar'd, fools?
It would be wondrous; rather beggar more;
Thou shalt have heirs enow, thou keep'st a whore: 30
And here comes kindred too with no mean purses,
Yet strive to be still blest with clients' curses.

Music playing, enter the other three Terms, the first bring-
    ing in a fellow poor, which the other two advanceth,
    giving him rich apparel, a page, and a pander : he
    then goes out.

    Mich. T. What subtility have we here? a fellow
Shrugging for life's kind benefits, shift and heat,
Crept up in three terms, wrapt in silk and silver,
So well appointed too with page and pander!
It was a happy gale that blew him hither.

First T. Thou father of the Terms, hail to thee !
Sec. T. May much contention still keep with thee !
Third T. Many new fools come up and fee thee !   40
Sec. T. Let 'em pay dear enough that see thee !
First T. And like asses use such men ;
When their load's off, turn 'em to graze agen.
   Sec. T. And may our wish have full effect,
Many a suit, and much neglect !
   Third T. And as it hath been often found,
Let the clients' cups come round !
   Sec. T. Help your poor kinsmen, when you ha' got
          'em ;
You may drink deep, leave us the bottom.
   Third T. Or when there is a lamb fall'n in,   50
Take you the lamb, leave us the skin.[1]
   Mich. T. Your duty and regard hath mov'd us ;
Never till now we thought you lov'd us.
Take comfort from our words, and make no doubt
You shall have suits come sixteen times about.
   All Three. We humbly thank the patron of our hopes.
                                [Exeunt.
   Mich. T. With what a vassal-appetite they gnaw
On our reversions, and are proud
Coldly to taste our meats, which eight returns
Serve in to us as courses !   60
One day our writs, like wild-fowl, fly abroad,
And then return o'er cities, towns, and hills,

---

[1] A punning allusion is intended (I suppose) to " lambswool "—a tipple composed of ale and roasted apples.

With clients, like dried straws, between their bills;
And 'tis no few birds pick to build their neasts,[1]
Nor no small money that keeps drabs and feasts!
But, gentlemen, to spread myself open unto you, in
cheaper terms I salute you; for ours have but sixpenny
fees all the year long; yet we despatch you in two hours,
without demur; your suits hang not long here after
candles be lighted. Why we call this play by such a
dear and chargeable title, *Michaelmas Term*, know it
consents happily to our purpose, though perhaps faintly
to the interpretation of many; for he that expects any
great quarrels in law to be handled here will be fondly
deceived; this only presents those familiar accidents
which happened in town in the circumference of those
six weeks whereof Michaelmas Term is lord. *Sat
sapienti:* I hope there's no fools i' th' house. 78
[*Exit with* Boy.

---

[1] "*i.e.* nests—for the sake of the rhyme. So Brome:
'That the tipling *feast*,
With the Doxie in the *neast*,' &c.
A Jovial Crew, 1652 (acted 1641), sig. F. 4."—*Dyce.*

ACT I.

SCENE I.

The Middle Aisle of St. Paul's.[1]

Enter REARAGE *meeting* SALEWOOD.

Sale. What, master Rearage?

Rear. Master Salewood? exceedingly well met in town. Comes your father up this term?

Sale. Why, he was here three days before the Exchequer gaped.

Rear. Fie, such an early termer?

Sale. He's not to be spoke withal; I dare not ask him blessing till the last of November.

Rear. And how looks thy little venturing cousin?

Sale. Faith, like a lute that has all the strings broke; nobody will meddle with her. 11

---

[1] The place of action is not marked in the old eds.; but it is plain from the mention of the "bills" (p. 225), as Dyce pointed out, that the scene takes place in the middle aisle of Paul's, where servants out of employment came to find masters, and gossips to chatter. Dyce refers to *Every Man out of his Humour*, i. i. Cf. Earle's *Characters* :—" The visitants are all men without exception, but the principal inhabitants and possessors are stale knights and captains out of service; men of long rapiers and breeches, which after all turn merchants here and traffic for news."—*Paul's Walk.*

Rear. Fie, there are doctors enow in town will string her again, and make her sound as sweet as e'er she did. Is she not married yet?

Sale. Sh'as no luck; some may better steal a horse than others look on: I have known a virgin of five bastards wedded. Faith, when all's done, we must be fain to marry her into the north, I'm afraid.

Rear. But will she pass so, think you?

Sale. Pooh, anything that is warm enough is good enough for them: so it come in the likeness, though the devil be in't, they'll venture the firing.   22

Rear. They're worthy spirits, i'faith. Heard you the news?

Sale. Not yet.

Rear. Mistress Difficult is newly fallen a widow.

Sale. Say true; is master Difficult, the lawyer, dead?

Rear. Easily dead, sir.

Sale. Pray, when died he?

Rear. What a question's that! when should a lawyer die but in the vacation? he has no leisure to die in the term-time; beside, the noise there would fetch him again.

Sale. Knew you the nature of his disease?   33

Rear. Faith, some say he died of an old grief he had, that the vacation was fourteen weeks long.

Sale. And very likely: I knew 'twould kill him at last; 't'as troubled him a long time. He was one of those that would fain have brought in the heresy of a fifth term; often crying, with a loud voice, O why should we lose Bartholomew week?   40

Rear. He savours; stop your nose; no more of him.

Enter COCKSTONE *meeting* EASY.

Cock. Young master Easy, let me salute you, sir.
When came you?

Easy. I have but inn'd my horse since, master Cockstone.

Cock. You seldom visit London, master Easy;
But now your father's dead, 'tis your only course:
Here's gallants of all sizes, of all lasts;
Here you may fit your foot, make choice of those
Whom your affection may rejoice in.

Easy. You've easily possess'd [1] me, I am free:		50
Let those live hinds that know not liberty!

Cock. Master Rearage?

Easy. Good master Salewood, I am proud of your
society.

Rear. What gentleman might that be?

Cock. One master Easy; has good land in Essex;
A fair, free-breasted gentleman, somewhat
Too open—bad in man, worse in woman,
The gentry-fault at first:—he is yet fresh,
And wants the city powdering. But what news?		60
Is't yet a match 'twixt master Quomodo's
The rich draper's daughter and yourself?

Rear. Faith, sir, I am vildly rivall'd.

Cock. Vildly? by whom?

Rear. One Andrew Lethe, crept to a little warmth,
And now so proud that he forgets all storms;

---

[1] Convinced.

One that ne'er wore apparel, but, like ditches,
'Twas cast before he had it; now shines bright
In rich embroideries.   Him master Quomodo affects,
The daughter him, the mother only me :
I rest most doubtful, my side being weakest.   70
    Cock. Yet the mother's side
Being surer than the father's, it may prove,
Men plead for money best, women for love.
    Rear. 'Slid, master Quomodo !
    Cock. How then ? afraid of a woollen-draper !
    Rear. He warned me his house, and I hate he should
see me abroad.   [*They all retire.*

Enter QUOMODO, *with his two spirits,* SHORTYARD
and FALSELIGHT.

    Quo. O my two spirits, Shortyard and Falselight,
you that have so enricht me ! I have industry for you
both.   80
    Sho. Then do you please us best, sir.
    Quo. Wealthy employment.
    Sho. You make me itch, sir.
    Quo. You, Falselight, as I have directed you—
    Fal. I am nimble.
    Quo. Go, make my coarse commodities look sleek ;[1]
With subtle art beguile the honest eye :
Be near to my trap-window, cunning Falselight.
    Fal. I never fail'd it yet.

---

[1] So ed. 2.—Ed. 1 "looke, seeke."

Quo. I know thou didst not.—[*Exit* FALSELIGHT.
But now to thee, my true and secret Shortyard,   90
Whom I dare trust e'en with my wife;
Thou ne'er didst mistress harm, but master good:
There are too few of thy name gentlemen,
And that we feel, but citizens abundance:
I have a task for thee, my pregnant spirit,
To exercise thy pointed wits upon.
   Sho. Give it me, for I thirst.
   Quo. Thine ear shall drink it.
Know, then, I have not spent this long vacation
Only for pleasure's sake:—give me the man
Who out of recreation culls advantage,   100
Dives into seasons, never walks but thinks,
Ne[1] rides but plots:—my journey was toward Essex——
   Sho. Most true.
   Quo. Where I have seen what I desire.
   Sho. A woman?
   Quo. Pooh, a woman! yet beneath her,
That which she often treads on, yet commands her;
Land, fair neat land.
   Sho. What is the mark you shoot at?
   Quo. Why, the fairest to cleave the heir in twain,
I mean his title; to murder his estate,
Stifle his right in some detested prison:
There are means and ways enow to hook in gentry,   110
Besides our deadly enmity, which thus stands,
They're busy 'bout our wives, we 'bout their lands.

---

[1] Old form of "Nor."

Sho. Your revenge is more glorious.
To be a cuckold is but for one life ;
When land remains to you, your heir, or wife.

Quo. Ah, sirrah, do we sting 'em ? This fresh gallant
Rode newly up before me.

Sho. I beseech his name.

Quo. Young master Easy.

Sho. Easy ? it may fall right.   120

Quo. I have inquired his haunt—stay,—hah ! ay,
that 'tis, that's he, that's he !

Sho. Happily !

Quo. Observe, take surely note of him ; he's fresh and
free : shift thyself speedily into the shape of gallantry :
I'll swell thy purse with angels. Keep foot by foot with
him, outdare his expenses, flatter, dice, and brothel to
him ; give him a sweet taste of sensuality ; train him to
every wasteful sin, that he may quickly need health, but
especially money ; ravish him with a dame or two,—be
his bawd for once, I'll be thine for ever ;—drink drunk [1]
with him, creep into bed to him, kiss him, and undo him,
my sweet spirit.   133

Sho. Let your care dwell in me ; soon shall it shine :
What subtilty's in man that is not mine ?

Quo. O my most cheerful spirit ! go, despatch.

[*Exit* SHORTYARD.

Gentry is the chief fish we tradesmen catch.   [*Exit.*

Easy. What's here ?

---

[1] Cf. Samuel Rowlands' *Letting of Humour's Blood in the Head Vaine*, 1600 :—
    "*Drink drunk* in kindness for good fellowship." (Epigr. 7).

Sale. O, they are bills [1] for chambers.

Easy [*reads*]. *Against St. Andrew's, at a painter's house, there's a fair chamber ready furnished to be let ; the house not only endued with a new fashion forepart, but, which is more convenient for a gentleman, with a very provident back door.*   144

Sale. Why, here's virtue still : I like that thing that's necessary as well as pleasant.

Cock. What news in yonder paper ?

Rear. Hah ! seek you for news ? there's for you !

Enter LETHE, *who remains behind reading the bills.*⟩

Sale. Who's this ? [2]
In the name of the black angels, Andrew Gruel !   150

Rear. No, Andrew Lethe.

Sale. Lethe ?

Rear. Has forgot his father's name,
Poor Walter Gruel, that begot him, fed him,
And brought him up.

Sale. Not hither.

Rear. No ;
'Twas from his thoughts ; he brought him up below.

Sale. But does he pass for Lethe ?

Rear. 'Mongst strange eyes,
That no more know him than he knows himself,   160
That's nothing now ; for master Andrew Lethe.
A gentleman of most received parts,
Forgetfulness, lust, impudence, and falsehood,

And one especial courtly quality,
To wit, no wit at all.   I am his rival
For Quomodo's daughter; but he knows it not.

 Sale. Has spied us o'er his paper.

 Rear. O, that's a warning
To make our duties ready.

  Cock. Salute him? hang him!

 Rear. Pooh, wish his health awhile; he'll be laid
   shortly:

Let him gorge venison for a time, our doctors   170
Will bring him to dry mutton.   Seem respective,[1]
To make his pride swell like a toad with dew.

         [LETHE *comes forward.*

 Sale. Master Lethe.

 Rear. Sweet master Lethe.

 Let. Gentlemen, your pardon; I remember you not.

 Sale. Why, we supt with you last night, sir.

 Let. O, cry you mercy! 'tis so long ago,
I'd quite forgot you; I must be forgiven.
Acquaintance, dear society, suits, and things,
Do so flow to me,   180
That had I not the better memory,
'Twould be a wonder I should know myself.
Esteem is made of such a dizzy metal;
I have receiv'd of many gifts o'er night,
Whom I've forgot ere morning: meeting the men,
I wish'd 'em to remember me agen:
They do so; then if I forget agen,

---

[1] Respectful.

I know what help'd before, that will help then :
This is my course ; for memory I've been told
Twenty preserves ; the best I find is gold ;   190
Ay, truly !   Are you not knights yet, gentlemen?

Sale. Not yet.

Let. No? that must be looked into ; 'tis your own
fault.   I have some store of venison : where shall we
devour it, gentlemen ?

Sale. The Horn were a fit place.

Let. For venison fit :
The horn having chas'd it,
At the Horn we'll——
Rhyme to that ?   200

Cock. Taste it.

Sale. Waste it.

Rear. Cast [1] it.

Let. That's the true rhyme indeed ! we hunt our venison
twice, I tell you ; first out a' th' park, next out a' th'
belly.

Cock. First dogs take pains to make it fit for men,
Then men take pains [2] to make it fit for dogs.

Let. Right.

Cock. Why, this [is] kindness ; a kind gallant you, 210
And love to give the dogs more than their due :
We shall attend you, sir.

Let. I pray do so.

Sale. The Horn.

---

[1] Vomit.

[2] So ed. 2.—Ed. 1 "payne."

Let. Easily remember'd that, you know.

[*Exeunt all except* LETHE.

But now unto my present business. The daughter yields,
and Quomodo consents ; only my mistress Quomodo,
her mother, without regard runs full against me, and
sticks hard. Is there no law for a woman that will run
upon a man at her own apperil ?[1] Why should not she
consent, knowing my state, my sudden fortunes ? I can
command a custard, and other bake-meats, death of
sturgeon :[2] I could keep house with nothing. What
friends have I ! how well am I beloved ! e'en quite
throughout the scullery. Not consent ? 'tis e'en as I
have writ : I'll be hanged, and she love me not herself,
and would rather preserve me, as a private friend, to her
own pleasures, than any way advance her daughter upon
me to beguile herself. Then how have I relieved her in
that point ? let me peruse this letter. [*Reads*]—*Good
mistress Quomodo, or rather, as I hope ere the term end,
mother Quomodo, since only your consent keeps aloof off,*[3]
*and hinders the copulation of your daughter, what may I
think, but that it is a mere affection in you, doating upon
some small inferior virtue of mine, to draw me in upon
yourself ? If the case stand so, I have comfort for you ; for*

---

[1] Peril.

[2] The text seems corrupt. Perhaps we should read " Death of
sturgeon ! I could keep house," &c.—taking the words " Death of
sturgeon ! " as a kind of silly half-oath ; for which compare Marston's
Fawn, ii. 1 :—

　　　　　　" As for me, why, *death a sense,*
　　　　I court the lady ! "

[3] So in iii. 1 :—" Since only her consent kept *aloof off,*" &c.

this you may well assure yourself, that by the marriage of your daughter I have the better means and opportunity to yourself, and without the least suspicion.—This is moving stuff, and that works best with a citizen's wife: but who shall I get to convey this now? My page I ha' lent forth; my pander I have employed about the country to look out some third sister, or entice some discontented gentlewoman from her husband, whom the laying out of my appetite shall maintain. Nay, I'll deal like an honourable gentleman, I'll be kind to women; that which I gather i' th' day, I'll put into their purses at night. You shall have no cause to rail at me; no, faith: I'll keep you in good fashion, ladies; no meaner men than knights shall ransom home your gowns and recover your smocks: I'll not dally with you.—Some [1] poor widow woman would come as a necessary bawd now! and see where fitly comes—   252

Enter MOTHER GRUEL.

my mother! Curse of poverty! does she come up to shame me, to betray my birth, and cast soil upon my new suit? Let her pass me; I'll take no notice of her,— scurvy murrey kersey! [2]

Moth. G. By your leave, and like your worship——

Let. Then I must proudly venture it.—To me, good woman?

Moth. G. I beseech one word with your worship.   260

---

[1] *i.e.* Would that some, &c.

[2] Dyce in his "Addenda" quotes from the *Two Merry Milk Maids*, 1620 :—" Foolish *scurvy, coarse kersey*, dirty-tail'd dangling dug-cow."

Let. Prithee, be brief then.

Moth. G. Pray, can your worship tell me any tidings of one Andrew Gruel, a poor son of mine own?

Let. I know a gallant gentleman of the name, one master Andrew Gruel, and well received amongst ladies.

Moth. G. That's not he, then : he is no gentleman that I mean.

Let. Good woman, if he be a Gruel, he's a gentleman i' th' mornings, that's a gentleman a' th' first ; you cannot tell me.　　　　　　　　　　　　　　　　　270

Moth. G. No, truly ; his father was an honest, upright tooth-drawer.

Let. O my teeth!

Moth. G. An't please your worship, I have made a sore journey out, all this vacant time, to come up and see my son Andrew.　Poor Walter Gruel, his father, has laid his life, and left me a lone woman ; I have not one husband in all the world : therefore my coming up is for relief, an't like your worship, hoping that my son Andrew is in some place about the kitchen.　　　　　　　　280

Let. Kitchen! pooh, faugh!

Moth. G. Or a serving-man to some knight of worship.

Let. O, let me not endure her! [*Aside.*]—Know you not me, good woman?

Moth. G. Alas, an't please your worship, I never saw such a glorious suit since the hour I was kersened.[1]

Let. Good, she knows me not; my glory does dis-
　　　　guise[2] me ;
Beside, my poorer name being drench'd in Lethe,

---

[1] Christened.　　　　　　　　[2] Old eds. "disguire."

She'll hardly understand me. What a fresh air can do!
I may employ her as a private drudge,   290
To pass my letters and secure my lust;
And ne'er be noted mine, to shame my blood,
And drop my staining birth upon my raiment.—[*Aside.*
Faith, good woman, you will hardly get to the speech of
master Andrew, I tell you.

Moth. G. No? marry, hang him! and like your worship, I have known the day when nobody cared to speak
to him.

Let. You must take heed how you speak ill of him, I
can tell you, now; he's so employed.   300

Moth. G. Employed? for what?

Let. For his 'haviour, wisdom, and other virtues.

Moth. G. He, virtues? no, 'tis well known his father
was too poor a man to bring him up to any virtues; he
can scarce write and read.

Let. He's the better regarded for that amongst courtiers,
for that's but a needy quality.

Moth. G. If it be so, then he'll be great shortly, for
he has no good parts about him.

Let. Well, good woman, or mother, or what you
will——   311

Moth. G. Alack the day! I know your worship scorns
to call me mother; 'tis not a thing fit for your worship
indeed, such a simple old woman as I am.

Let. In pity of thy long journey, there's sixpence
British: tend upon me; I have business for you.

Moth. G. I'll wait upon your worship.

Let. Two pole off at least.

Moth. G. I am a clean old woman, an't like your
worship.   320

Let. It goes not by cleanness here, good woman; if
you were fouler, so you were braver,[1] you might come
nearer.   [*Exit.*

Moth. G. Nay, and that be the fashion, I hope I shall
get it shortly; there's no woman so old but she may
learn : and as an old lady delights in a young page or
monkey, so there are young courtiers will be hungry upon
an old woman, I warrant you.   [*Exit.*

SCENE II.

A Street.

Enter DICK HELLGILL[2] *and Country Wench.*

Hell. Come, leave your puling and sighing.

Coun. W. Beshrew you now, why did you entice me
from my father?

Hell. Why? to thy better advancement. Wouldst thou,
a pretty, beautiful, juicy squall,[3] live in a poor thrummed[4]
house i' th' country, in such servile habiliments, and may

---

[1] More handsomely attired.

[2] Old eds. " Lethes Pandar."

[3] A term of endearment.

[4] " Seems here to mean thatched : the father of the Country Wench,
speaking of her (act ii. sc. 2), says—

        " O, if she knew
    The danger that attend on women's lives,
    She'd rather lodge under a poor *thatch'd roof*," &c.

Thrum is, properly, the tuft at the end of the warp in weaving."—*Dyce.*

well pass for a gentlewoman i' th' city? does not five
hundred do so, thinkest thou, and with worse faces?
O, now in these latter days, the devil reigning, 'tis an age
for cloven creatures! But why sad now? yet indeed 'tis
the fashion of any courtesan to be sea-sick i' th' first
voyage; but at next she proclaims open wars, like a beaten
soldier. Why, Northamptonshire lass, dost dream of
virginity now? remember a loose-bodied gown,[1] wench,
and let it go; wires and tires, bents and bums,[2] felts and
falls, thou that shalt deceive the world, that gentlewomen
indeed shall not be known from others. I have a master,
to whom I must prefer thee after the aforesaid deckening;
Lethe by name, a man of one most admired property;
he can both love thee, and for thy better advancement,
be thy pander himself; an excellent spark of humility. 21

Coun. W. Well, heaven forgive you! you train me
up to't.

Hell. Why, I do acknowledge it, and I think I do you
a pleasure in't.

Coun. W. And if I should prove a harlot now, I should
be bound to curse you.

Hell. Bound? nay, and you prove a harlot, you'll be
loose enough.

Coun. W. If I had not a desire to go like a gentlewoman, you should be hanged ere you should get me
to't, I warrant you. 32

---

[1] Loose-bodied gowns were worn by courtesans.

[2] "Bum-rolls. Stuffed cushions, used by women of middling rank to
make their petticoats swell out, in lieu of the farthingales, which were
more expensive."—*Nares.*

Hell. Nay, that's certain, nor a thousand more of you ; I know you are all chaste enough till one thing or other tempt you : deny [1] a satin gown and you dare now?

Coun. W. You know I have no power to do't, and that makes you so wilful ; for what woman is there such a beast that will deny any thing [2] that is good?

Hell. True ; they will not, most [3] dissembler.

Coun. W. No ; and she bear a brave mind, she will not, I warrant you.   41

Hell. Why, therefore, take heart, faint not at all ;
Women ne'er rise but when they fall :
Let a man break, he's gone, blown up ;
A woman's breaking sets her up :
Virginity is no city trade,
You're out a' th' freedom when you're a maid :
Down with the lattice, 'tis but thin ;
Let coarser beauties work within,
Whom the light mocks ; thou art fair and fresh ;   50
The gilded flies will light upon thy flesh.

Coun. W. Beshrew your sweet enchantments, you have won !

Hell. How easily soft women are undone !
So farewell wholesome weeds, where treasure pants ; [4]
And welcome silks, where lies disease and wants !

[*Aside.*

---

[1] Refuse.

[2] So ed. 2.—Ed. 1 " things."

[3] *i.e.* thorough dissembler.

[4] " ' Qy. haunts?' says a friend ; but I believe the text is right : for the sake of the rhyme, *pants* is used in the forced sense of—breathes, exists, dwells."—*Dyce.*

Come, wench; now flow thy fortunes in to bless
    thee;
I'll bring thee where thou shalt be taught to dress
    thee.

  Coun. W. O, as soon as may be! I am in a swoon
till I be a gentlewoman; and you know what flesh is
man's meat till it be dressed?   60

  Hell. Most certain, no more; a woman.   *[Exeunt.*

ACT II.

SCENE I.

An Ordinary.[1]

REARAGE, SALEWOOD, LETHE, EASY, *and* SHORTYARD,
discovered at dice: Boy attending.

Rear. Gentlemen, I ha' sworn I'll change the room.
Dice? devils!

Let. You see I'm patient, gentlemen.

Sale. Ay, the fiend's in't! you're patient; you put
up all.

Rear. Come, set me, gentlemen!

Sho. An Essex gentleman, sir.

Easy. An unfortunate one, sir.

---

[1] I have followed Dyce in marking the place of action "An Ordinary."
George Whetstone, in the second part of *The Enemie to Unthryftinesse*
(1586), denounces the gambling that was carried on at ordinaries :—
" The nurses of these (worse than heathenish) hellish exercises are places
called *Ordinary tables :* of which there are in London more in number to
honour the devil than churches to serve the living God." Stubbes
in the *Anatomy of Abuses* writes in a similar strain.

Sho. I'm bold to salute you, sir : you know not master
Alsup there?	10

Easy. O, entirely well.

Sho. Indeed, sir?

Easy. He's second to my bosom.

Sho. I'll give you that comfort then, sir, you must not
want money as long as you are in town, sir.

Easy. No, sir?

Sho. I am bound in my love to him to see you furnished; and in that comfort I recover my salute again,
sir.

Easy. Then I desire to be more dear unto you.	20

Sho. I rather study to be dear unto you. [*Aside.*]—
Boy, fill some wine.—I knew not what fair impressure [1]
I received at first, but I began to affect your society very
speedily.

Easy. I count myself the happier.

Sho. To master Alsup, sir; to whose remembrance I
could love to drink till I were past remembrance.

[*Drinks.*

Easy. I shall keep Christmas with him, sir, where your
health shall likewise undoubtedly be remembered; and
thereupon I pledge you. [*Drinks.*] I would sue for
your name, sir.	31

Sho. Your suit shall end in one term, sir; my name
is Blastfield.

Easy. Kind master Blastfield, your dearer acquain-
tance.	[*Drinks.*

---

[1] Old eds. "impressier."

Rear. Nay, come, will ye draw in, gentlemen? set me.

Easy. Faith, I'm scattered.

Sho. Sir, you shall not give out so meanly of yourself
in my company for a million : make such privy to your
disgrace ! you're a gentleman of fair fortunes ; keep me
your reputation : set 'em all; there's crowns for you.   41
                                           [*Giving him money.*

Easy. Sir, you bind me infinitely in these courtesies.

Sho. You must always have a care of your reputation
here in town, master Easy : although you ride down with
nothing, it skills not.

Easy. I'm glad you tell me that yet, then I'm indifferent.—Well, come; who throws? I set all these.

Sho. Why, well said.

Sale. This same master Lethe here begins to undo us
again.   50

Let. Ah, sir, I came not hither but to win !

Sho. And then you'll leave us; that's your fashion.

Let. He's base that visits not his friends.

Sho. But he's more base that carries out his winnings;
None will do so but those have base beginnings.

Let. It is a thing in use, and ever was.
I pass this time.

Sho. I wonder you should pass,
And that you're suffer'd.

Let. Tut, the dice are ours ;
Then wonder not at those that have most powers.

Rear. The devil and his angels !

Let. Are these they?   60

Welcome, dear angels![1] where you're curs'd ne'er stay.

Sale. Here's luck!

Easy. Let's search him, gentlemen; I think he wears a smock.[2]

Sho. I knew the time he wore not half a shirt,
Just like a pea.

Easy. No? how did he for the rest?

Sho. Faith, he compounded with a couple of napkins at Barnet, and so trussed up the lower parts.

Easy. 'Twas a pretty shift, i'faith!   70

Sho. But master Lethe has forgot that too.

Easy. A mischief on't, to lose all! I could——

Sho. Nay, but, good master Easy, do not do yourself that tyranny, I beseech you; I must not ha' you alter your body now for the purge of a little money: you undo me, and you do.

Easy. 'Twas all I brought up with me, I protest, master Blastfield; all my rent till next quarter.

Sho. Pox of money! talk not on't, I beseech you,— what said I to you? mass, I am out of cash myself too.—Boy.   81

Boy. Anon, sir.

Sho. Run presently to master Gum the mercer, and will[3] him to tell out two or three hundred pound for me, or more, according as he is furnished: I'll visit him 'i th' morning, say.

---

[1] See note 2, p. 32.

[2] Dyce thought that the expression "wears a smock" was equivalent to—is a knave; but the quotation he adduces is hardly to the point.

[3] Desire.

Boy. It shall be said, sir.   [*Going.*

Sho. Do you hear, boy?

Boy. Yes, sir.

Sho. If master Gum be not sufficiently ready, call upon master Profit the goldsmith.   91

Boy. It shall be done, sir.   [*Going.*

Sho. Boy.

Boy. I knew[1] I was not sent yet; now is the time.
[*Aside.*

Sho. Let them both rest till another occasion; you shall not need to run so far at this time; take one nigher hand; go to master Quomodo the draper, and will him to furnish me instantly.

Boy. Now I go, sir.   [*Exit.*

Easy. It seems you're well known, master Blastfield, and your credit very spacious here i' th' city.   101

Sho. Master Easy, let a man bear himself portly, the whorsons will creep to him a' their bellies, and their wives a' their backs: there's a kind of bold grace expected throughout all the parts of a gentleman. Then for your observances, a man must not so much as spit but within line and fashion. I tell you what I ha' done: sometimes I carry my water all London over only to deliver it proudly at the Standard;[2] and do I pass altogether unnoted, think you? no, a man can no sooner peep out his head but there's a bow bent at him out of some watchtower or other.   112

---

[1] Old eds. "know."

[2] A conduit in Cheapside set up by John Wells, mayor, in 1430.

Easy. So readily, sir?

Sho. Push,[1] you know a bow's quickly ready, though
a gun be long a-charging, and will shoot five times to his
once.   Come, you shall bear yourself jovially : take heed
of setting your looks to your losses, but rather smile upon
your ill luck, and invite 'em to-morrow to another breakfast of bones.

Easy. Nay, I'll forswear dicing.

Sho. What? peace, I am ashamed to hear you: will
you cease in the first loss? show me one gentleman that
e'er did it.   Fie upon't, I must use you to company, I
perceive ; you'd be spoiled else.   Forswear dice ! I would
your friends heard you, i'faith !   125

Easy. Nay, I was but in jest, sir.

Sho. I hope so : what would gentlemen say of you?
there goes a gull that keeps his money !   I would not
have such a report go on you for the world, as long as you
are in my company.   Why, man, fortune alters in a minute ;
I ha' known those have recovered so much in an hour,
their purses were never sick after.   132

Rear. O, worse than consumption of the liver ! consumption of the patrimony !

Sho. How now ?   Mark their humours, master Easy.

Rear. Forgive me, my posterity yet ungotten !

Sho. That's a penitent maudlin dicer.

Rear. Few know the sweets that the plain life allows :
Vild son that surfeits of his father's brows !

Sho. Laugh at him, master Easy.   140

---

[1] Pish.

Easy. Ha, ha, ha!

Sale. I'll be damned, and these be not the bones of some quean that cozened me in her life, and now consumes me after her death.

Sho. That's the true wicked, blasphemous, and soul-shuddering dicer, that will curse you all service-time, and attribute his ill luck always to one drab or other!

Enter HELLGILL.

Let. Dick Hellgill? the happy news.

Hell. I have her for you, sir.

Let. Peace : what is she?　　　　　　　　　　　150

Hell. Young, beautiful, and plump; a delicate piece of sin.

Let. Of what parentage?

Hell. O, a gentlewoman of a great house.

Let. Fie, fie.

Hell. She newly came out of a barn—yet too good for a tooth-drawer's son.　　　　　　　　　　　[*Aside.*

Let. Is she wife or maid?

Hell. That which is daintiest, maid.

Let. I'd rather she'd been a wife.　　　　　　　160

Hell. A wife, sir? why?

Let. O, adultery is a great deal sweeter in my mind.

Hell. Diseases gnaw thy bones!　　　　　　　[*Aside.*
I think she has deserv'd to be a wife, sir.

Let. That will move well.

Hell. Her firstlings shall be mine :
Swine look but for the husks; the meat be thine.

Re-enter Boy.

Sho. How now, boy?

Boy. Master Quomodo takes your worship's greeting exceeding kindly, and in his commendations returns this answer, that your worship shall not be so apt to receive it as he willing to lend it.   171

Sho. Why, we thank him, i'faith.

Easy. Troth, and you ha' reason to thank him, sir; 'twas a very friendly answer.

Sho. Push, a gentleman that keeps his days even here i' th' city, as I myself watch to do, shall have many of those answers in a twelvemonth, master Easy.

Easy. I promise you, sir, I admire your carriage, and begin to hold a more reverend respect of you.

Sho. Not so, I beseech you; I give my friends leave to be inward[1] with me.—Will you walk, gentlemen? 181

Let. We're for you.—

Present her with this jewel, my first token.

[*Giving jewel to* HELLGILL.

Enter Drawer.

Dra. There are certain countrymen without, inquiring for master Rearage and master Salewood.

Rear. Tenants?

Sale. Thou revivest us, rascal.

Rear. When's our next meeting, gentlemen?

Sho. To-morrow night;

---

[1] Intimate.

This gentleman, by me, invites you all.—
Do you not, master Easy?

    Easy. Freely, sir.   191

    Sale. We do embrace your love.—A pure, fresh gull.
                                                                [*Aside.*

    Sho. Thus make you men at parting dutiful,
And rest beholding to you; 'tis the slight,
To be remember'd when you're out of sight.

    Easy. A pretty virtue!   [*Exeunt.*

SCENE II.

A Street.

Enter the Country Wench's Father.

    Fath. Where shall I seek her now?   O, if she knew
The dangers that attend on women's lives,
She'd rather lodge under a poor thatch'd roof
Than under carved ceilings!   She was my joy,
And all content that I receiv'd from life,
My dear and only daughter.
What says the note she left? let me again
With staider grief peruse it.
[*Reads.*] *Father, wonder not at my so sudden departure,
without your leave or knowledge. Thus, under pardon, I
excuse it: had you had knowledge of it, I know you would
have sought to restrain it, and hinder me from what I have
long desired. Being now happily preferred to a gentleman's
service in London, about Holborn, if you please to send, you
may hear well of me.*   15

As false as she is disobedient !
I've made larger inquiry, left no place
Where gentry keeps [1] unsought, yet cannot hear ;
Which drives me most into a shameful fear.
Woe worth th' infected cause that makes me visit   20
This man-devouring city ! where I spent
My unshapen youth, to be my age's curse,
And surfeited away my name and state
In swinish riots, that now, being sober,
I do awake a beggar : I may hate her :
Whose youth voids wine, his age is curs'd with water.
O heavens, I know the price of ill too well !
What the confusions are in whom they dwell,
And how soon maids are to their ruins won,
One minute, and eternally undone ;   30
So in mine may it : may it not be thus !
Though she be poor, her honour's precious.
May be my present form, and her fond fear,
May chase her from me, if her eye should get me ;
And therefore, as my love and wants advise,
I'll serve, until I find her, in disguise.
Such is my care to fright her from base evils,
I leave calm state to live amongst you, devils.   [*Exit.*

---

[1] Dwells.

SCENE III.

QUOMODO's *Shop.*

Enter THOMASINE [1] *and* MOTHER GRUEL.

Tho. Were these fit words, think you, to be sent to any citizen's wife,—to enjoy the daughter, and love the mother too for a need? I would foully scorn that man that should love me only for a need, I tell you. And here the knave writes again, that by the marriage of my daughter 'a has the better means and opportunity to myself: he lies in his throat, like a villain; he has no opportunity of me for all that; 'tis for his betters to have opportunity of me, and that he shall well know. A base, proud knave! 'a has forgot how he came up and brought two of his countrymen to give their words to my husband for a suit of green kersey; 'a has forgot all this: and how does he appear to me when his white satin suit's on, but like a maggot crept out of a nutshell—a fair body and a foul neck: those parts that are covered of him looks indifferent well, because we cannot see 'em; else, for all his cleansing, pruning, and paring, he's not worthy a broker's daughter; and so tell him.   18

Moth. G. I will indeed, forsooth.

Tho. And as for my child, I hope she'll be ruled in time, though she be foolish yet, and not be carried away

---

[1] Old eds. "Quomodo's Wife."

with a cast of manchets,[1] a bottle of wine, or a custard :[2] and so, I pray, certify him.

Moth. G. I'll do your errand effectually.

Tho. Art thou his aunt,[3] or his——

Moth. G. Alas, I am a poor drudge of his !

Tho. Faith, and thou wert his mother, he would make thee his drudge, I warrant him.

Moth. G. Marry, out upon him ! sir-reverence of your mistress-ship.   30

Tho. Here's somewhat for thy pains : fare thee well.
                                              [*Giving money.*

Moth. G. 'Tis more than he gave me since I came to him.   [*Exit.*

Enter QUOMODO *and* SUSAN.

Quo. How now ? what prating have we here ? whispers ? dumbshows ? Why, Thomasine, go to : my shop is not altogether so dark [4] as some of my neighbours', where a man may be made cuckold at one end, while he's measuring with his yard at t'other.

Tho. Only commendations sent from master Lethe, your worshipful son-in-law that should be.   40

---

[1] " Cast of manchets," a couple of fine white rolls.

[2] Custards were not uncommon love-presents.

[3] A cant term for procuress.

[4] It was a common charge against dishonest tradesmen that they used " dark lights,"—darkened their shops in order to palm off goods of an inferior quality on unsuspecting customers. Stubbes, in his *Display of Corruptions*, says :—" Then have they their shops, and places where they sell their cloth, commonly very dark and obscure, of purpose to deceive the buyers."

Quo. O, and that you like not ! he that can make us rich in custom, strong in friends, happy in suits ; bring us into all the rooms a' Sundays, from the leads to the cellar ; pop us in with venison till we crack again, and send home the rest in an honourable napkin : this man you like not, forsooth.

Sus. But I like him, father.

Quo. My blessing go with thy liking !

Sus. A number of our citizens hold our credit by't, to come home drunk, and say, we ha' been at court : then how much more credit is't to be drunk there indeed ! 51

Quo. Tut, thy mother's a fool.—Pray, what's master Rearage, whom you plead for so ?

Tho. Why, first, he is a gentleman.

Quo. Ay, he's often first a gentleman that's last a beggar.

Sus. My father tells you true : what should I do with a gentleman ? I know not which way to lie with him.

Quo. 'Tis true, too. Thou knowest, beside, we undo gentlemen daily. 61

Tho. That makes so few of 'em marry with our daughters, unless it be one green fool or other. Next, master Rearage has land and living ; t'other but his walk i' th' street, and his snatching diet : he's able to entertain you in a fair house of his own ; t'other in some nook or corner, or place us behind the cloth,[1] like a company of puppets : at his house you shall be served curiously, sit

---

[1] Arras.

down and eat your meat with leisure ; there we must be
glad to take it standing, and without either salt, cloth, or
trencher, and say we are befriended too.   71

Quo. O, that gives a citizen a better appetite than his
garden.

Sus. So say I, father ; methinks it does me most good
when I take it standing: I know not how all women's
minds are.

Enter FALSELIGHT.

Quo. Faith, I think they are all of thy mind for that
thing.—How now, Falselight?

Fal. I have descried my fellow Shortyard, alias Blastfield, at hand with the gentleman.   80

Quo. O my sweet Shortyard!—Daughter, get you up
to your virginals.[1]   [*Exit* SUSAN.]   By your leave,
mistress Quomodo——

Tho. Why, I hope I may sit i' th' shop, may I not?

Quo. That you may, and welcome, sweet honey-thigh,
but not at this season ; there's a buck to be struck.

Tho. Well, since I'm so expressly forbidden, I'll watch
above i' th' gallery, but I'll see your knavery.

[*Aside, and exit.*

Quo. Be you prepared as I tell you.

Fal. You ne'er feared me.   [*Retires.*[2]   90

Quo. O that sweet, neat, comely, proper, delicate,
parcel of land ! like a fine gentlewoman i' th' waist, not
so great as pretty, pretty ; the trees in summer whistling,

---

[1] Sèe note, 2, p. 63.   [2] Old eds. " Exit."

the silver waters by the banks harmoniously gliding.   I
should have been a scholar ; an excellent place for a
student ; fit for my son that lately commenced at Cambridge, whom now I have placed at inns of court.   Thus
we that seldom get lands honestly, must leave our heirs
to inherit our knavery : but, whist ;[1] one turn about my
shop, and meet with 'em.   100

Enter EASY *and* SHORTYARD.

Easy. Is this it, sir ?

Sho. Ay ; let me see ; this is it ; sign of Three
Knaves ; 'tis it.

Quo. Do you hear, sir ? what lack you,[2] gentlemen ?
see good kerseys or broadcloths here ; I pray come near
—master Blastfield !

Sho. I thought you would know me anon.

Enter THOMASINE *above.*

Quo. You're exceeding welcome to town, sir : your
worship must pardon me ; 'tis always misty weather in
our shops here ; we are a nation the sun ne'er shines
upon.   Came this gentleman with you ?   111

Sho. O, salute him fairly ; he's a kind gentleman, a
very inward [3] of mine.

Quo. Then I cry you mercy, sir ; you're especially
welcome.

Easy. I return you thanks, sir.

---

[1] Hush.

[2] The ordinary form of address used by shopkeepers to customers.

[3] Intimate friend.

Quo. But how shall I do for you now, master Blast-field?

Sho. Why, what's the matter?

Quo. It is my greatest affliction at this instant, I am not able to furnish you.   121

Sho. How, master Quomodo? pray, say not so; 'slud, you undo me then.

Quo. Upon my religion, master Blastfield, bonds lie forfeit in my hands; I expect the receipt of a thousand every hour, and cannot yet set eye of a penny.

Sho. That's strange, methinks.

Quo. 'Tis mine own pity that plots against me, master Blastfield; they know I have no conscience to take the forfeiture, and that makes 'em so bold with my mercy.

Easy. I am sorry for this.   131

Quo. Nevertheless, if I might entreat your delay but the age of three days, to express my sorrow now, I would double the sum, and supply you with four or five hundred.

Sho. Let me see; three days?

Quo. Ay, good sir, and it may be possible.

Easy. Do you hear, master Blastfield?

Sho. Hah?

Easy. You know I've already invited all the gallants to sup with me to-night.   141

Sho. That's true, i'faith.

Easy. 'Twill be my everlasting shame if I have no money to maintain my bounty.

Sho. I ne'er thought upon that.—I looked still when that should come from him. [*Aside.*]—We have strictly examined our expenses; it must not be three days, master Quomodo.

Quo. No? then I'm afraid 'twill be my grief, sir.

Easy. Master Blastfield, I'll tell you what you may do now.   151

Sho. What, good sweet bedfellow? [1]

Easy. Send to master Gum, [2] or master Profit, the mercer and goldsmith.

Sho. Mass, that was well remembered of thee.—I perceive the trout will be a little troublesome ere he be catched. [*Aside.*]—Boy.

Enter Boy.

Boy. Here, sir.

Sho. Run to master Gum, or master Profit, and carry my present occasion of money to 'em.   160

Boy. I run, sir.   [*Exit.*

Quo. Methinks, master Blastfield, you might easily attain to the satisfaction of three days: here's a gentleman, your friend, I dare say will see you sufficiently possessed till then.

Easy. Not I, sir, by no means: master Blastfield knows I'm further in want than himself: my hope rests all upon him; it stands upon the loss of my credit to-night, if I walk [3] without money.

---

[1] " It was formerly common for men (even those of the highest rank) to sleep together; and the custom was still prevalent in the time of Cromwell: see the notes of Steevens and Malone on Shakespeare's *Henry V.*, act ii. sc. 2 ; and Clarendon's *Hist. of the Rebellion*, vol. vii. p. 34, ed. 1826."—*Dyce.*

[2] Old eds. " Goome."   [3] Go away.

Sho. Why, master Quomodo, what a fruitless motion have you put forth ! you might well assure yourself this gentleman had it not, if I wanted it : why, our purses are brothers; we desire but equal fortunes : in a word, we're man and wife ; they can but lie together, and so do we.   175

 Easy. As near as can be, i'faith.

Sho. And, to say truth, 'tis more for the continuing of this gentleman's credit in town, than any incitement from mine own want only, that I covet to be so immediately furnished : you shall hear him confess as much himself.

Easy. 'Tis most certain, master Quomodo.   181

Re-enter Boy.

Sho. O, here comes the boy now.—How now, boy? what says master Gum or master Profit?

Boy. Sir, they're both walked forth this frosty morning to Brainford,[1] to see a nurse-child.

Sho. A bastard be it ! spite and shame !

Easy. Nay, never vex yourself, sweet master Blastfield.

Sho. Bewitched, I think.

Quo. Do you hear, sir? you can persuade with him?

Easy. A little, sir.   190

Quo. Rather than he should be altogether destitute, or be too much a vexation to himself, he shall take up a commodity [2] of cloth of me, tell him.

---

[1] Brentford.—A noted place for assignations.

[2] It was a very common practice (not yet extinct) for money-lenders to force a client to take a part of the sum he wanted to borrow in goods (commodities),—brown paper, lute strings, pins, &c. " If he

Easy. Why, la! by my troth, 'twas kindly spoken.

Quo. Two hundred pounds' worth, upon my religion, say.

Sho. So disastrously!

Easy. Nay, master Blastfield, you do not hear what master Quomodo said since, like an honest, true citizen, i'faith; rather than you should grow diseased [1] upon't, you shall take up a commodity of two hundred pounds' worth of cloth.   202

Sho. The mealy moth consume it! would he ha' me turn pedlar now? what should I do with cloth?

Quo. He's a very wilful gentleman at this time, i'faith: he knows as well what to do with it as I myself, i-wis.[2] There's no merchant in town but will be greedy upon't, and pay down money upo' th' nail; they'll despatch it over to Middleburgh presently, and raise double commodity by exchange: if not, you know 'tis term time, and Michaelmas term too, the drapers' harvest for foot-cloths,[3] riding-suits, walking-suits, chamber-gowns, and hall-gowns.   213

---

borrow an hundred pounds, he shall have forty in silver, and three score in wares, as lute strings, hobby horses, or brown paper."—Greene's *Quip for an Upstart Courtier.* Nashe, in *Christ's Tears over Jerusalem,* inveighs bitterly against the practice:—" This I will prove, that never in any city (since the first assembly of societies), was ever suffered such notorious cozenage and villany as is shrouded under this seventy-fold usury of commodities. It is a hundred times more hateful than coney-catching: it is the nurse of sins, without the which the fire of them all would be extinguished and want matter to feed on."

[1] Uneasy, troubled.
[2] Assuredly.
[3] See note, p. 196.

Easy. Nay, I'll say that, it comes in as fit a time as can be.

Quo. Nay, take me with you [1] again ere you go, sir : I offer him no trash, tell him, but present money, say : where I know some gentlemen in town ha' been glad, and are glad at this time, to take up commodities in hawks' hoods and brown paper.   220

Easy. O horrible ! are there such fools in town ?

Quo. I offer him no trash, tell him ; upon my religion, you may say.—Now, my sweet Shortyard ; now the hungry fish begins to nibble ; one end of the worm is in his mouth, i'faith.   [*Aside.*

Tho. Why stand I here (as late our graceless dames,[2]
That found no eyes), to see that gentleman
Alive, in state and credit, executed,
Help to rip up himself does all he can ?
Why am I wife to him that is no man ?
I suffer in that gentleman's confusion.   [*Aside.* 231

Easy. Nay, be persuaded in that, master Blastfield ; 'tis ready money at the merchant's : beside, the winter season and all falls in as pat as can be to help it.

Sho. Well, master Easy, none but you could have persuaded me to that.—Come, would you would despatch then, master Quomodo : where's this cloth ?

Quo. Full and whole within, all of this piece, of my

---

[1] " Take me with you "=understand me.
[2] " The allusion here is probably to the execution of Sir Everard Digby, who, for his share in the gunpowder plot, was drawn, hanged, and quartered, at the west end of St. Paul's Church, 30th January 1606 : see Stow's *Annales*, p. 882, ed. 1631."—*Dyce.*

religion, master Blastfield. Feel't; nay, feel't, and spare
not, gentlemen, your fingers and your judgment.   240

Sho. Cloth's good.

Easy. By my troth, exceeding good cloth; a good
wale [1] 't'as.

Quo. Falselight.

Fal. I'm ne'er out a' the shop, sir.

Quo. Go, call in a porter presently, carry away the
cloth with the star-mark.—Whither will you please to
have it carried, master Blastfield?

Sho. Faith, to master Beggarland, he's the only
merchant now; or his brother, master Stilliarddown;
there's little difference.   251

Quo. You've happened upon the money-men, sir;
they and some of their brethren, I can tell you, will not
stick to offer thirty thousand pound to be cursed still:
great monied men, their stocks lie in the poors' throats.
But you'll see me sufficiently discharged, master Blastfield,
ere you depart?

Sho. You have always found me righteous in that.

Quo. Falselight.

Fal. Sir?   260

Quo. You may bring a scrivener along with you.

Fal. I'll remember that, sir.   [*Exit.*

Quo. Have you sent for a citizen, master Blastfield?

Sho. No, faith, not yet.—Boy.

Easy. What must you do with a citizen, sir?

Sho. A custom they're bound to a' late by the default

---

[1] The ridge of threads in cloths; the texture.

of evil debtors; no citizen must lend money without two
be bound in the bond; the second man enters but for
custom sake.

Easy. No? and must he needs be a citizen?   270

Sho. By th' mass, stay; I'll learn that.—Master Quomodo——

Quo. Sir?

Sho. Must the second party, that enters into bond only
for fashion's sake, needs be a citizen? what say you to
this gentleman for one?

Quo. Alas, sir! you know he's a mere stranger to me:
I neither am sure of his going or abiding; he may inn
here to-night, and ride away to-morrow: although I
grant the chief burden lies upon you, yet we are bound
to make choice of those we know, sir.   281

Sho. Why, he's a gentleman of a pretty living, sir.

Quo. It may be so; yet, under both your pardons, I'd
rather have a citizen.

Easy. I hope you will not disparage me so: 'tis well
known I have three hundred pound a-year in Essex.

Sho. Well said; to him thyself, take him up roundly.

Easy. And how doubtfully soe'er you account of me,
I do not think but I might make my bond pass for a
hundred pound i' th' city.   290

Quo. What, alone, sir?

Easy. Alone, sir? who says so? perhaps I'd send
down for a tenant or two.

Quo. Ay, that's another case, sir.

Easy. Another case let it be then.

Quo. Nay, grow not into anger, sir.

VOL. I.   R

Easy. Not take me into a bond ! as good as you shall, goodman goosecap.

Quo. Well, master Blastfield, because I will not disgrace the gentleman, I'm content for once ; but we must not make a practice on't.　　　　　　　　　　　301

Easy. No, sir, now you would, you shall not.

Quo. Cuds me, I'm undone ! he's gone again. [*Aside.*

Sho. The net's broke.　　　　　　　　　　　[*Aside.*

Tho. Hold there, dear gentleman !　　　　　[*Aside.*

Easy. Deny me that small courtesy ! 'S foot, a very Jew will not deny it me.

Sho. Now must I catch him warily.　　　　　[*Aside.*

Easy. A jest indeed ! not take me into a bond, quo' they.　　　　　　　　　　　　　　　　　310

Sho. Master Easy, mark my words : if it stood not upon the eternal loss of thy credit against supper——

Easy. Mass, that's true.

Sho. The pawning of thy horse for his own victuals——

Easy. Right, i'faith.

Sho. And thy utter dissolution amongst gentlemen for ever——

Easy. Pox on't !

Sho. Quomodo should hang, rot, stink——

Quo. Sweet boy, i'faith !　　　　　　　　[*Aside.* 320

Sho. Drop, damn.

Quo. Excellent Shortyard !　　　　　　　　[*Aside.*

Easy. I forgot all this : what meant I to swagger before I had money in my purse ?—How does master Quomodo? is the bond ready ?

Quo. O sir !

Enter DUSTBOX.

Easy. Come, we must be friends ; here's my hand.

Quo. Give it the scrivener : here he comes.

Dust. Good day, master Quomodo ; good morrow, gentlemen.   330

Quo. We must require a little aid from your pen, good master Dustbox.

Dust. What be the gentlemen's names that are bound, sir?

Quo. [*while* DUSTBOX *writes*]. Master John Blastfield, esquire, i' th' wild[1] of Kent : and—what do they call your bedfellow's name?

Sho. Master Richard Easy ; you may easily hit on't.

Quo. Master Richard Easy, of Essex, gentleman, both bound to Ephestian Quomodo, citizen and draper, of London ; the sum, two hundred pound.—What time do you take, master Blastfield, for the payment?   341

Sho. I never pass my month, you know.

Quo. I know it, sir : October sixteenth to-day ; sixteenth of November, say.

Easy. Is it your custom to return so soon, sir?

Sho. I never miss you.

Enter FALSELIGHT, *disguised as a Porter, sweating.*

Fal. I am come for the rest of the same piece,[2] master Quomodo.

---

[1] *i.e.* Weald of Kent. Cf. the ballad of *The fortunate sailor and the farmer's daughter* in De Vaynes' *Kentish Garland*, p. 177 :—

> " A sailor courted a Farmer's Daughter,
> Whose living was in the *Wild* of Kent."

[2] Old eds. "price." The emendation was suggested by Dyce.

Quo. Star-mark ; this is it : are all the rest gone ?

Fal. They're all at master Stilliarddown's by this time.

Easy. How the poor rascal's all in a froth !   351

Sho. Push,[1] they're ordained to sweat for gentlemen : porters' backs and women's bellies bear up the world.

[*Exit* FALSELIGHT *with the remainder of the cloth.*

Easy. 'Tis true, i'faith ; they bear men and money, and that's the world.

Sho. You've found it, sir.

Dust. I'm ready to your hands, gentlemen.

Sho. Come, master Easy.

Easy. I beseech you, sir.

Sho. It shall be yours, I say.   360

Easy. Nay, pray, master Blastfield.

Sho. I will not, i'faith.

Easy. What do you mean, sir ?

Sho. I should show little bringing up, to take the way of a stranger.

Easy. By my troth, you do yourself wrong though, master Blastfield.

Sho. Not a whit, sir.

Easy. But to avoid strife, you shall have your will of me for once.   370

Sho. Let it be so, I pray.

Quo. [*while* EASY *signs the bond*]. Now I begin to set one foot upon the land : methinks I am felling of trees already : we shall have some Essex logs yet to keep Christmas with, and that's a comfort.

---

[1] Pish.

Tho. Now is he quartering out; the executioner
Strides over him : with his own blood he writes :
I am no dame that can endure such sights.

       [Aside, and exit above.

Sho. So, his right wing is cut ; will not fly far
Past the two city hazards, Poultry and Wood Street.[1]

       [Aside.

Easy. How like you my Roman hand, i'faith ? 381

Dust. Exceeding well, sir, but that you rest too much
upon your R, and make your ease too little.

Easy. I'll mend that presently.

Dust. Nay, 'tis done now, past mending. [SHORTYARD
signs the bond.]—You both deliver this to master Quomodo as your deed ?

Sho. We do, sir.

Quo. I thank you, gentlemen.

Sho. Would the coin would come away now ! we have
deserved for't. 391

  Re-enter FALSELIGHT *disguised as before.*[2]

Fal. By your leave a little, gentlemen.

Sho. How now ? what's the matter ? speak.

Fal. As fast as I can, sir : all the cloth's come back
again.

Quo. How?

Sho. What's the news ?

Fal. The passage to Middleburgh is stopt, and there-

---

[1] The counter prisons in the Poultry and Wood Street.

[2] Old eds. " *with the cloath.* '

fore neither master Stilliarddown nor master Beggarland, nor any other merchant, will deliver present money upon't. 401

Quo. Why, what hard luck have you, gentlemen !

[*Exit* FALSELIGHT.

Easy. Why, master Blastfield !

Sho. Pish !

Easy. You're so discontented too presently, a man cannot tell how to speak to you.

Sho. Why, what would you say ?

Easy. We must make somewhat on't now, sir.

Sho. Ay, where ? how ? the best is, it lies all upon my neck.—Master Quomodo, can you help me to any money for't ? speak. 411

Quo. Troth, master Blastfield, since myself is so unfurnished, I know not the means how : there's one i' th' street, a new setter up ; if any lay out money upon't, 'twill be he.

Sho. His name ?

Quo. Master Idem : but you know we cannot give but greatly to your loss, because we gain and live by't.

Sho. 'S foot, will he give anything ?

Easy. Ay, stand upon that. 420

Sho. Will he give anything ? the brokers will give nothing : to no purpose.

Quo. Falselight.

Re-enter FALSELIGHT *above.*

Fal. Over your head, sir.

Quo. Desire master Idem to come presently, and look
upo' th' cloth.

Fal. I will, sir.   [*Exit above.*

Sho. What if he should offer but a hundred pound?

Easy. If he want twenty on't, let's take it.

Sho. Say you so?

Easy. Master Quomodo, he[1] will have four or five
hundred pound for you of his own within three or four
days.   432

Enter THOMASINE.

Sho. 'Tis true, he said so indeed.

Easy. Is that your wife, master Quomodo?

Quo. That's she, little Thomasine.

Easy. Under your leave, sir, I'll show myself a gentleman.

Quo. Do, and welcome, master Easy.

Easy. I have commission for what I do, lady, from
your husband.   [*Kisses her.* 440

Tho. You may have a stronger commission for the
next, an't please you, that's from myself.

Enter SIM.

Easy. You teach me the best law, lady.

Tho. Beshrew my blood, a proper springall[2] and a
sweet gentleman.   [*Aside, and exit.*

Quo. My son, Sim Quomodo :—here's more work for

---

[1] *i.e.* Quomodo.—So ed. 2 ; ed. 1 " we."

[2] So Dyce for " proper, springfull " of the old eds. " Springall "=
youth : "probably from the old French, in which *espringaller* or
springaller means to leap, dance, or sport."—*Nares.*

you, master Easy; you must salute him too,—for he's
like to be heir of thy land, I can tell thee.   [*Aside.*

Sim. Vim, vitam, spemque salutem.

Quo. He shows you there he was a Cambridge man,
sir; but now he's a Templar: has he not good grace to
make a lawyer?   452

Easy. A very good grace to make a lawyer.

Sho. For indeed he has no grace at all.   [*Aside.*

Quo. Some gave me counsel to make him a
divine——

Easy. Fie, fie.

Quo. But some of our livery think it an unfit thing,
that our own sons should tell us of our vices: others
to make him a physician; but then, being my heir, I'm
afraid he would make me away: now, a lawyer they're
all willing to, because 'tis good for our trade, and in-
creaseth the number of cloth gowns; and indeed 'tis the
fittest for a citizen's son, for our word is, What do ye
lack? and their word is, What do you give?   465

Easy. Exceeding proper.

Re-enter FALSELIGHT *disguised as* IDEM.

Quo. Master Idem, welcome.

Fal. I have seen the cloth, sir.

Quo. Very well.

Fal. I am but a young setter up; the uttermost I
dare venture upon't is threescore pound.   471

Sho. What?

Fal. If it be for me so, I am for it; if not, you have
your cloth, and I have my money.

Easy. Nay, pray, master Blastfield, refuse not his kind offer.

Sho. A bargain then, master Idem, clap hands.—He's finely cheated ! [*Aside.*]—Come, let's all to the next tavern and see the money paid.

Easy. A match.   480

Quo. I follow you, gentlemen ; take my son along with you. [*Exeunt all but* QUOMODO.]—Now to my keys : I'm master Idem, he [1] must fetch the money. First have I caught him in a bond for two hundred pound, and my two hundred pounds' worth a' cloth again for threescore pound. Admire me, all you students at inns of cozenage.   [*Exit.*

---

[1] *i.e.* he who.

ACT III.

SCENE I.

The Country Wench's Lodging.

The Country Wench [1] *discovered, dressed gentlewoman-like, in a new-fashioned gown : the Tailor points* [2] *it ; while* MISTRESS COMINGS, *a tirewoman,* [3] *is busy about her head :* HELLGILL *looking on.*

Hell. You talk of an alteration : here's the thing itself. What base birth does not raiment make glorious ? and what glorious births do not rags make infamous ? Why should not a woman confess what she is now, since the finest are but deluding shadows, begot between tirewomen and tailors ? for instance, behold their parents !

Mis. C. Say what you will, this wire becomes you best. —How say you, tailor ?

Tai. I promise you 'tis a wire would draw me from my work seven days a-week.   10

---

[1] " To her speeches in this scene, and in all the subsequent scenes where she appears, is prefixed ' *Curt*,' *i.e.* courtesan ; and in the stage-direction safter this scene she is called ' *Courtesan*' or '*Harlot*.'"—*Dyce.*

[2] Ties the laces.—Millinery was formerly an occupation of men.

[3] One who arranged the head-dresses of ladies.

Coun. W. Why, do you work a' Sundays, tailor?

Tai. Hardest of all a' Sundays, because we are most forbidden.

Coun. W. Troth, and so do most of us women; the better day the better deed, we think.

Mis. C. Excellent, exceeding, i' faith! a narrow-eared wire sets out a cheek so fat and so full: and if you be ruled by me, you shall wear your hair still like a mock-face behind: 'tis such an Italian world, many men know not before from behind.   20

Tai. How like you the sitting of this gown now, mistress Comings?

Mis. C. It sits at marvellous good ease and comely discretion.

Hell. Who would think now this fine sophisticated squall [1] came out of the bosom of a barn, and the loins of a hay-tosser?

Coun. W. Out, you saucy, pestiferous pander! I scorn that, i'faith.

Hell. Excellent! already the true phrase and style of a strumpet. Stay; a little more of the red, and then I take my leave of your cheek for four and twenty hours.— Do you not think it impossible that her own father should know her now, if he saw her?   34

Coun. W. Why, I think no less: how can he know me, when I scarce know myself?

Hell. 'Tis right.

---

[1] " *Obeseau,* a young minx or little proud *squall.*"—*Cotgrave.* We have had the word *squall* on p. 232 as a term of endearment.

Coun. W. But so well you lay wait for a man for me!

Hell. I protest I have bestowed much labour about it;
and in fit time, good news I hope.   40

Enter HELLGILL'S *Servant* [1] *bringing in the* Country
Wench's Father *disguised.* [2]

Ser. I've found one yet at last, in whose preferment I
hope to reap credit.

Coun. W. Is that the fellow?

Ser. Lady, it is.

Coun. W. Art thou willing to serve me, fellow?

Fath. So please you, he that has not the heart to serve
such a mistress as your beautiful self, deserves to be
honoured for a fool or knighted for a coward.

Coun. W. There's too many of them already. [3]

Fath. 'Twere sin then to raise the number.   50

Coun. W. Well, we'll try both our likings for a month,
and then either proceed or let fall the suit.

Fath. Be it as you have spoke, but 'tis my hope
A longer term.

Coun. W. No, truly; our term ends once a-month:
we should get more than the lawyers, for they have but
four terms a-year, and we have twelve, and that makes
'em run so fast to us in the vacation.

Fath. A mistress of a choice beauty! Amongst such
imperfect creatures I ha' not seen a perfecter. I should

---

[1] Old eds. "One."

[2] So Friscobaldo in the *Honest Whore* disguises himself and acts as
servant to his daughter.

[3] See note, p. 135.

have reckoned the fortunes of my daughter among the happiest, had she lighted into such a service ; whereas now I rest doubtful whom or where she serves. [*Aside.*

Coun. W. There's for your bodily advice, tailor ; and there's for your head-counsel [*giving money to the Tailor aud to* MISTRESS COMINGS] ; and I discharge you both till to-morrow morning again. 67

Tai. At which time our neatest attendance.

Mis. C. I pray, have an especial care, howsoever you stand or lie, that nothing fall upon your hair to batter your wire.

Coun. W. I warrant you for that. [*Exit* MIS. C. *with Tailor.*]—Which gown becomes me best now, the purple satin or this ?

Hell. If my opinion might rule over you——

Enter LETHE, REARAGE, *and* SALEWOOD.

Let. Come, gallants, I'll bring you to a beauty shall strike your eyes into your hearts : what you see, you shall desire, yet never enjoy.

Rear. And that's a villanous torment.

Sale. And is she but your underput, master Lethe ? 80

Let. No more, of my credit ; and a gentlewoman of a great house, noble parentage, unmatchable education, my plain pung.[1] I may grace her with the name of a courtesan, a backslider, a prostitution, or such a toy ; but when all comes to all, 'tis but a plain pung. Look you, gentlemen, that's she ; behold her !

---

[1] A variant (I suppose) of " punk."

Coun. W. O my beloved strayer! I consume in thy
absence.   88

Let. La, you now! You shall not say I'll be proud to
you, gentlemen; I give you leave to salute her.—I'm
afraid of nothing now, but that she'll utterly disgrace 'em,
turn tail to 'em, and place their kisses behind her. No,
by my faith, she deceives me; by my troth, sh'as kissed
'em both with her lips. I thank you for that music,
masters. 'Slid, they both court her at once; and see, if
she ha' not the wit to stand still and let 'em! I think
if two men were brewed into one, there is that woman
would drink 'em up both.   [*Aside.*

Rear. A coxcomb! he a courtier?   99

Coun. W. He says he has a place there.

Sale. So has the fool, a better place than he, and can
come where he dare not show his head.

Let. Nay, hear you me, gentlemen——

Sale. I protest you were the last man we spoke on;
we're a little busy yet; pray, stay there awhile; we'll come
to you presently.

Let. This is good, i'faith: endure this, and be a slave
for ever! Since you neither savour of good breeding nor
bringing up, I'll slice your hamstrings, but I'll make you
show mannerly. [*Aside.*]—Pox on you, leave courting:
I ha' not the heart to hurt an Englishman, i'faith or
else——   112

Sale. What else?

Let. Prithee, let's be merry; nothing else.—Here, fetch
some wine.

Coun. W. Let my servant go for't.

Let. Yours? which is he?

Fath.[1] This, sir.—But I scarce like my mistress now: the loins can ne'er be safe where the flies be so busy. Wit, by experience bought, foils wit at school :   120 Who proves a deeper knave than a spent fool? [*Aside.* I am gone for your worship's wine, sir.   [*Exit.*

Hell. Sir, you put up too much indignity; bring company to cut your own throat. The fire is not yet so hot, that you need two screens before it; 'tis but new kindled yet : if 'twere risse[2] to a flame, I could not blame you then to put others before you; but, alas, all the heat yet is comfortable; a cherisher, not a defacer!

Let. Prithee, let 'em alone; they'll be ashamed on't anon, I trow, if they have any grace in 'em.   130

Hell. I'd fain have him quarrel, fight, and be assuredly killed, that I might beg his place, for there's ne'er a one void yet.   [*Aside.*

Enter SHORTYARD *and* EASY.

Coun. W. You'll make him mad anon.

Sale. 'Tis to that end.

Sho. Yet at last master Quomodo is as firm as his promise.

Easy. Did I not tell you still he would?

Sho. Let me see; I am seven hundred pound in bond now to the rascal.   140

Easy. Nay, you're no less, master Blastfield; look to't.

---

[1] Old eds. "Sho."

[2] A common form of "risen" (which is the reading of ed. 2).

By my troth, I must needs confess, sir, you ha' been uncommonly kind to me since I ha' been in town : but master Alsup shall know on't.

Sho. That's my ambition, sir.

Easy. I beseech you, sir,—
Stay, this is Lethe's haunt; see, we have catch'd him.

Let. Master Blastfield and master Easy? you're kind gentlemen both.

Sho. Is that the beauty you famed so? 150

Let. The same.

Sho. Who be those so industrious about her?

Let. Rearage and Salewood : I'll tell you the unmannerliest trick of 'em that ever you heard in your life.

Sho. Prithee, what's that?

Let. I invited 'em hither to look upon her; brought 'em along with me; gave 'em leave to salute her in kindness : what do they but most saucily fall in love with her, very impudently court her for themselves, and, like two crafty attorneys, finding a hole in my lease, go about to defeat me of my right? 161

Sho. Ha' they so little conscience?

Let. The most uncivilest part that you have seen ! I know they'll be sorry for't when they have done; for there's no man but gives a sigh after his sin of women ; I know it by myself.

Sho. You parcel of a rude, saucy, and unmannerly nation——

Let. One good thing in him, he'll tell 'em on't roundly.
[*Aside.*

Sho. Cannot a gentleman purchase a little fire to thaw

his appetite by, but must you, that have been daily singed
in the flame, be as greedy to beguile him on't? How
can it appear in you but maliciously, and that you go
about to engross hell to yourselves? heaven forbid that
you should not suffer a stranger to come in! the devil
himself is not so unmannerly. I do not think but some
of them rather will be wise enough to beg offices there
before you, and keep you out; marry, all the spite will
be, they cannot sell 'em again.   179

Easy. Come, are you not to blame? not to give place,—
To us, I mean.

Let. A worse and a worse disgrace!

Coun. W. Nay, gentlemen, you wrong us both then:
stand from me; I protest I'll draw my silver bodkin
upon you.

Sho. Clubs, clubs![1]—Gentlemen, stand upon your
guard.

Coun. W. A gentlewoman must swagger a little now
and then, I perceive; there would be no civility in her
chamber else. Though it be my hard fortune to have
my keeper there a coward, the thing that's kept is a
gentlewoman born.   192

Sho. And, to conclude, a coward, infallible of your
side: why do you think, i'faith, I took you to be a coward?
do I think you'll turn your back to any man living?
you'll be whipt first.

Easy. And then indeed she turns her back to some
man living.

---

[1] "Clubs" was originally the popular cry to call out the apprentices
when any disturbance arose.

Sho. But that man shows himself a knave, for he dares not show his own face when he does it; for some of the common council in Henry the Eighth's days thought it modesty at that time that one vizzard should look upon another.   203

Easy. 'Twas honestly considered of 'em, i'faith.

Enter MOTHER GRUEL.

Sho. How now? what piece of stuff[1] comes here?

Let. Now, some good news yet to recover my repute, and grace me in this company. [*Aside.*]—Gentlemen, are we friends among ourselves?

Sho. United.

Re-enter Father *with wine.*

Let. Then here comes Rhenish to confirm our amity. —Wagtail,[2] salute them all; they are friends.   211

Coun. W. Then, saving my quarrel, to you all.

Sho. To's all.   [*They drink.*

Coun. W. Now beshrew your hearts, and you do not.

Sho. To sweet master Lethe.

Let. Let it flow this way, dear master Blastfield.— Gentlemen, to you all.

Sho. This Rhenish wine is like the scouring stick to a gun, it makes the barrel clear; it has an excellent virtue, it keeps all the sinks in man and woman's body sweet in June and July; and, to say truth, if ditches were not cast

---

1 " Buonarobba, as we say *good stuffe*, &c."—*Florio.*
2 A common term of endearment.

once a-year, and drabs once a-month, there would be no
abiding i' th' city.   223

Let. Gentlemen, I'll make you privy to a letter I sent.

Sho. A letter comes well after privy ; it makes amends.

Let. There's one Quomodo a draper's daughter in
town, whom for her happy portion I wealthily affect.

Rear. And not for love?—This makes for me his rival :
Bear witness.   [*To* SALEWOOD.

Let. The father does elect me for the man,   230
The daughter says the same.

Sho. Are you not well?

Let. Yes, all but for the mother ; she's my sickness.

Sho. Byrlady, and the mother [1] is a pestilent, wilful,
troublesome sickness, I can tell you, if she light upon
you handsomely.

Let. I find it so : she for a stranger pleads,
Whose name I ha' not learn'd.

Rear. And e'en now he called me by it.   [*Aside.*

Let. Now, as my letter told her, since only her consent
kept aloof off,[2] what might I think on't but that she
merely [3] doted upon me herself?   242

Sho. Very assuredly.

Sale. This makes still for you.

Sho. Did you let it go so, i'faith?

Let. You may believe it, sir.—Now, what says her
answer?

Sho. Ay, her answer.

---

        [1] Hysterical fit.   [2] See note 3, p. 228.
                [3] Wholly.

Moth. G. She says you're a base, proud knave, and
like your worship.   250

Let. How !

Sho. Nay, hear out her answer, or there's no goodness
in you.

Moth. G. You ha' forgot, she says, in what pickle your
worship came up, and brought two of your friends to
give their words for a suit of green kersey.

Let. Drudge, peace, or——

Sho. Show yourself a gentleman : she had the patience
to read your letter, which was as bad as this can be :
what will she think on't ? not hear her answer !—Speak,
good his drudge.   261

Moth. G. And as for her daughter, she hopes she'll be
ruled by her in time, and not be carried away with a cast
of manchets,[1] a bottle of wine, and a custard; which
once made her daughter sick, because you came by it
with a bad conscience.

Let. Gentlemen, I'm all in a sweat.

Sho. That's very wholesome for your body : nay, you
must keep in your arms.

Moth. G. Then she demanded of me whether I was
your worship's aunt [2] or no?   271

Let. Out, out, out !

Moth. G. Alas, said I, I am a poor drudge of his !
Faith, and thou wert his mother, quoth she, he'd make
thee his drudge, I warrant him.   Marry, out upon him,
quoth I, an't like your worship.

---

[1] "Cast of manchets."   See note 1, p. 247.
[2] See note 3, p. 247.

Let. Horror, horror! I'm smothered: let me go; torment me not.   [*Exit.*

Sho. And you love me, let's follow him, gentlemen.   280

Rear and Sale. Agreed.   [*Exeunt.*

Sho. I count a hundred pound well spent to pursue a good jest, master Easy.

Easy. By my troth, I begin to bear that mind too.

Sho. Well said, i'faith: hang money! good jests are worth silver at all times.

Easy. They're worth gold, master Blastfield.

[*Exeunt all except* Country Wench *and her* Father.

Coun. W. Do you deceive me so? Are you toward marriage, i'faith, master Lethe? it shall go hard but I'll forbid the banes:[1] I'll send a messenger into your bones, another into your purse, but I'll do't.   [*Exit.*   291

Fa. Thou fair and wicked creature, steept in art!
Beauteous and fresh, the soul the foulest part.
A common filth is like a house possest,
Where, if not spoil'd, you'll come out 'fraid at least.
This service likes not me: though I rest poor,
I hate the basest use to screen a whore.
The human stroke ne'er made him; he that can
Be bawd to woman never leapt from man;
Some monster won his mother.   300

---

[1] *i.e.* bans. Dyce compares Herrick:—
  "Whenere my heart Love's warmth but entertaines,
  O Frost! O Snow! O Haile forbid the *Banes*."
                          Hesperides, p. 42, ed. 1648.

I wish'd my poor child hither ; doubled wrong !
A month and such a mistress were too long.
Yet here awhile in others' lives I'll see
How former follies did appear in me.   [*Exit.*

SCENE II.

A Street.

Enter EASY *and* Boy.

Easy. Boy.

Boy. Anon, sir.

Easy. Where left you master Blastfield, your master, say you ?

Boy. An hour since I left him in Paul's, sir :—but you'll not find him the same man again next time you meet him.   [*Aside.*

Easy. Methinks I have no being without his company ; 'tis so full of kindness and delight : I hold him to be the only companion in earth.   10

Boy. Ay, as companions go now-a-days, that help to spend a man's money.   [*Aside.*

Easy. So full of nimble wit, various discourse, pregnant apprehension, and uncommon entertainment ! he might keep company with any lord for his grace.

Boy. Ay, with any lord that were past it.   [*Aside.*

Easy. And such a good, free-hearted, honest, affable kind of gentleman.—Come, boy, a heaviness will possess me till I see him.   [*Exit.*

Boy. But you'll find yourself heavier then, by a seven hundred pound weight.   Alas, poor birds that cannot keep the sweet country, where they fly at pleasure, but must needs come to London to have their wings clipt, and are fain to go hopping home again !   [*Exit.* 24

SCENE III.

A Street near St. Paul's.

Enter SHORTYARD *and* FALSELIGHT *disguised as a Sergeant and a Yeoman.*

Sho. So, no man is so impudent to deny that : spirits can change their shapes, and soonest of all into sergeants, because they are cousin-germans to spirits; for there's but two kind of arrests till doomsday,—the devil for the soul, the sergeant for the body; but afterward the devil arrests body and soul, sergeant and all, if they be knaves still and deserve it.   Now, my yeoman Falselight.

Fal. I attend you, good sergeant Shortyard.

Sho. No more master Blastfield now.   Poor Easy, hardly beset !   10

Fal. But how if he should go to prison? we're in a mad state then, being not sergeants.

Sho. Never let it come near thy belief that he'll take prison, or stand out in law, knowing the debt to be due, but still expect the presence of master Blastfield, kind master Blastfield, worshipful master Blastfield; and at the last——

Boy. [*within*]. Master Shortyard, master Falselight !

Sho. The boy? a warning-piece. See where he comes.

Enter EASY *and* Boy.

Easy. Is not in Paul's.   20

Boy. He is not far off sure, sir.

Easy. When was his hour, sayst thou ?

Boy. Two, sir.

Easy. Why, two has struck.

Boy. No, sir, they are now a-striking.

Sho. Master Richard Easy of Essex, we arrest you.

Easy. Hah ?

Boy. Alas, a surgeon ! he's hurt i' th' shoulder. [*Exit*.

Sho. Deliver your weapons quietly, sir.

Easy. Why, what's the matter ?   30

Sho. You're arrested at the suit of master Quomodo.

Easy. Master Quomodo ?

Sho. How strange you make it ! You're a landed gentleman, sir, I know ;[1] 'tis but a trifle, a bond of seven hundred pound.

 Easy. La, I knew[2] you had mistook ; you should arrest

One master Blastfield ; 'tis his bond, his debt.

 Sho. Is not your name there ?

 Easy. True, for fashion's sake.

 Sho. Why, and 'tis for fashion's sake that we arrest you.

 Easy. Nay, and it be no more, I yield to that : I know

---

[1] So ed. 2—Ed. 1 " knew."

[2] Old eds. "know."

master Blastfield will see me take no injury as long as
I'm in town, for master Alsup's sake.   42

Sho. Who's that, sir.

Easy. An honest gentleman in Essex.

Sho. O, in Essex? I thought you had been in London,
where now your business lies : honesty from Essex will
be a great while a-coming, sir ; you should look out an
honest pair of citizens.

Easy. Alas, sir, I know not where to find 'em !

Sho. No? there's enow in town.   50

Easy. I know not one, by my troth ; I am a mere
stranger for these parts : master Quomodo is all, and the
honestest that I know.

Sho. To him then let's set forward.—Yeoman Spider-
man, cast an eye about for master Blastfield.

Easy. Boy.—Alas, the poor boy was frighted away at
first !

Sho. Can you blame him, sir? we that daily fray
away knights, may fright away boys, I hope.   [*Exeunt.*

SCENE IV.

QUOMODO'S *Shop.*

Enter QUOMODO *and* Boy ; THOMASINE *watching above.*

Quo. Ha ! have they him, sayst thou ?

Boy. As sure as——

Quo. The land's mine : that's sure enough, boy.
Let me advance thee, knave, and give thee a kiss :
My plot's so firm, I dare it now to miss.

Now shall I be divulg'd a landed man
Throughout the livery : one points, another whispers,
A third frets inwardly ; let him fret and hang !
Especially his envy I shall have
That would be fain, yet cannot be a knave ;   10
Like an old lecher[1] girt in a[2] furr'd gown,
Whose mind stands stiff, but his performance down.
Now come my golden days in.   Whither is the worship-
ful master Quomodo and his fair bed-fellow rid forth ?
To his land in Essex.   Whence comes those goodly
load[s] of logs ?   From his land in Essex.   Where
grows this pleasant fruit, says one citizen's wife in the
Row ?[3]   At master Quomodo's orchard in Essex.   O,
O, does it so ?   I thank you for that good news, i'faith.

    Boy. Here they come with him, sir.   [*Exit.*

    Quo. Grant me patience in my joys, that being so
great, I run not mad with 'em !   22

    Enter SHORTYARD *and* FALSELIGHT *disguised as before,*
             bringing in EASY.

    Sho. Bless master Quomodo !

    Quo. How now, sergeants? who ha' you brought me
here ?—Master Easy !

    Easy. Why, la you now, sergeants ; did I not tell you
you mistook ?

    Quo. Did you not hear me say, I had rather ha' had
master Blastfield, the more sufficient man a great deal ?

---

[1] Old eds. " leather."
[2] So ed. 2.—Not in ed. 1.
[3] Probably Goldsmith's Row in Cheapside.

Sho. Very true, sir; but this gentleman lighting into
our hands first——   31

Quo. Why did you so, sir?

Sho. We thought good to make use of that opportunity, and hold him fast.

Quo. You did well in that, I must needs say, for
your own securities : but 'twas not my mind, master
Easy, to have you first; you must needs think so.

Easy. I dare swear that, master Quomodo.

Quo. But since you are come to me, I have no reason
to refuse you ; I should show little manners in that, sir.

Easy. But I hope you spake not in that sense, sir, to
impose the bond upon me?   42

Quo. By my troth, that's my meaning, sir ; you shall
find me an honest man ; you see I mean what I say.
Is not the day past, the money untendered? you'd ha'
me live uprightly, master Easy?

Easy. Why, sir, you know master Blastfield is the
man.

Quo. Why, sir, I know master Blastfield is the man ;
but is he any more than one man? Two entered into
bond to me, or I'm foully cozened.   51

Easy. You know my entrance was but for fashion
sake.

Quo. Why, I'll agree to you : you'll grant 'tis the
fashion likewise, when the bond's due, to have the money
paid again.

Sho. So we told him, sir, and that it lay in your
worship's courtesy to arrest which you please.

Quo. Marry, does it, sir—these fellows know the law

—beside, you offered yourself into bond to me, you know, when I had no stomach to you : now beshrew your heart for your labour ! I might ha' had a good substantial citizen, that would ha' paid the sum roundly, although I think you sufficient enough for seven hundred pound : beside the forfeiture, I would be loath to disgrace you so much before sergeants.   66

Easy. If you would ha' the patience, sir, I do not think but master Blastfield is at carrier's to receive the money.

Quo. He will prove the honester man then, and you the better discharged. I wonder he should break with me ; 'twas never his practice. You must not be angry with me now, though you were somewhat hot when you entered into bond ; you may easily go in angrily, but you cannot come out so.

Eas. No, the devil's in't for that !

Sho. Do you hear, sir ? a' my troth, we pity you : ha' you any store of crowns about you ?

Easy. Faith, a poor store ; yet they shall be at their service that will strive to do me good.—We were both drunk last night, and ne'er thought upon the bond.   81
        [*Aside.*

Sho. I must tell you this, you have fell into the hands of a most merciless devourer, the very gull a' the city : should you offer him money, goods or lands now, he'd rather have your body in prison, he's a' such a nature.

Easy. Prison ? we're undone then !

Sho. He's a' such a nature, look ; let him owe any

man a spite, what's his course? he will lend him money
to-day, a' purpose to 'rest him to-morrow.

Easy. Defend me!   90

Sho. Has at least sixteen at this instant proceeded in
both the counters; some bachelors,[1] some masters, some
doctors of captivity of twenty years' standing; and he
desires nothing more than imprisonment.

Easy. Would master Blastfield would come away!

Sho. Ay, then things would not be as they are. What
will you say to us, if we procure you two substantial
subsidy citizens to bail you, spite on's heart, and set you
at liberty to find out master Blastfield?

Easy. Sergeant, here, take all; I'll be dear to you, do
but perform it.   101

Sho. Much![2]

Easy.[3] Enough, sweet sergeant; I hope I understand
thee.

Sho. I love to prevent the malice of such a rascal;
perhaps you might find master Blastfield to-night.

Easy. Why, we lie together, man; there's the jest
on't.

Sho. Fie: and you'll seek to secure your bail, because
they will be two citizens of good account, you must do
that for your credit sake.   111

Easy. I'll be bound to save them harmless.

Sho. A pox on him, you cut his throat then: no
words.

---

[1] So ed. 2.—Ed. 1 "batchler."
[2] See note 4, p. 40.
[3] In the old eds. Falselight is the speaker.

Easy. What's it you require me, master Quomodo?

Quo. You know that before this time, I hope, sir; present money, or present imprisonment.

Sho. I told you so.

Easy. We ne'er had money of you.

Quo. You had commodities, an't please you.   120

Easy. Well, may I not crave so much liberty upon my word, to seek out master Blastfield?

Quo. Yes, and you would not laugh at me: we are sometimes gulls to gentlemen, I thank 'em; but gentlemen are never gulls to us, I commend 'em.

Sho. Under your leave, master Quomodo, the gentleman craves the furtherance of an hour; and it sorts well with our occasion at this time, having a little urgent business at Guildhall; at which minute we'll return, and see what agreement is made.   130

Quo. Nay, take him along with you, sergeant.

Easy. I'm undone then!

Sho. He's your prisoner; and being safe in your house at your own disposing, you cannot deny him such a request: beside, he hath a little faith in master Blastfield's coming, sir.

Quo. Let me not be too long delayed, I charge you.

Easy. Not an hour, i'faith, sir.

[*Exeunt* SHORTYARD *and* FALSELIGHT.

Quo. O master Easy, of all men living I never dreamed you would ha' done me this injury! make me wound my credit, fail in my commodities, bring[1] my

---

[1] So ed. 2.—Ed. 1 " ring."

state into suspicion ! for the breaking of your day to me
has broken my day to others.   143

Easy. You tell me of that still which is no fault of
mine, master Quomodo.

Quo. O, what's a man but his honesty, master Easy ?
and that's a fault amongst most of us all.   Mark but this
note ; I'll give you good counsel now.   As often as you
give your name to a bond, you must think you christen
a child, and take the charge on't, too ; for as the one,
the bigger it grows, the more cost it requires, so the
other, the longer it lies, the more charges it puts you to.
Only here's the difference ; a child must be broke, and
a bond must not ; the more you break children, the
more you keep 'em under ; but the more you break
bonds, the more they'll leap in your face ; and therefore,
to conclude, I would never undertake to be gossip [1] to
that bond which I would not see well brought up.   158

Easy. Say you so, sir ?   I'll think upon your counsel
hereafter for't.

Quo. Ah fool, thou shouldest ne'er ha' tasted such
wit, but that I know 'tis too late !   [*Aside.*

Tho. The more I grieve.   [*Aside.*

Quo. To put all this into the compass of a little
hoop-ring,—
Make this account, come better days or worse,
So many bonds abroad, so many boys at nurse.

Easy. A good medicine for a short memory : but

---

[1] Sponsor.

since you have entered so far, whose children are desperate debts, I pray? 170

Quo. Faith, they are like the offsprings of stolen lust,
put to the hospital: their fathers are not to be found;
they are either too far abroad, or too close within: and
thus for your memory's sake,—

The desperate debtor hence derives his name,
One that has neither money, land, nor fame;
All that he makes prove bastards, and not bands:[1]
But such as yours at first are born to lands.

Easy. But all that I beget hereafter I'll soon disinherit, master Quomodo. 180

Quo. In the meantime, here's a shrewd knave will
disinherit you. [*Aside.*

Easy. Well, to put you out of all doubt, master
Quomodo, I'll not trust to your courtesy; I ha' sent for
bail.

Quo. How? you've cozened me there, i'faith!

Easy. Since the worst comes to the worst, I have
those friends i' th' city, I hope, that will not suffer me to
lie for seven hundred pound.

Quo. And you told me you had no friends here at all:
how should a man trust you now? 191

Easy. That was but to try your courtesy, master
Quomodo.

Quo. How unconscionably he gulls himself! [*Aside.*]
—They must be wealthy subsidy-men, sir, at least forty

---

[1] So Dyce for "bonds" of the old eds. The forms "bands" and
"bonds" were used indifferently.

pound i' th' king's books, I can tell you, that do such a feat for you.

Re-enter Shortyard *and* Falselight *disguised as wealthy citizens in satin suits.*

Easy. Here they come, whatsoe'er they are.

Quo. Byrlady, alderman's deputies !—I am very sorry for you, sir ; I cannot refuse such men.   200

Sho. Are you the gentleman in distress ?

Easy. None more than myself, sir.

Quo. He speaks truer than he thinks ; for if he knew the hearts that owe [1] those faces !   A dark [2] shop's good for somewhat.   [*Aside.*

Easy. That was all, sir.

Sho. And that's enough ; for by that means you have made yourself liable to the bond, as well as that Basefield.

Easy. Blastfield, sir.   210

Sho. O, cry you mercy ; 'tis Blastfield indeed.

Easy. But, under both your worships' favours I know where to find him presently.

Sho. That's all your refuge.

Re-enter Boy.

Boy. News, good news, master Easy !

Easy. What, boy ?

Boy. Master Blastfield, my master, has received a thousand pound, and will be at his lodging at supper.

---

[1] Own.   [2] See note 4, p. 247.

Easy. Happy news! Hear you that, master Quo-
modo?   220

Quo. 'Tis enough for you to hear that; you're the
fortunate man, sir.

Easy. Not now, I beseech your good worships.

Sho. Gentleman, what's your t'other name?

Easy. Easy.

Sho. O, master Easy. I would we could rather
pleasure you otherwise, master Easy; you should soon
perceive it. I'll speak a proud word: we have pitied
more gentlemen in distress than any two citizens within
the freedom; but to be bail to seven hundred pound
action is a matter of shrewd weight.   231

Easy. I'll be bound to secure you.

Sho. Tut, what's your bond, sir?

Easy. Body, goods, and lands, immediately before
master Quomodo.

Sho. Shall we venture once again, that have been so
often undone by gentlemen?

Fal. I have no great stomach to't; it will appear in
us more pity than wisdom.

Easy. Why should you say so, sir?   240

Sho. I like the gentleman's face well; he does not look
as if he would deceive us.

Easy. O, not I, sir!

Sho. Come, we'll make a desperate voyage once again;
we'll try his honesty, and take his single bond, of body,
goods, and lands.

Easy. I dearly thank you, sir.

Sho. Master Quomodo——

Quo. Your worships.

Sho. We have took a course to set your prisoner free.

Quo. Your worships are good bail; you content me.

Sho. Come, then, and be a witness to a recullisance.[1]

Quo. With all my heart, sir.   253

Sho. Master Easy, you must have an especial care now to find out that Blastfield.

Easy. I shall have him at my lodging, sir.

Sho. The suit will be followed against you else; master Quomodo will come upon us, and forsake you.

Easy. I know that, sir.

Sho. Well, since I see you have such a good mind to be honest, I'll leave some greater affairs, and sweat with you to find him myself.   262

Easy. Here then my misery ends:
A stranger's kindness oft exceeds a friend's.

                                        [*Exeunt.*

Tho. Thou art deceiv'd; thy misery but begins:
To beguile goodness is the core of sins.
My love is such unto thee, that I die
As often as thou drink'st up injury;
Yet have no means to warn thee from't, for he
That sows in craft does reap in jealousy.   270

                                        [*Exit above.*

---

[1] A corruption of *recognisance.* See the article *Cullisen* in Nares' Glossary.

SCENE V.

A Street.

Enter REARAGE *and* SALEWOOD.

Rear. Now the letter's made up and all; it wants but the print of a seal, and away it goes to master Quomodo. Andrew Lethe is well whipt in't; his name stands in a white sheet here, and does penance for him.

Sale. You have shame enough against him, if that be good.

Rear. First, as a contempt of that reverend ceremony he has in hand, to wit, marriage.

Sale. Why do you say, to wit, marriage, when you know there's none will marry that's wise?

Rear. Had it not more need then to have wit to put to't, if it be grown to a folly?   11

Sale. You've won; I'll give't you.

Rear. 'Tis no thanks now: but, as I was saying, as a foul contempt to that sacred ceremony, he most audaciously keeps a drab in town, and, to be free from the interruption of blue beadles [1] and other bawdy officers, he most politicly lodges her in a constable's house.

Sale. That's a pretty point, i'faith.

Rear. And so the watch, that should fetch her out, are her chiefest guard to keep her in.   20

---

[1] Blue coats were worn by beadles. Hence the term "blue-bottle rogue" in 2 *Henry IV.* v. 4.

Sale. It must needs be; for look, how the constable plays his conscience, the watchmen will follow the suit.

Rear. Why, well then.

Enter EASY, *and* SHORTYARD *disguised as before.*[1]

Easy. All night from me? he's hurt, he's made away!

Sho. Where shall we seek him now? you lead me fair jaunts, sir.

Easy. Pray, keep a little patience, sir; I shall find him at last, you shall see.

Sho. A citizen of my ease and substance to walk so long a-foot!   30

Easy. You should ha' had my horse, but that he has eaten out his head, sir.

Sho. How? would you had me hold him by the tail, sir, then?

Easy. Manners forbid! 'tis no part of my meaning, sir. O, here's master Rearage and master Salewood: now we shall hear of him presently.—Gentlemen both.

Sale. Master Easy? how fare you, sir?

Easy. Very well in health. Did you see master Blastfield this morning?   40

Sale. I was about to move it to you.

Rear. We were all three in a mind then.

Sale. I ha' not set eye on him these two days.

Rear. I wonder he keeps so long from us, i'faith.

Easy. I begin to be sick.

Sale. Why, what's the matter?

---

[1] *i.e.* as a rich citizen, in a satin suit.

Easy. Nothing in troth, but a great desire I had to have seen him.

Rear. I wonder you should miss on't lately ; you're his bedfellow.   50

Easy. I lay alone to-night, i'faith, I do not know how. O, here comes master Lethe ; he can despatch me.—

Enter LETHE.

Master Lethe.

Let. What's your name, sir ? O, cry you mercy, master Easy.

Easy. When parted you from master Blastfield, sir ?

Let. Blastfield's an ass : I have sought him these two days to beat him.

Easy. Yourself all alone, sir ?

Let. Ay, and three more.   [*Exit.* 60

Sho. I am glad I am where I am, then ; I perceive 'twas time of all hands.   [*Aside.*

Rear. Content, i'faith ; let's trace him.

[*Exit with* SALEWOOD.

Sho. What, have you found him yet ? neither ? what's to be done now ? I'll venture my body no further for any gentleman's pleasure : I know not how soon I may be called upon, and now to overheat myself——

Easy. I'm undone !

Sho. This is you that slept with him ! you can make fools of us ; but I'll turn you over to Quomodo for't. 70

Easy. Good sir——

Sho. I'll prevent mine own danger.

Easy. I beseech you, sir——

Sho. Though I love gentlemen well, I do not mean to be undone for 'em.

Easy. Pray, sir, let me request you, sir; sweet sir, I beseech you, sir ——   [*Exeunt.*

ACT IV.

SCENE I.

QUOMODO'S *Shop.*

Enter QUOMODO, SHORTYARD *and* FALSELIGHT *his disguised spirits,*[1] *after whom* EASY *follows hard.*

Sho. Made fools of us ! not to be found !

Quo. What, what ?

Easy. Do not undo me quite, though, master Quomodo.

Quo. You're very welcome, master Easy : I ha' nothing to say to you ; I'll not touch you ; you may go when you please ; I have good bail here, I thank their worships.

Easy. What shall I say, or whom shall I beseech ?

Sho. Gentlemen ! 'slid, they were born to undo us, I think : but, for my part, I'll make an oath before master Quomodo here, ne'er to do gentlemen good while I live.

Fal. I'll not be long behind you.   12

Sho. Away ! if you had any grace in you, you would be ashamed to look us i' th' face, i-wis :[2] I wonder with

---

what brow you can come amongst us. I should seek
my fortunes far enough, if I were you ; and neither return
to Essex, to be a shame to my predecessors, nor remain
about London, to be a mock to my successors.

Quo. Subtle Shortyard !   [*Aside.*

Sho. Here are his lands forfeited to us, master Quomodo ; and to avoid the inconscionable trouble of law, all
the assurance he made to us we willingly resign to you. 22

Quo. What shall I do with rubbish ? give me money :
'tis for your worships to have land, that keep great houses;
I should be hoisted.

Sho. But, master Quomodo, if you would but conceive
it aright, the land would fall fitter to you than to us.

Easy. Curtsying about my land !   [*Aside.*

Sho. You have a towardly son and heir, as we hear.

Quo. I must needs say, he is a Templar indeed.   30

Sho. We have neither posterity in town, nor hope for
any abroad : we have wives, but the marks have been out
of their mouths these twenty years ; and, as it appears,
they did little good when they were in. We could not
stand about it, sir; to get riches and children too, 'tis
more than one man can do : and I am of those citizens'
minds that say, let our wives make shift for children and
they will, they get none of us ; and I cannot think, but
he that has both much wealth and many children has
had more helps coming in than himself.   40

Quo. I am not a bow[1] wide of your mind, sir ; and

---

[1] *i.e.* a bow-length wide. In archery the distance at which arrows
fell from the mark was measured by bow-lengths.

for the thrifty and covetous hopes I have in my son and heir, Sim Quomodo, that he will never trust his land in wax and parchment, as many gentlemen have done before him——

Easy. A by-blow for me.   [*Aside.*

Enter THOMASINE.

Quo. I will honestly discharge you, and receive it in due form and order of law, to strengthen it for ever to my son and heir, that he may undoubtedly enter upon't without the let or molestation of any man, at his or our pleasure whensoever.   51

Sho. 'Tis so assured unto you.

Quo. Why, then, master Easy, you're a free man, sir; you may deal in what you please, and go whither you will.—Why, Thomasine, master Easy is come from Essex; bid him welcome in a cup of small beer.

Tho. Not only vild, but in it tyrannous.   [*Aside.*

Quo. If it please you, sir, you know the house; you may visit us often, and dine with us once a-quarter.

Easy. Confusion light on you, your wealth, and heir! Worm gnaw your conscience as the moth your ware! I am not the first heir that robb'd or begg'd.   [*Exit.*

Quo. Excellent, excellent, sweet spirits!   63
                    [*Exit* THOMASINE.

Sho. Landed master Quomodo!

Quo. Delicate Shortyard, commodious Falselight, Hug and away, shift, shift:
'Tis slight, not strength, that gives the greatest lift.
                    [*Exeunt* SHORTYARD *and* FALSELIGHT.

Now my desires are full,—for this time.
Men may have cormorant wishes, but, alas,
A little thing, three hundred pound a-year,   70
Suffices nature, keeps life and soul together !—
I'll have 'em lopt[1] immediately ; I long
To warm myself by th' wood.
A fine journey in the Whitsun holydays, i'faith, to ride
down with a number of citizens and their wives, some
upon pillions, some upon side-saddles, I and little
Thomasine i' th' middle, our son and heir, Sim Quomodo, in a peach-colour taffeta jacket, some horse-
length, or a long yard before us ;—there will be a fine
show on's, I can tell you ;—where we citizens will laugh
and lie down,[2] get all our wives with child against a
bank, and get up again.   Stay ; hah ! hast thou that
wit, i'faith ? 'twill be admirable : to see how the very
thought of green fields puts a man into sweet inventions !
I will presently possess Sim Quomodo of all the land : I
have a toy[3] and I'll do't : and because I see before
mine eyes that most of our heirs prove notorious rioters
after our deaths, and that cozenage in the father wheels
about to folly in the son, our posterity commonly foiled
at the same weapon at which we played rarely ; and
being the world's beaten[4] word,—what's got over the
devil's back (that's by knavery) must be spent under his[92

---

[1] "Something seems to have dropt out before these words."—*Dyce.*
The abruptness is probably intentional.   He is resuming the reflections in which he had indulged on p. 287.

[2] See note 1, p. 54.

[3] Whim.

[4] Well-worn, trite.

belly (that's by lechery) : being awake in these knowings, why should not I oppose 'em now, and break Destiny of her custom, preventing that by policy, which without it must needs be destiny? And I have took the course : I will forthwith sicken, call for my keys, make my will, and dispose of all; give my son this blessing, that he trust no man, keep his hand from a quean and a scrivener, live in his father's faith, and do good to nobody : then will I begin to rave like a fellow of a wide conscience, and, for all the world, counterfeit to the life that which I know I shall do when I die; take on [1] for my gold, my lands, and my writings, grow worse and worse, call upon the devil, and so make an end. By this time I have indented with a couple of searchers,[2] who, to uphold my device, shall fray them out a' th' chamber with report of sickness ; and so, la, I start up, and recover again ! for in this business I will trust, no, not my spirits, Falselight and Shortyard, but, in disguise, note the condition of all ; how pitiful my wife takes my death, which will appear by November in her eye, and the fall of the leaf in her body, but especially by the cost she bestows upon my funeral, there shall I try her love and regard ; my daughter's marrying to my will and liking ; and my son's affection after my disposing : for, to conclude, I am as jealous of this land as of my wife, to know what would become of it after my decease.　118

[*Exit.*

---

[1] " Take on " = grieve. The expression is still heard in the mouths of uneducated people.

[2] "*i.e.* persons appointed officially to examine bodies and report the cause of death."—*Dyce.*

SCENE II.

The Country Wench's Lodging.

Enter Country Wench *and* Father.

Fa. Though I be poor, 'tis my glory to live honest.

Coun. W. I prithee, do not leave me.

Fa. To be bawd !

Hell has not such an office.

I thought at first your mind had been preserv'd

In virtue and in modesty of blood ;

That such a face had not been made to please

Th' unsettled appetites of several men ;

Those eyes turn'd up through prayer, not through lust :

But you are wicked, and my thoughts unjust.   9

Coun. W. Why, thou art an unreasonable fellow, i'faith. Do not all trades live by their ware, and yet called honest livers ? do they not thrive best when they utter[1] most, and make it away by the great?[2] is not whole-sale the chiefest merchandise ? do you think some merchants could keep their wives so brave[3] but for their whole-sale? you're foully deceived and you think so.

Fa. You are so glu'd to punishment and shame,

Your words e'en deserve whipping.

To bear the habit of a gentlewoman,

And be in mind so distant !   20

Coun. W. Why, you fool you, are not gentlewomen

---

[1] Sell.   [2] By the gross.   [3] Finely dressed.

sinners? and there's no courageous sinner amongst us
but was a gentlewoman by the mother's side, I warrant
you : besides, we are not always bound to think those
our fathers that marry our mothers, but those that lie
with our mothers ; and they may be gentlemen born,
and born again for ought we know, you know.

Fa. True :
Corruption may well be generation's first ;
We're bad by nature, but by custom worst. [*Exeunt.* 30

SCENE III.

Quomodo's *Shop.*[1]

Tho. [*within*]. O, my husband !
Sim. [*within*]. My father, O, my father !
Fal. [*within*]. My sweet master, dead !

Enter Shortyard *and* Boy.

Sho. Run, boy; bid 'em ring out; he's dead, he's
    gone.
Boy. Then is as arrant a knave gone as e'er was
called upon.   [*Exit.*
Sho. The happiest good that ever Shortyard felt !
I want to be express'd, my mirth is such.
To be struck now e'en when his joys were high !
Men only kiss their knaveries, and so die ;   10
I've often mark'd it.

---

[1] Old eds. print in advance the stage-direction "*A Bell toales, a
Confused crie within.*"

He was a famous cozener while he liv'd,
And now his son shall reap't; I'll ha' the lands,
Let him study law after; 'tis no labour
To undo him for ever: but for Easy,
Only good confidence did make him foolish,
And not the lack of sense; that was not it:
'Tis worldly craft beats down a scholar's wit.
For this our son and heir now, he
From his conception was entail'd an ass,   20
And he has kept it well, twenty-five years now:
Then the slightest art will do't; the lands lie fair:
No sin to beggar a deceiver's heir.   [*Exit.*
                                                 [*Bell tolls.*

Enter THOMASINE *and* WINEFRED *in haste.*

Tho. Here, Winefred, here, here, here; I have always found thee secret.

Win. You shall always find me so, mistress.

Tho. Take this letter and this ring—— [*Giving them.*

Win. Yes, forsooth.

Tho. O, how all the parts about me shake!—inquire for one master Easy, at his old lodging i' the Blackfriars.

Win. I will indeed, forsooth.   31

Tho. Tell him, the party that sent him a hundred pound t'other day to comfort his heart, has likewise sent him this letter and this ring, which has that virtue to recover him again for ever, say: name nobody, Winefred.

Win. Not so much as you, forsooth.

Tho. Good girl! thou shalt have a mourning-gown at the burial of mine honesty.

Win. And I'll effect your will a' my fidelity. [*Exit.* 40

Tho. I do account myself the happiest widow that ever counterfeited weeping, in that I have the leisure now both to do that gentleman good and do myself a pleasure; but I must seem like a hanging moon, a little waterish awhile.

Enter REARAGE *and* Country Wench's Father.

Rear. I entertain both thee and thy device;
'Twill put 'em both to shame.

Fa. That is my hope, sir;
Especially that strumpet.

Rear. Save you, sweet widow!
I suffer for your heaviness.

Tho. O master Rearage, I have lost the dearest husband that ever woman did enjoy! ·   51

Rear. You must have patience yet.

Tho. O, talk not to me of patience, and you love me, good master Rearage.

Rear. Yet, if all tongues go right, he did not use you so well as a man mought.[1]   56

Tho. Nay, that's true indeed, master Rearage; he ne'er used me so well as a woman might have been used, that's certain; in troth, 't'as been our greatest falling out, sir; and though it be the part of a widow to show herself a woman for her husband's death, yet when I remember

---

[1] Might.

all his unkindness, I cannot weep a stroke, i'faith, master
Rearage : and, therefore, wisely did a great widow in this
land comfort up another ; Go to, lady, quoth she, leave
blubbering ; thou thinkest upon thy husband's good parts
when thou sheddest tears ; do but remember how often
he has lain from thee, and how many naughty slippery
turns he has done thee, and thou wilt ne'er weep for him.
I warrant thee.   You would not think how that counsel
has wrought with me, master Rearage ; I could not dis-
pend another tear now, and you would give me ne'er so
much.   72

Rear. Why, I count you the wiser, widow ; it shows
you have wisdom when you can check your passion :[1]
for mine own part, I have no sense to sorrow for his
death, whose life was the only rub[2] to my affection.

Tho. Troth, and so it was to mine : but take courage
now ; you're a landed gentleman, and my daughter is
seven hundred pound strong to join with you.

Rear. But Lethe lies i' th' way.

Tho. Let him lie still :   80
You shall tread over him, or I'll fail in will.

Rear. Sweet widow !   [*Exeunt.*

---

[1] Sorrow.
[2] Obstacle.—A term borrowed from the bowling-alley.

SCENE IV.

Before QUOMODO'S *door.*

Enter QUOMODO *disguised as a Beadle.*

Quo. What a beloved man did I live! My servants
gall their fingers with ringing, my wife's cheeks smart
with weeping, tears stand in every corner,—you may
take water in my house. But am not I a wise fool now?
what if my wife should take my death so to heart that
she should sicken upon't, nay, swoon, nay, die? When
did I hear of a woman do so? let me see; now I remember me, I think 'twas before my time; yes, I have
heard of those wives that have wept, and sobbed, and
swooned; marry, I never heard but they recovered
again; that's a comfort, la, that's a comfort; and I hope
so will mine. Peace; 'tis near upon the time, I see:
here comes the worshipful Livery; I have the hospital
boys;[1] I perceive little Thomasine will bestow cost of
me.   15
I'll listen to the common censure[2] now,
How the world tongues me when my ear lies low.

Enter the Livery, *&c.*

First Liveryman. Who, Quomodo? merely enrich'd
        by shifts
And cozenages, believe it.

---

[1] "Compare Brome: 'He is indeed my brother, and has been one of
the true blew *Boyes of the Hospitall; one of the sweet singers to the City
Funeralls* with a two penny loafe under his arme.'—*The City Wit*, act
ii. sc. I.—(*Five New Playes*, 1653)."—*Dyce.*   [2] Judgment.

Quo. I see the world is very loath to praise me ; 20
'Tis rawly friends with me : I cannot blame it,
For what I've done has been to vex and shame it.
Here comes my son, the hope, the landed heir,
One [1] whose rare thrift will say, men's tongues you lie,
I'll keep by law what was got craftily.

Enter SIM.

Methinks I hear him say so :
He does salute the Livery with good grace
And solemn gesture.   [*Aside.*
O my young worshipful master, you have parted from a
dear father, a wise and provident father !   30
    Sim. Art thou grown an ass now?
    Quo. Such an honest father——
    Sim. Prithee, beadle, leave thy lying; I am scarce
able to endure thee, i'faith : what honesty didst thou e'er
know by my father, speak ?   Rule your tongue, beadle,
lest I make you prove it; and then I know what will
become of you : 'tis the scurviest thing i' th' earth to
belie the dead so, and he's a beastly son and heir that
will stand by and hear his father belied to his face ; he
will ne'er prosper, I warrant him.   Troth, if I be not
ashamed to go to church with him, I would I might be
hanged ; I hear [2] such filthy tales go on him.   O, if I
had known he had been such a lewd [3] fellow in his life,
he should ne'er have kept me company !   44

---

[1] So ed. 2.—Ed. 1 " Ont."
[2] So ed. 2.—Ed. 1 " feare."
[3] Base.

Quo. O, O, O!   [*Aside.*

Sim. But I am glad he's gone, though 'twere long first:
Shortyard and I will revel it, i'faith; I have made him
my rent-gatherer already.

Quo. He shall be speedily disinherited, he gets not a
foot, not the crown of a mole-hill: I'll sooner make a
courtier my heir, for teaching my wife tricks, than thee,
my most neglectful son.   52
O, now the corse; I shall observe yet farther.   [*Aside.*

A coffin [1] *brought in followed by* THOMASINE, SUSAN,
THOMASINE'S Mother, *and other mourners.*

O my most modest, virtuous, and remembering wife! she
shall have all when I die, she shall have all.   [*Aside.*

Enter EASY.

Tho. Master Easy? 'tis: O, what shift shall I make
now? [*Aside*]—O!
    [*Falls down in a feigned swoon, while the coffin is
        carried out; the mourners, except* THOMASINE'S
        Mother, *following it.*

Quo. Sweet wife, she swoons: I'll let her alone, I'll
have no mercy at this time; I'll not see her, I'll follow
the corse.   [*Aside, and exit.* 60
Easy. The devil grind thy bones, thou cozening rascal!
T.'s Moth. [2] Give her a little more air; tilt up her

---

[1] Old eds. "*A counterfet Coarse brought in, Tomazin and al the
mourners equally counterfeit.*"
[2] Old eds. simply give the prefix "*Moth.*" to her speeches.

head.—Comfort thyself, good widow; do not fall like a
beast for a husband : there's more than we can well tell
where to put 'em, good soul.

   Tho. O, I shall be well anon.

   T.'s Moth. Fie, you have no patience, i'faith : I have
buried four husbands, and never offered 'em such abuse.

   Tho. Cousin,[1] how do you?

   Easy. Sorry to see you ill, coz.

   Tho. The worst is past, I hope.

[*Pointing after the coffin.*

   Easy. I hope so too.   70

   Tho. Lend me your hand, sweet coz; I've troubled
      you.

   T.'s Moth. No trouble indeed, forsooth.—Good cousin,
have a care of her, comfort her up as much as you can,
and all little enough, I warrant ye.   [*Exit.*

   Tho. My most sweet love !

   Easy. My life is not so dear.

   Tho. I've always pitied you.

   Easy. You've shown it here,
And given the desperate hope.

   Tho. Delay not now; you've understood my love;
I've a priest ready; this is the fittest season.
No eye offends us : let this kiss   80
Restore thee to more wealth, me to more bliss.

   Easy. The angels have provided for me.   [*Exeunt.*

---

[1] Merely a familiar mode of address.

ACT V.

SCENE I.

QUOMODO'S *Shop*.

Enter SHORTYARD *with writings, having cozen'd*
SIM QUOMODO.

Sho. I have not scope enough within my breast
To keep my joys contain'd : I'm Quomodo's heir ;
The lands, assurances, and all are mine :
I've tript his son's heels up above the ground
His father left him : had I not encouragement ?
Do not I know, what proves the father's prey,
The son ne'er looks on't, but it melts away ?
Do not I know, the wealth that's got by fraud,
Slaves share it, like the riches of a bawd ?
Why, 'tis a curse unquenchable, ne'er cools ;   10
Knaves still commit their consciences to fools,
And they betray who ow'd 'em.   Here's all the bonds,
All Easy's writings : let me see.   [*Reads.*

Enter THOMASINE *and* EASY.[1]

Tho. Now my desires wear crowns.

---

[1] Old eds. "*Enter Quomodoes wife marryed to Easie.*"

Easy. My joys exceed :
Man is ne'er healthful till his follies bleed.
    Tho. O,
Behold the villain, who in all those shapes
Confounded your estate !
    Easy. That slave ! that villain !
    Sho. So many acres of good meadow——
    Easy. Rascal !
    Sho. I hear you, sir.   20
    Easy. Rogue, Shortyard, Blastfield, sergeant, deputy,
        cozener !
    Sho. Hold, hold !
    Easy. I thirst the execution of his ears.
    Tho. Hate you that office.
    Easy. I'll strip him bare for punishment and shame.
    Sho. Why, do but hear me, sir ; you will not think
What I've done for you.
    Easy. Given his son my lands !
    Sho. Why, look you, 'tis not so ; you're not told
        true :
I've cozen'd him again merely for you,
Merely for you, sir ; 'twas my meaning then   30
That you should wed her, and have all agen.
A' my troth, it's true, sir : look you then here, sir :
                        [Giving the writings.
You shall not miss a little scroll, sir.   Pray, sir,
Let not the city know me for a knave ;
There be richer men would envy my preferment,
If I should be known before 'em.
    Easy. Villain, my hate to more revenge is drawn :

When slaves are found, 'tis their base art to fawn.—
Within there!

     Enter Officers [1] *with* FALSELIGHT *bound.*

  Sho. How now? fresh warders!   40
  Easy. This is the other, bind him fast.—Have I found
       you,
Master Blastfield?   [Officers *bind* SHORTYARD.
  Sho. This is the fruit of craft:
Like him that shoots up high, looks for the shaft,
And finds it in his forehead, so does hit
The arrow of our fate; wit destroys wit;
The head the body's bane and his own bears.—
You ha' corn enough, you need not reap mine ears,
Sweet master Blastfield!

  Easy. I loathe his voice; away!

    [*Exeunt* Officers *with* SHORTYARD *and* FALSELIGHT.

  Tho. What happiness was here! but are you sure you
have all?   50

  Easy. I hope so, my sweet wife.

  Tho. What difference there is in husbands! not only
in one thing but in all.

  Easy. Here's good deeds and bad deeds; the writings
that keep my land [2] to me, and the bonds that gave it
away from me.

---

   1 "The old eds. have no stage-direction here. From the words
which presently follow, 'This is the other,' it seems that Falselight had
been previously taken into custody; and as they both afterwards make
their appearance together at the justice's house, I have thought it best to
despatch them thither in company."—*Dyce.*
   2 Old eds. "lands."

These, my good deeds, shall to more safety turn,
And these, my bad, have their deserts and burn.
I'll see thee again presently : read there.   [*Exit.*   59
    Tho. Did he want all, who would not love his care ?
                              [*Reads the writings.*

Enter QUOMODO *disguised as before.*

Quo. What a wife hast thou, Ephestian Quomodo ! so
loving, so mindful of her duty ; not only seen to weep,
but known to swoon ! I knew a widow about Saint
Antling's [1] so forgetful of her first husband, that she
married again within the twelvemonth ; nay, some, byrlady, within the month : there were sights to be seen !
Had they my wife's true sorrows, seven [months] nor
seven years would draw 'em to the stake.   I would most
tradesmen had such a wife as I : they hope they have ;
we must all hope the best : thus in her honour,—   70
A modest wife is such a jewel,
    Every goldsmith cannot show it :
He that's honest and not cruel
    Is the likeliest man to owe [2] it—
and that's I : I made it by myself ; and coming to her
as a beadle for my reward this morning, I'll see how she
takes my death next her heart.   [*Aside.*
    Tho. Now, beadle.

---

[1] " For an account of the church and parish so called, see Stow's
Survey of London : ' First you have the fair Parish Church of St.
Anthonines, in Budge Row (more vulgarly known by the name of St.
Antlins),' &c.—B. iii. p. 15, &c. ed. 1720."—*Dyce.*
[2] Own.

Quo. Bless your mistresship's eyes from too many tears, although you have lost a wise and worshipful gentle-man. 81

Tho. You come for your due, beadle, here i' th' house?

Quo. Most certain; the hospital money, and mine own poor forty pence.

Tho. I must crave a discharge from you, beadle.

Quo. Call your man; I'll heartily set my hand to a memorandum.

Tho. You deal the truelier.

Quo. Good wench still. [*Aside.*

Tho. George! 90

Enter Servant.

here is the beadle come for his money; draw a memo-randum that he has received all his due he can claim here i' th' house after this funeral.

Quo. [*Aside, while the* Servant *writes the memorandum*]. What politic directions she gives him, all to secure her-self! 'tis time, i'faith, now to pity her: I'll discover my-self to her ere I go; but came it off with some lively jest now, that were admirable. I have it: after the memorandum is written and all, I'll set my own name to't, Ephestian Quomodo; she'll start, she'll wonder how Ephestian Quomodo came hither,[1] that was buried yester-day: you're beset,[2] little Quomodo. 101

Tho. [*running over the memorandum*]. Nineteen, twenty, —five pound, one, two, three and fourpence.

---

[1] So ed 2.—Ed. 1 "thether."
[2] Perplexed.

Quo. [*signing it*]. So ; we shall have good sport when 'tis read.   [*Aside.*]   [*Exit* Servant.

Enter EASY, *as* THOMASINE *is giving the money to* QUOMODO.

Easy. How now, lady? paying away money so fast ?

Tho. The beadle's due here, sir.

Quo. Who's this ? [1]

'Tis Easy ! what makes Easy in my house?

He is not my wife's overseer, I hope.   [*Aside.* 110

    Easy. What's here?

    Quo. He makes me sweat !   [*Aside.*

    Easy [*reads*]. *Memorandum, that I have received of Richard Easy all my due I can claim here i' th' house, or any hereafter for me* : *in witness wherof I have set to mine own hand,* EPHESTIAN QUOMODO.

    Quo. What have I done ! was I mad ?   [*Aside.*

    Easy. Ephestian Quomodo ?

    Quo. Ay ; well, what then, sir ? get you out of my house first,

You master prodigal Had-land ; [2] away !   120

    Tho. What, is the beadle drunk or mad ?

Where are my men to thrust him out a' doors ?

    Quo. Not so, good Thomasine, not so.

    Tho. This fellow must be whipt.

---

[1] Ed. 1 " Whose? tis."—Ed. 2 " Whose? this."

[2] Old eds. " Had land."—Cf. *Trick to catch the Old One*, i. 2— " What's the news, bully *Had-land* ?"   There is a black-letter broadside ballad (printed circ. 1635) by R[ichard] C[limsell] entitled " John Hadland's Adviee."

Quo. Thank you, good wife.

Easy. I can no longer bear him.

Tho. Nay, sweet husband.

Quo. Husband? I'm undone, beggared, cozened, confounded for ever! married already? [*Aside.*]—Will it please you know me now, mistress Harlot and master Horner? who am I now? [*Discovers himself.*

Tho. O, he's as like my t'other husband as can be! 132

Quo. I'll have judgment; I'll bring you before a judge: you shall feel, wife, whether my flesh be dead or no; I'll tickle you, i'faith, i'faith. [*Exit.*

Tho. The judge that he'll solicit knows me well.

Easy. Let's on then, and our grievances first tell.

[*Exeunt.*

SCENE II.

A Street.

Enter REARAGE *and* SUSAN.

Rear. Here they come.

Sus. O, where?

Enter Officers [1] *with* LETHE *and* Country Wench *in custody;* SALEWOOD, HELLGILL, *and* MOTHER GRUEL.

Let. Heart of shame!

Upon my wedding morning so disgrac'd!

---

1 " The only stage-direction of the old eds. in this scene is, ' *Enter Lethe with Officers, taken with his Harlot:*' that the additions which I have made to it are necessary, the following scene will show."—*Dyce.*

Have you so little conscience, officers,
You will not take a bribe?

Coun. W. Master Lethe, we may lie together lawfully
hereafter, for we are coupled together before people enow,
i'faith.

> [*Exeunt* Officers *with* LETHE *and* Country
> Wench, *&c.*

Rear. There goes the strumpet!   10

Sus. Pardon my wilful blindness, and enjoy me;
For now the difference appears too plain
'Twixt [1] a base slave and a true gentleman.

Rear. I do embrace thee in the best of love.—
How soon affections fail, how soon they prove!

> [*Exeunt.*

SCENE III.

An Apartment in the Judge's *House.*

Enter Judge, EASY *and* THOMASINE *in talk with him:*
SHORTYARD *and* FALSELIGHT *in the custody of* Officers.

Jud. His cozenages are odious: he the plaintiff!
Not only fram'd deceitful in his life,
But so to mock his funeral!

Easy. Most just:
The Livery all assembled, mourning weeds
Throughout his house e'en down to his last servant,
The herald richly hir'd to lend him arms
Feign'd from his ancestors (which I dare swear knew

---

[1] Old eds. "Betwixt."

No other arms but those they labour'd with),
All preparations furnish'd, nothing wanted
Save that which was the cause of all, his death,—   10
If he be living!

 Jud. 'Twas an impious part.

 Easy. We are not certain yet it is himself,
But some false spirit that assumes his shape,
And seeks still to deceive me.

Enter QUOMODO.

 Quo. O, are you come?—
My lord, they're here.—Good-morrow, Thomasine.

 Jud. Now, what are you?

 Quo. I'm Quomodo, my lord, and this my wife;
Those my two men, that are bound wrongfully.

 Jud. How are we sure you're he?

 Quo. O, you cannot miss, my lord!   20

 Jud. I'll try you:
Are you the man that liv'd the famous cozener?

 Quo. O no, my lord!

 Jud. Did you deceive this gentleman of his right,
And laid nets o'er his land?

 Quo. Not I, my lord.

 Jud. Then you're not Quomodo, but a counterfeit.—
Lay hands on him, and bear him to the whip.

 Quo. Stay, stay a little,
I pray.—Now I remember me, my lord,
I cozen'd him indeed; 'tis wondrous true.   30

 Jud. Then I dare swear this is no counterfeit:
Let all doubts cease; this man is Quomodo.

Quo. Why, la, you now, you would not believe this?
I am found what I am.

Jud. But setting these thy odious shifts apart,
Why did that thought profane enter thy breast,
To mock the world with thy supposed death?

Quo. Conceive you not that, my lord? a policy.

Jud. So.

Quo. For having gotten the lands, I thirsted still
To know what fate would follow 'em——   41

Jud. Being ill got.

Quo. Your lordship apprehends me.

Jud. I think I shall anon.

Quo. And thereupon,
I, out of policy, possess'd my son,
Which since I have found lewd ; and now intend
To disinherit him for ever.
Not only this was in my death set down,
But thereby a firm trial of my wife,
Her constant sorrows, her rememb'ring virtues ;
All which are dews ; the shine of a next morning
Dries 'em up all, I see't.   51

Jud. Did you profess wise cozenage, and would
       dare
To put a woman to her two days' choice,
When oft a minute does it?

Quo. Less, a moment,
The twinkling of an eye, a glimpse, scarce something
       does it.
Your lordship yet will grant she is my wife?

Tho. O heaven !

Jud. After some penance and the dues of law,
I must acknowledge that.

Quo. I scarce like   60
Those dues of law.

Easy. My lord,
Although the law too gently 'lot his wife,
The wealth he left behind he cannot challenge.

Quo. How?

Easy. Behold his hand against it. [*Showing writings.*

Quo. He does devise all means to make me mad,
That I may no more lie with my wife
In perfect memory; I know't: but yet
The lands will maintain me in my wits;   70
The land[s] will do so much for me.

Jud. [*reads*]. *In witness whereof I have set to mine
own hand*, EPHESTIAN QUOMODO.
'Tis firm enough your own, sir.

Quo. A jest, my lord; I did I knew not what.

Jud. It should seem so: deceit is her own foe;
Craftily gets, and childishly lets go.
But yet the lands are his.

Quo. I warrant ye.

Easy. No, my good lord, the lands know the right
          heir;
I am their master once more.

Quo. Have you the lands?   80

Easy. Yes, truly, I praise heaven.

Quo. Is this good dealing?
Are there such consciences abroad?   How,
Which way could he come by 'em?

Sho. My lord,
I'll quickly resolve you that it comes to me.
This cozener, whom too long I call'd my patron,
To my thought dying, and the fool his son
Possess'd of all, which my brain partly sweat for,
I held it my best virtue, by a plot
To get from him what for him was ill got——   90
   Quo. O beastly Shortyard !
   Sho. When, no sooner mine,
But I was glad more quickly to resign.
   Jud. Craft once discover'd shows her abject line.
   Quo. He hits me everywhere ; for craft once known
Does teach fools wit, leaves the deceiver none.
My deeds have cleft me, cleft me !   [*Aside.*

Enter Officers *with* LETHE *and the* Country Wench ;
    REARAGE, SUSAN, SALEWOOD, HELLGILL, *and*
    MOTHER GRUEL.

   First Off. Room there.
   Quo. A little yet to raise my spirit,
Here master Lethe comes to wed my daughter :
That's all the joy is left me.—Hah ! who's this?
   Jud. What crimes have those brought forth?
   Sale.[1] The shame of lust :   100
Most viciously on this his wedding morning
This man was seiz'd in shame with that bold strumpet.

---

[1] "Old eds. '*Gent. :* ' for which I have substituted *Salewood*, who,
as we may gather from act iii. sc. 5, was privy to the design of exposing
Lethe."—*Dyce.*

Jud. Why, 'tis she he means to marry.

Let. No, in truth.

Jud. In truth you do :

Who for his wife his harlot doth prefer,

Good reason 'tis that he should marry her.

  Coun. W. I crave it on my knees ; such was his vow
   at first.

  Hell. I'll say so too, and work out mine own safety.—

                 [*Aside.*

Such was his vow at first indeed, my lord,

Howe'er his mood has chang'd him.

  Let. O vild slave !   110

  Coun. W. He says it true, my lord.

  Jud. Rest content,

He shall both marry and taste punishment.

  Let. O, intolerable ! I beseech your good lordship, if
I must have an outward punishment, let me not marry
an inward, whose lashes[1] will ne'er out, but grow worse
and worse. I have a wife stays for me this morning with
seven hundred pound in her purse : let me be speedily
whipt and be gone, I beseech your lordship.

  Sale.[2] He speaks no truth, my lord : behold the virgin,
Wife to a well-esteemed gentleman,   120
Loathing the sin he follows.

  Let. I was betray'd ; yes, faith.

  Rear. His own mother,[3] my lord,

---

[1] So ed. 2.—Ed. 1 "lustes."

[2] Old eds. "*Gent.*"

[3] Something seems to have dropped out before this speech.

Which he confess'd through ignorance and disdain,
His name so chang'd to abuse the world and her.

Let. Marry a harlot, why not? 'tis an honest man's
fortune.   I pray, did not one of my countrymen marry
my sister? why, well then, if none should be married
but those that are honest, where should a man seek a
wife after Christmas?   I pity that gentleman that has
nine daughters to bestow, and seven of 'em seeded
already; they will be good stuff [1] by that time.   131
I do beseech your lordship to remove
The punishment; I am content to marry her.

Jud. There's no removing of your punishment——

Let. O, good my lord!

Jud. Unless one here assembled,
Whom you have most unnaturally abus'd,
Beget your pardon.

Let. Who should that be?
Or who would do't that has been so abus'd?
A troublesome penance!—Sir——

Quo. Knave in your face! leave your mocking, Andrew;
marry your quean, and be quiet.   141

Let. Master Easy——

Easy. I'm sorry you take such a bad course, sir.

Let. Mistress [2] Quomodo——

Tho. Inquire my right name again [3] next time; now
go your ways like an ass as you came.

---

[1] See note 1, p. 274.
[2] So ed. 2.—Ed. 1 " Maister."
[3] Against.

Let. Mass, I forget my mother all this while; I'll make her do't at first.—Pray, mother, your blessing for once.

Moth. G. Call'st me mother? out, I defy[1] thee, slave !   151

Let. Call me slave as much as you will, but do not shame me now : let the world know you are my mother.

Moth. G. Let me not have this villain put upon me, I beseech your lordship.

Jud. He's justly curs'd : she loathes to know him
        now,
Whom he before did as much loathe to know.—
Wilt thou believe me, woman ?

Moth. G. That's soon done.

Jud. Then know him for a villain; 'tis thy son.   160

Moth. G. Art thou Andrew, my wicked son Andrew ?

Let. You would not believe me, mother.

Moth. G. How art thou changed ! Is this suit fit for thee, a tooth-drawer's son ? This country has e'en spoiled thee since thou camest hither : thy manners [were] better than thy clothes, but now whole clothes and ragged manners : it may well be said that truth goes naked; for when thou hadst scarce a shirt, thou hadst more truth about thee.

Jud. Thou art thine own affliction, Quomodo.   170
Shortyard, we banish [thee] ; it is our pleasure.

---

[1] Renounce.

Sho. Henceforth no woman shall complain for
    measure.

Jud. And that all error from our works may stand,
We banish Falselight evermore the land.

                                   [*Exeunt omnes.*

END OF VOL. I